Teacher Quality 2.0

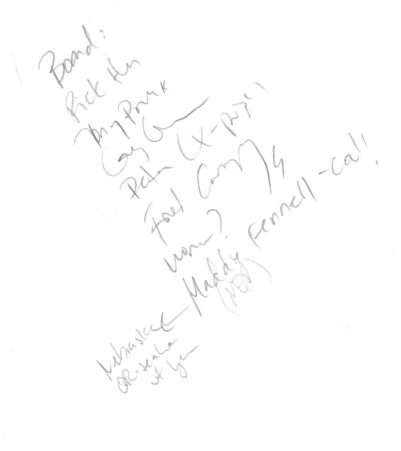

THE EDUCATIONAL
INNOVATIONS SERIES

The Educational Innovations series explores a wide range of current school reform efforts. Individual volumes examine entrepreneurial efforts and unorthodox approaches, highlighting reforms that have met with success and strategies that have attracted widespread attention. The series aims to disrupt the status quo and inject new ideas into contemporary education debates.

Series edited by Frederick M. Hess

Other books in this series:

Teacher Quality 2.0

Toward a New Era in Education Reform

Frederick M. Hess
Michael Q. McShane
Editors

Harvard Education Press
Cambridge, Massachusetts

Library of Congress Control Number 2014932483
Paperback ISBN 978-1-61250-699-9
Library Edition 978-1-61250-700-2

Published by Harvard Education Press,
an imprint of the Harvard Education Publishing Group

Harvard Education Press
8 Story Street
Cambridge, MA 02138

Cover Design: Deborah Hodgdon

The typefaces used in this book are Meridien LT Std and Myriad Pro

Contents

Introduction

MICHAEL Q. McSHANE, FREDERICK M. HESS,
AND TARYN HOCHLEITNER

In an age of dizzying technological advances and a rapidly evolving knowledge economy, students must know and be able to do more than ever before in order to compete. The task of preparing them for this increasingly demanding landscape falls largely to teachers, who must lead a rapid evolution of their own profession.

U.S. Secretary of Education Arne Duncan, May 6, 2013

IN A THIRD GRADE CLASSROOM in southeast Washington, DC, it's time for math. In many ways, this may seem like a typical classroom, like any you'd find in Boise, Idaho, or Poughkeepsie, New York. There are about twenty-five or twenty-six students, all roughly eight or nine years old, with one teacher in charge. The students are working on rounding, a task drawn from the "number sense and operations" strand of the third grade math standards. At the end of the year, they will take a standardized test to demonstrate their knowledge of rounding, and much else, just like the other kids in the district. But this classroom is different.

When the bell rings, the teacher divides the class into three groups. The first heads to a bank of computers along one wall. They sit down, put on headphones, and get to work on ST Math, an online program that allows them to practice concepts at a pace automatically adapted for their skill level. The second group moves

1

to a cluster of desks to work collaboratively on a more in-depth problem-solving challenge related to the week's material. The final group gathers around the teacher at a table in the front of the room for direct instruction. The teacher has divided the groups by ability, using data from the online program as well as her personal assessment of the students' progress. Before long, the class is buzzing.

This classroom offers a peek at the change sweeping through the American education system. Across the country, innovative teachers and school leaders are redesigning their schools. Some are using technology to share the task of instruction. Some are choosing to give teachers unique responsibilities that better complement their strengths. Many are asking teachers to cooperate with analytic software to use data to drive their instruction. Some transformations are more extreme than others, but all involve reimagining the role of the teacher.

Decades of research attest to what anyone who has been a student knows intuitively: teachers matter. In a 2013 Associated Press poll of parents of children in grades K–12, 96 percent cited teacher quality as an extremely or very important factor in a student's education.[1] In a seminal 2011 study, economists Raj Chetty, John Friedman, and Jonah Rockoff analyzed data from 2.5 million students and found that better teachers increase student test scores, the likelihood that students will attend college, and students' early career earnings.[2] These findings align with a robust literature on the positive effects of high-quality teachers.[3]

With increasing use of technology and innovative staffing arrangements to "disrupt" the familiar education system, expectations of the teaching role are also evolving. The question is, Are all of our efforts to improve the quality of our nation's teachers failing to keep up with these innovations or, worse, holding them back?

Teacher Quality: From 0.0 to 2.0

Quality teaching has been a priority since the American school system's earliest days. In 1873 Horace Mann, father of the Common School movement and the first secretary of education for the state of Massachusetts, dubbed teaching "the most difficult of all arts, and the profoundest of all sciences."[4] He helped create the first normal, or teacher preparatory, college in the country in Framingham, Massachusetts, two years later. Mann pioneered one era of teacher quality reform; for the sake of classification, and in the spirit of the digital age, we might call his efforts and those of the ensuing 150 years *teacher quality 0.0*. The 0.0 reforms saw the establishment of the profession, creation of new institutions to train and certify teachers, and development of a canon of standards for practice.

In the mid-1990s, access to new data from standardized tests and the computing power to process vast numbers of student records began to advance new ideas for policy and practice—*teacher quality 1.0*. States no longer needed to rely on blunt measures of quality like the number of courses taken or relevant certifications earned; instead, they could consider a teacher's impact on student performance when evaluating his or her capabilities.

As detailed by Sara Mead, Andrew Rotherham, and Rachael Brown in chapter 1, improving policies governing teacher quality has been a central concern of education reformers for the past two decades. After the National Commission on Teaching and America's future, led by former North Carolina governor James B. Hunt and Stanford professor Linda Darling-Hammond released *What Matters Most: Teaching for America's Future* in 1996, it became accepted wisdom that teacher knowledge and skill are important; recruiting, preparing, and retaining good teachers is central to improving schools; and school reform is predicated on the ability to create conditions that allow teachers to teach.[5] The release of The New Teacher Project's 2009 report "The Widget Effect"—which famously found that 99 percent of tenured teachers were rated "satisfactory" in districts with binary rating systems and 94 percent were rated in the top two categories in those with multiple categories—demonstrated just how far current systems were from achieving that goal.[6]

As a result, teacher quality 1.0 reforms have garnered significant attention in public debates about education across the past half-decade. The Obama administration has promoted changes in teacher evaluation in its offered waivers from the requirements of the 2001 No Child Left Behind Act (NCLB). Forty-six states (all but Montana, North Dakota, Nebraska, and California) and the

District of Columbia have agreed to create teacher evaluation systems that include student performance on standardized assessments as a waiver condition.[7] In the political realm, both the Democratic and Republican 2012 election platforms spoke of remaking teacher policy. While Democrats called for "carefully crafted evaluation systems that give struggling teachers a chance to succeed and protect due process if another teacher has to be put in the classroom," Republicans stated that, if elected, they would "correct the current law provision which defines a 'highly qualified teacher' merely by his or her credentials, not results in the classroom."[8] The media has also become entranced by the topic. From August 2008 to August 2013, more than 1,450 U.S. newspaper headlines mentioned "teacher evaluation." That number is more than double the 550 headlines containing the same term published between 1998 and 2003, a period that marked the end of the Clinton presidency and the birth of No Child Left Behind.[9]

Today, we face the makings of a new era in teacher quality policy—*teacher quality 2.0.*

Teacher Quality 2.0: New Schools, New Measures?

While education reformers have advocated for changes to how teachers are prepared, evaluated, supported, and compensated, entrepreneurial school and system leaders have added a new wrinkle into the teacher quality discussion. Driven by a belief that the shortcomings of our current system of education are as much a result of the *organization* of schools as the composition of the teaching force, many have pushed for redesigning the classroom and schoolhouse. This has led to the growth of 2.0 schools—or those that adopt a nontraditional arrangement of staff or delivery of the learning experience. No longer wedded to the regimented, age-graded school of Mann's time, schools are leveraging technology by using adaptive, computer-based software to give students a customized learning experience. Some are choosing to use staff differently, breaking down teaching into component roles that can be spread across different, specialized individuals. Many eschew the building altogether and provide a virtual learning environment that allows both teachers and students to work from home.

Some examples might be helpful.

ONLINE SCHOOLS

In thirty states, students are able to complete their education entirely online through full-service virtual schools.[10] One of these, the Florida Virtual School (FLVS), offers more than 120 courses to over 12,000 students across the country and the world. Students enrolled in traditional schools can sign up to take one or two courses to supplement their in-person education or access a class that their school is unable to provide at the time they need it, or students can attend FLVS full time. Full-time, state-certified teachers lead the classes, which provide all necessary materials online. Students are able to call, text, e-mail, or instant message their teachers any time between 8:00 a.m. and 8:00 p.m. while they are enrolled in the class, and they can take the course at any time and move as quickly as they are able to work through the material.

HYBRID SCHOOLS

Students enrolled in Carpe Diem Public Collegiate High School and Middle School in Yuma, Arizona, spend the majority of their day in a "learning center," a large farm of cubicles in which they progress through customized curricula on computers. A small number of teachers circulate throughout the room monitoring student progress. Four times a day, students participate in small teacher-led "workshops" in classrooms that ring the cubicle room. These workshops provide extra help for students struggling with content that the computer program has not succeeded in teaching. They also allow a forum for discussions, labs, or demonstrations of topics in math, science, literature, and history.

Leveraging technology allows the school to employ fewer teachers than the average school; in fact, there is only one teacher in each subject for almost 250 students in grades 7–12. This means, theoretically, that each student has the same subject matter teacher for his or her entire career. Not only does this allow teachers a unique opportunity to gain an intimate understanding of a student's strengths and weaknesses, it dramatically drives down the cost of providing education, even with the capital costs of the technological infrastructure. Carpe Diem reports that it spends only $5,300 per student per year, more than $2,000 less than the average public school in Arizona.[11]

ELEMENTARY SCHOOL SPECIALIZATION

Some schools experiment with ways to take advantage of teachers' diverse skills. At Ingenuity Prep in Washington, DC, elementary school teachers, like their middle and high school counterparts, specialize in subject matters. Rather than employing elementary teachers that teach every subject for a given set of students for a school year, Ingenuity Prep utilizes math specialists, reading specialists, and dedicated teachers in the other subject matters that loop with a given cohort of students for three years as they progress through their studies. Students have the same math teacher, for example, for grades K–2, then another for grades 3–5, and another for grades 6–8.

MULTI-CLASSROOM LEADERSHIP

Other schools have explored what education research firm Public Impact has termed *multi-classroom leadership*, a model in which high-performing teachers lead a team of developing teachers by modeling strong teaching practice. In this model, used at schools like City Charter in Pittsburgh, the teacher team leader divides tasks, assigns classes, leads instructional planning, reviews and helps develop assessment, and operates relatively autonomously to guide the teaching and learning in a particular "pod" in the school.

ROTATION MODEL

In the School of One, a middle school math program in New York City, students rotate through a series of stations throughout open, 2,000-square-foot "classrooms" along a predesigned plan developed by a computer program. Stations include teacher-led instruction, independent practice online, and peer-to-peer practice as befitting each individual student's learning needs and preferences. At the end of each day, students take a short assessment that gauges their mastery of the day's subject, the results of which the School of One computer program uses to build that student's customized lesson plan for the following day. In this model, teachers are responsible for particular stations, teaching certain skills to a mix of different students every day. The school has automated most of the organizational tasks related to teaching, like grading and attendance, so teachers focus solely on developing particular lessons for particular skills or a piece of content knowledge for that day.

In 2011, School of One's Joel Rose and Christopher Rush created New Classrooms Innovation Partners to bring a similar version of this model, dubbed "Teach to One: Math," to more schools. In contrast to entirely hybrid schools, Teach to One, which currently operates in fifteen schools in five cities, brings a hybrid learning experience to one part of a student's day, while the rest is spent in traditional classrooms.[12]

On one hand, states across the country are creating a policy environment that is friendlier to the development of innovative models. Nevada, New Hampshire, Oklahoma, Pennsylvania, South Carolina, Utah, and Wisconsin provide flexibility in their charter laws to allow hybrid or virtual schools to exist under the auspices of a charter school. States like Arizona, Wisconsin, Indiana, and Louisiana have taken school reorganization a step further by allowing K–12 students to "unbundle" their coursework and take classes from a mixture of in-person and online resources with state support.[13] In addition to programs like course choice, four states require students to have taken at least one course online in order to graduate from high school.[14]

But at the same time, today's 1.0 teacher quality reforms—multiple-measure evaluations, teacher tenure reform, and calls for more rigorous preparation—still assume a 0.0 organization of schools and classrooms and can threaten to stymie new models. They rely on the conditions that teachers will take a traditional path through a college of education to the front of the classroom, where they will take on traditional responsibilities—teaching a lesson to a group of age-graded students at varying levels of competency for a specified period of time each day. In order for teacher quality–driven policies to have their desired effect, however, they must be adaptable to the conditions they are meant to govern. Teacher quality 2.0 reformers, then, would take care to anticipate and leave room for innovative developments in today's, and tomorrow's, schools.

How 1.0 Reform Stymies 2.0 Schooling

1.0 policy proposals concerning evaluation, preparation, and compensation, intended to be applied to all schools, may clash with those that do not fit the traditional mold. This clash can occur for two reasons. First, 1.0 policies can *emphasize skills that are not relevant to innovative models of schooling.* Consider classroom management, which can look quite different for an online school or a hybrid school, that utilizes a station-rotation model where students are split into small groups. Lesson planning might also differ in a 2.0 schooling context, if a teacher works in a school that uses a master teacher to set the scope and sequence of instruction. Second, 1.0 policies might *fail to acknowledge the skills teachers in 2.0 schools need,* which may not be relevant in a more traditional context. Such skills might include product selection, data analysis, nontraditional time management, or communication skills for new media, like chat rooms or comment threads. Proposed reforms to teacher preparation, professional development, or evaluation might not adequately take these job functions into account.

EVALUATION

New school models can conflict with what states have promised as a condition of their NCLB waivers. One provision specifically waives the "highly qualified teacher" requirements if states have acceptable evaluation programs. Florida's waiver application, for example, is extremely specific about the use of student growth in teacher evaluations. All school districts must adopt the state's method for teacher evaluation in "all courses associated with statewide assessment and must select an equally appropriate formula for measuring learning goals for all grades and subjects." Specifically, "the student learning growth portion of the evaluation must include growth data for students assigned to the teacher over the course of at least three years." If that is not available, "the years for which data are available must be used and the percentage of the evaluation . . . may be reduced to not less than 40 percent." This hinges on the phrase "students assigned to the teacher."[15] What does it mean to have a student "assigned to a teacher" in a school with a new model? How would a teacher at School of One, say, be evaluated when a student spends some portion of their time learning from a teacher, some under virtual instruction, and some under peer-to-peer review?

Similarly, provisions for collaborative learning goals chafe with alternative environments, like those outlined above. In a school that divides the teaching role among multiple individuals, who is responsible for establishing the goals? Would all of the teachers on the team need to pick the same set of outcomes to be evaluated by? Does that make sense when they are teaching different subjects or performing different tasks?

But perhaps more difficult is the use of "established frameworks" for monitoring teacher performance. The push for best practices of teacher evaluation has widely validated frameworks like that of renowned teacher effectiveness consultant Charlotte Danielson. Danielson's *Framework for Teaching* measures teacher practice in four domains: planning and preparation, the classroom environment, instruction, and professional responsibilities. Under each domain are specific indicators of teacher practice and rubrics for classifying teachers as "unsatisfactory," "basic," "proficient," or "distinguished."[16]

Few, if any, of these frameworks have been designed to take into account alternative school models. For example, in the Danielson framework:

- Domain 1c is "setting instructional outcomes." Teachers are expected to demonstrate value, sequence, and alignment in content taught, as well as clarity, balance, and suitability for diverse students. This responsibility may look different when a computer program is helping to automatically customize content based on a student's performance completing online tasks.
- Domain 1e, "Designing Coherent Instruction," poses the same issue. If computers or a master teacher team leader are designing

the learning activities, producing instructional materials, dividing students into instructional groups, and structuring the lessons and units, this particular evaluation tool doesn't work.

- What does "respect and rapport" (Domain 2a) look like in a chat room?
- What do classroom procedures (Domain 2c) look like in an online school? How do we measure how students manage transitions, materials and supplies, or classroom routines like the framework calls for?
- Standards for management of student behavior (Domain 2d) emphasize "maintaining order" through posting classroom rules, "silently and subtly monitor(ing) student behavior," and preventing things like "objects flying through the air" is simply not relevant for many 2.0 schools.

The Danielson framework is but one common example. All over, teacher evaluation models that assume 1.0 classrooms are being included in legislation, and districts and schools are grading teachers on an increasingly outdated model.

PREPARATION

Today's teachers are not being prepared to teach in 2.0 schools. The Council for Accreditation of Educator Preparation (a joint venture of the National Council for Accreditation of Teacher Education and the Teacher Accreditation Council) accredits almost half of all teacher education programs (about 800 of the more than 1,600 total).[17] It relies on the Interstate Teacher Assessment and Support Consortium (InTASC) standards to set the benchmarks for what prospective teachers should know and be able to do. It is clear that many of these skills and dispositions have little relevance for teachers that teach in 2.0 schools.

- Standard #6, "Assessment," for example, says that a successful teacher "understands and uses multiple methods of assessment to engage learners in their own growth, to monitor learner progress, and to guide the teacher's and learner's decision making." What if a computer does the brunt of this?

- Similarly, Standard #7, "Planning for Instruction," says that a successful teacher "plans instruction that supports every student in meeting rigorous learning goals by drawing upon knowledge of content areas, curriculum, cross-disciplinary skills, and pedagogy, as well as knowledge of learners and the community context." Again, it is unclear how this applies to an online school.
- Finally, Standard #8, "Instructional Strategies," wherein a teacher is evaluated in how he or she "understands and uses a variety of instructional strategies to encourage learners to develop deep understanding of content areas and their connections, and to build skills to apply knowledge in meaningful ways," is not necessarily applicable to teachers in these new models.[18]

If these are the standards by which accreditation agents judge the quality of teacher preparation programs, it is not clear that they will do a good job assessing schools that prepare teachers for 2.0 model schools.

COMPENSATION

Changing what it means to be a teacher may require rethinking how teachers are compensated. One of the most popular education reforms of the past half-decade has been the movement to abolish tenure and rethink the step-and-lane pay scales that have been used to compensate teachers since the late 1800s.[19] Where these reforms have been successful, old systems have been replaced with merit-based systems that base compensations and continued employment on performance, not years of experience or degrees attained. There is legitimate debate about both the ability of these systems to improve student achievement and the best way to structure merit-based incentives. Regardless of the resolution, it is clear that many of these programs use the same definitions of teaching and teaching success as the evaluation programs mentioned above.

Take the District of Columbia Public School's (DCPS) IMPACT teacher evaluation system, for example. IMPACT allows a teacher to earn bonuses based on her evaluation. That evaluation is 50 percent student performance on the district's standardized test, 40 percent measurement of instructional expertise on the Teaching and Learning Framework, and 10 percent on a measure of commitment to the school community. This compensation model suffers from many of the same issues that evaluations based on 1.0 models encounter. Value-added can be hard to assign to a particular teacher. The DCPS's Teaching and Learning Framework includes large sections for "classroom environment," "classroom procedures and routines," and "classroom behavior management" that do not apply as neatly in nontraditional classrooms. Similarly, it does not have a means of assessing commitment to a school community that might be virtual.

This proliferation of new models fundamentally increases the need for teachers to be able to match themselves with the type of school that best fits their teaching skills and style. Perhaps the same teacher that thrives moderating an online class will not be the same that thrives in front of a traditional lecture-based classroom. In a school that differentiates roles, not every teacher will be the best lesson planner or the best assessment developer. The idea of specialization is predicated on the belief that some people do some things better than others. In order for a system like this to work, teachers need to be able to select where they work, and school leaders need to be able to select who teaches in their schools. This is not always the case.

CONTRACTS

Contracts and collective bargaining agreements codify the norms and expectations of teachers and school systems. They specify work conditions such as class and day length and student-teacher ratios. For example, the contract between the Chicago Teachers Union and the Chicago Public Schools specifies that for an elementary school teacher, "each teacher's day shall be comprised of no more than 296 minutes of instruction, 15 minutes of non-classroom supervision and 64 minutes of continuous duty-free preparation," and student-teacher ratios will not exceed twenty-eight students at the primary level and thirty-one at the intermediate and upper levels.[20] As schools move away from traditional classrooms, these terms and their attendant requirements run the risk of holding back innovation. If there is a cap on the number of students a teacher can teach, a program that increases their reach through technology could conflict with those limits. For example, rigid instructional time requirements could prevent teachers from finding more efficient ways to deliver instruction by condensing some lessons to create more space for others. If schools are going to change, contracts, collective bargaining, and the definitions they rely on will have to change as well.

A Broader Lens

Encouraging flexibility in teacher evaluation, preparation, compensation, professional development, and contracts might establish the conditions necessary for 2.0 schools to exist, but to help them thrive involves looking at teacher quality with a broader lens. Enabling the next generation of new school models also involves a reimagining of many of the norms that have come to define teacher policy.

First, when we redefine what it means to be a teacher, we shock a system of professionalization that has been in development over the past one hundred years. Over that time period, educators and scholars have attempted to develop a body of knowledge around what students should know and what practices are more useful in helping students develop that knowledge. Teacher educators and labor unions have worked to establish professional norms for preparation and practice, all of which can be upset by new models and new schools. These new schools redefine what we know as "teachers," and thus our norms and expectations will need to evolve as well.

Second, we will need to create a new research base. Serious, quantitative research formed the backbone of the Teacher Quality 1.0 agenda. The work of Eric Hanushek, Dan Goldhaber, Raj Chetty, and many others established the causal links between teacher quality and student success. A new generation of research, spearheaded by Harvard's Tom Kane and the Bill & Melinda Gates Foundation's Measures of Effective Teaching project are unpacking classroom practice in an attempt to measure different teaching practices for their impact on student learning. New schools and their new teaching roles have implications for understanding not only practice but how to effectively prepare, select, compensate, and retain individuals with the skills necessary to thrive in new schools.

Third, we will need to find new exemplars of innovation. No country in the world has mastered creating technology-rich or innovatively staffed schools. Paeans to Finland, South Korea, and Singapore are unhelpful, as most of their classrooms are still organized in what we would consider to be traditional ways. Where we find inspiration and new ideas will have to change as well.

The Book Ahead

This volume opens with an illustration of the risks of 1.0 policy making from Sara Mead and Andy Rotherham of Bellwether Education Partners, and Rachael Brown of District of Columbia Public Schools. The chapter describes the foundations of the 1.0 agenda and the risks posed by its swift adoption into long-standing policy. After establishing the context for the teacher quality 2.0 discussion, the book proceeds in two parts.

Part I explores how the 0.0 model of teaching might evolve. In chapter 2, Bryan Hassel, Emily Ayscue Hassel, and Sharon Kebschull Barrett of Public Impact describe schools that are using talent in innovative ways. In chapter 3, Michael DeArmond and Betheny Gross of the Center for Reinventing Public Education look at four high-performing schools across the charter and traditional public sectors to identify promising talent management practices and show how other schools can learn from them. Recognizing that 2.0 schools necessitate a different kind of teacher, Billie Gastic, director of research at Relay Graduate School of Education, explores in chapter 4 how we might build preparation programs that better equip teachers to excel in new environments. On the other end of the professional pipeline, Jal Mehta of Harvard University and Steven Teles of Johns Hopkins University conclude Part I by sketching a new vision for teacher professionalism that could better serve a more diverse landscape of schools.

In Part II, the contributing authors dig into the policy issues that intersect with the practices discussed in the first half of the book. Dennis Beck and Robert Maranto of the University of Arkansas offer in chapter 6 a perspective on how new teacher quality-driven policies might impact virtual schools through a case study of cyber charter schools in Pennsylvania. In chapter 7, Katharine Strunk of the University of Southern California shares the results of her survey of the provisions of more than five hundred California collective bargaining agreements, concluding with a discussion about how they could evolve to better accommodate new reforms. In chapter 8, Matthew Di Carlo of the Albert Shanker Institute takes a deep look into the world of value-added modeling: Now that there seems to be a widespread appetite to use them in the evaluation of teachers, how can we best use them and what are their limits? International education expert and University of Connecticut professor Jonathan Plucker asks in chapter 9 what we can learn from "innovative" approaches to talent management abroad. Finally, Dan Goldhaber of the University of Washington Bothell concludes the volume by outlining a next-generation teacher policy research agenda.

In concluding the volume, we highlight several recurring themes gleaned from the chapters and offer some concrete steps policy makers, school leaders, and philanthropists can take to help promote reform that does not stifle innovation.

PART I

From Teacher Quality 0.0 to Teacher Quality 2.0

CHAPTER 1

The Hangover

The Unintended Consequences of the Nation's Teacher Evaluation Binge

SARA MEAD, ANDREW ROTHERHAM,
AND RACHAEL BROWN

TEACHER EVALUATION IS HOT THESE DAYS. In the past two years, more than twenty states have passed legislation changing teacher evaluation systems to include evidence of teachers' impact on student achievement. This fevered pace of legislation was sparked by the federal Race to the Top (RTTT) program, which called on states to "design and implement rigorous, transparent, and fair evaluation systems for teachers and principals that differentiate effectiveness." And the Department of Education's Elementary and Secondary Education Act (ESEA) flexibility waiver process built momentum by demanding such policies as a condition for a waiver from No Child Left Behind (NCLB) requirements. Media attention has added to the clamor; newspapers in New York and Los Angeles even published individual teacher value-added ratings as major stories.

After years of policies that ignored differences in teacher effectiveness, the pendulum is swinging in the other direction. By and large, this is progress; research shows that teachers affect student achievement more than any other within-school factor. Decades of inattention to teacher performance have been costly for students, teachers, and the credibility of the teaching profession. Addressing this problem is critical to improving public education outcomes and raising the status of teaching, and neither the issues raised in this paper nor technical concerns about the design and mechanisms of evaluation systems should be viewed as reasons not to move toward a more performance-oriented public education culture that gives teachers meaningful feedback about the quality and impact of their work.

Yet the recent evaluation binge is not without risks. By nature, education policy making tends to lurch from inattention to over-reach. When a political moment appears, policy makers and advocates rush to quickly take advantage, knowing opportunities for real change are fleeting. This is understandable, and arguably necessary, given the nature of our political system. But headlong rushes inevitably produce unintended consequences—something akin to a policy hangover as ideas move from conception to implementation.

Welcome to teacher evaluation's morning after. States are beginning to design and implement ambitious statewide evaluation systems, and it is clear that many are struggling with technical and political challenges. On their list of challenges are systematically evaluating personnel for whom evaluations have long been cursory; incorporating value-added measures of student learning into evaluations for teachers in tested grades and subjects; grappling with the even greater challenge of how to measure impact on student learning for the majority of teachers who teach nontested grades and subjects; and coping with insufficient managerial capacity. In the process, many are running up against the limits of the carefully constructed systems that well-meaning policy wonks told them were critical to effective teacher evaluation systems.

And we are not even beginning to see the greatest of these challenges. The current range of teacher evaluation policies is designed for our education system as it currently exists, even as technological innovation, blended learning, and the growth of charter and portfolio models in many urban areas are fundamentally changing the way the system works. If we are not careful, new teacher evaluations will become another Ice Nine–like element in education, freezing in place what they touch and ultimately becoming as much of an impediment to progress as the old, inadequate systems they displaced.

The current attention to teacher evaluation is long overdue, and the nation has yet to wrestle honestly with the issue of teacher quality. Yet, one can acknowledge that and still worry about what is happening today. We do.

So how did we get here?

Historical Context

Current efforts to establish teacher evaluation systems must be understood as the most recent in a series of reforms—stretching back to the origins of public schooling—that sought to improve the quality of teaching in public schools. These historical efforts emphasized different indicators of teacher quality and mechanisms for improvement, but research suggests many of these mechanisms and indicators have little relationship to improved student learning. Proponents of new teacher evaluation systems fixated on these findings not because they "hate" teachers, as some suggest, but because the existing evidence indicates that teachers' actual performance in the classroom is a far better indicator of quality than the proxy indicators—certification, years of experience, postgraduate credentials—on which our educational system currently relies.

For over a century, efforts to improve the quality of teaching largely focused on a "professionalism" agenda, seeking to improve quality through increasing state regulation and formal training requirements for teacher certification and licensure.[1] Beginning in the 1980s, standards-based reformers also called for greater rigor in teacher preparation programs, which reformers argued placed too much emphasis on pedagogical theories and too little on ensuring teachers had deep content knowledge in the subjects they taught. Massachusetts, for example, enacted reforms that required all teachers to hold a major in a subject area rather than education and to pass rigorous licensure exams of communication and literacy skills and academic content knowledge.[2]

Building on this concern, NCLB also emphasizes teachers' subject matter content knowledge. The law's "highly qualified teacher" provisions require all teachers to hold a bachelor's degree and state licensure and to demonstrate knowledge of the subject they teach through a college major, by passing a certification exam, or, for veteran teachers, by meeting a state-defined "highly objective, uniform state standard of evaluation." These provisions were designed to ensure that teachers have subject matter knowledge in the subjects they teach, to reduce the rate of "out of field" teaching in middle and secondary schools, and to improve equity in the distribution of qualified teachers for poor and minority students. But while the "highly qualified teacher" provisions were designed with the best of intentions, they ultimately fell short, creating paperwork hoops for teachers and schools without necessarily improving the quality of instruction. Because the definition of a "highly qualified teacher" relies almost entirely on a teacher's subject matter knowledge, the standard does not guarantee teacher effectiveness in improving student achievement.[3] Similarly, reliance on the "highly qualified teacher" standard undercuts NCLB's provisions requiring states to ensure low-income and minority students equitable access to quality teachers.

Many indicators policy makers historically relied on as measures of teacher quality are, at best, very weak predictors of teachers' effectiveness in improving student learning. Indeed, studies that account for the range of characteristics perceived as external indicators of teacher quality indicate that these characteristics explain only a small percentage of the observed variation in teacher impact on student learning.[4] Research shows that holding a master's degree—a proxy for quality that most teacher compensation systems reward—has no positive correlation with improved student learning, with the exception of secondary math and science teachers who hold master's degrees in those subjects.[5] As this finding suggests, indicators of subject knowledge are correlated with improved effectiveness for some teachers, but content knowledge alone does not ensure teacher effectiveness. Research also shows that while experience does matter in teacher quality, the majority of teacher improvement comes in the first few years of teaching, and returns diminish beyond that point.[6] A wide body of research also finds little relationship between a teacher's licensure credentials and certification and her impact on student performance; the variation in effectiveness among teachers from the same preparation pathway is much greater than the difference between pathways.[7] Given the lack of evidence that many common indicators of quality actually correlate with improved performance, it is not surprising that the last century of teacher quality efforts has often proved disappointing.

But even as policy makers and advocates for low-income and minority students have grown disillusioned with NCLB's "highly qualified teacher" provisions and other policies that rely on teacher credentials, NCLB's annual testing requirements in grades 3–8 are generating abundant student achievement data that are transforming the national debate on teacher quality. Systems in a growing number of states link student achievement data to teachers, making it possible to calculate individual teachers' impact on student learning.

The Growth of Value-Added

Value-added measures of teacher effectiveness have been used to some extent for many years. In the early 1980s, two statisticians at the University of Tennessee, William Sanders and Robert McLean, experimented with statistical methodologies to better assess teacher and school effectiveness using data from Tennessee school districts. Their "value-added" method found that there are significant measurable differences in schools' and teachers' impacts on student learning, and estimates of school and teacher effectiveness tend to be consistent from year to year. Value-added research also showed that these differences could have significant implications for student learning, potentially large enough to meaningfully narrow or widen achievement gaps.[8]

In 1991, the Tennessee legislature passed the Education Improvement Act, which created a new statewide school accountability system, a major component of which was the Tennessee Value-Added Assessment System, based on Sanders' and McLean's work. This model had clear advantages for improving school and teacher accountability, yet it remained largely unknown outside of Tennessee and a small circle of education policy wonks for several years, in part because many states lacked the annual assessments and robust data-tracking systems needed to replicate the Tennessee model.[9]

- Instructional expertise (measured through formal classroom observations)
- Collaboration and commitment to school community
- Professionalism (which includes attendance, on-time arrival, following policies and procedures, and treating colleagues and students with respect).

For teachers in grades and subjects that take the DC assessment, impact on student achievement comprises 50 percent of a teacher's evaluation (35 percent based on value-added and 15 percent based on learning goals determined by a teacher and his or her principal). Professionalism is not scored, but failure to meet standards for professionalism can reduce a teacher's rating. Based on their performance, teachers are rated highly effective, effective, minimally effective, or ineffective.

These ratings have implications for both teachers' compensation and continued employment. Teachers who are rated highly effective can receive a bonus of up to $25,000; those who are rated as such for two consecutive years may receive a base pay increase of up to $20,000. Teachers rated as effective advance normally on the pay scale. Teachers rated minimally effective receive targeted professional development to help them improve, and those who do not improve after two years may be dismissed. Finally, teachers rated ineffective are subject to dismissal. With strong encouragement from the federal government, IMPACT became the model for a new wave of state and district teacher evaluation systems in states like Florida and Illinois.

The move toward new systems of teacher evaluation gained additional steam in July 2009, when the U.S. Department of Education released draft application guidelines for Race to the Top. RTTT was initially a $4.35 billion pot of money created as part of the $787 billion American Recovery and Reinvestment Act, which authorized the Department of Education to use RTTT funds to develop competitive grants to states making progress in four "assurance areas":

- Making progress toward rigorous college- and career-ready standards and high-quality assessments that are valid and reliable

for all students, including English language learners and students with disabilities
- Establishing pre-K to college and career data systems that track progress and foster continuous improvement
- Improving teacher effectiveness and equitable distribution of qualified teachers for all students, particularly the highest-need students
- Providing intensive support and effective interventions for the lowest-performing schools.

Within those parameters, the department had broad latitude to define specific application criteria and priorities for RTTT. It chose to use RTTT guidance to promote the development of new teacher evaluation systems that reflected recommendations in "The Widget Effect." The "Great Teachers and Leaders" component of RTTT accounted for more points than any other section of the application—more than one-quarter of the total. The largest component of that section (worth over 10 percent of the application) required states to articulate their plans for developing annual teacher and principal evaluation systems; include student achievement growth as a significant factor in teacher evaluations; differentiate teacher effectiveness in multiple categories; and use teacher evaluation results to inform key personnel decisions, including professional development, compensation, promotion, retention, tenure, certification, and dismissal. The department also stipulated within RTTT that any state that established statutory barriers to using student achievement data in teacher evaluation was ineligible to compete.[14]

RTTT instigated a flurry of state activity around teacher evaluation.[15] By the first round of applications in early 2010, eleven states passed legislation to eliminate statutory barriers to using student achievement data in teacher evaluations, established new standards for school and district teacher evaluations, or created new state teacher evaluation systems.[16] Additional states followed in the next two years, bringing the total to more than twenty by the end of 2012. Other states accomplished similar results through regulatory action. To support states in establishing teacher evaluation policies that met RTTT criteria, TNTP published "Teacher Evaluation 2.0," a report drawing on extant research to outline six key design features for teacher evaluation systems, including:[17]

1. Annual (at least) evaluations, including evaluations of veteran teachers
2. Clear, rigorous expectations that prioritize student learning
3. Multiple measures of performance, primarily the teacher's impact on student academic growth
4. Multiple rating levels (at least four) with clear descriptions and expectations at each level
5. Frequent observations and ongoing constructive critical feedback
6. Use in employment decisions, including bonuses, tenure, compensation, promotion, and dismissal.

These features became the grammar of the evaluation conversation; most of the recent state laws overhauling teacher evaluation requirements reflect them. But as multiple ratings of state teacher evaluation laws show, the degree of reflection depends on the state.[18] The focus of each rating varies, but all reflect the six design principles articulated in "Teacher Evaluation 2.0." Further, some of them go well beyond the six design principals, specifying how state teacher evaluation systems should address a number of topics, including teacher input in evaluation development, choosing evaluators, and appeal or mediation processes.

Most recently, the U.S. Department of Education's ESEA flexibility waiver process, which allows states to request a waiver of key NCLB provisions, requires states applying for a waiver to commit to "develop, adopt, pilot, and implement" teacher and principal evaluation systems that

- Evaluate educators on a regular basis
- Support instructional improvement
- Differentiate performance using at least three levels
- Incorporate multiple measures of educator performance, including student growth as a significant factor

- Provide clear, timely, and useful feedback to inform professional development
- Inform personnel decisions.

States applying for a waiver must develop and adopt guidelines for these systems and require local educational agencies to develop and implement evaluation systems that comply with those guidelines.[19] Given frustrations with NCLB, the waiver requirements create a powerful incentive for states to adopt new teacher evaluation requirements aligned with federal guidelines, making it likely that "Teacher Evaluation 2.0" will increasingly displace "The Widget Effect" as the norm for teacher evaluation throughout the country over the next few years.

Tensions and Trade-Offs

Recent state and district policy changes are leading to new evaluation systems that have the potential to provide teachers more useful feedback about their performance, inform professional development, and ultimately improve teacher practice. The information these systems produce can also help policy makers address persistent inequities in teacher distribution; improve the quality of pre-service teacher preparation; better align compensation and resource allocation decisions to what matters most for student learning; identify, reward, and retain high performers through meaningful career ladders; and identify and remediate underperforming teachers and, when necessary, exit them from the system. In short, improved teacher evaluation policies and systems have much to offer.

That said, much of the teacher evaluation debate is framed in either-or terms that obscure, rather than illuminate, real tensions inherent in these efforts. Too often the choices presented are to adopt policies that mandate the six "Teacher Evaluation 2.0" design elements across all schools and districts or to defend teacher evaluation systems that rate nearly everyone "satisfactory" and, therefore, provide little useful feedback.

Debates about teacher evaluation tend to veer between the technical (implementation, issues with the validity and stability of value-added measures, or evaluating teachers in nontested grades and subjects) and the ideological (the fairness of holding teachers accountable for student learning, the extent to which test scores truly measure their most important contributions). But the emphasis on technical and ideological questions elides fundamental tensions and trade-offs in the development of teacher evaluation systems, which deserve greater consideration than they currently receive. Here we address four key tensions of the new generation of teacher evaluation systems—flexibility versus control, the role of teacher evaluation in an evolving education system, how evaluations are designed and used, and what it means to evaluate teachers as professionals—and discuss two models, developed independently from current state policy reforms, that encompass many elements of "Teacher Evaluation 2.0" but also serve to illustrate what may be lost if states implement evaluation system requirements without caution.

FLEXIBILITY VERSUS CONTROL

Tensions related to centralization, flexibility, and control of key decisions are inherent in the structure of our education system, which vests multiple levels of government—school district, state, federal—with the power to influence what happens in schools and classrooms. Over time, policy approaches have oscillated between emphasizing centralization as a means of quality control and prioritizing flexibility to place decision making with those closest to the child. During the Progressive Era, for example, reformers sought to centralize decision making at the state and urban district level; decades later, site-based management and charter school reforms sought to devolve power to school-level leaders. These shifts reflect the tension between recognition that school- and local-level leaders often have the best insight into their specific needs and skepticism of those leaders' ability or will to make the right decisions.

Flexibility and control are not inherently in tension. It is possible for state and federal policies to be, to borrow Secretary of Education Arne Duncan's formulation, "tight" in defining accountability and outcomes goals for schools and "loose" on the specifics of how they get there. In practice, though, it can be difficult to delineate exactly where the boundary falls between the ends and means.

Teacher evaluation is a clear demonstration. On one hand, the recent emphasis on teacher evaluations seems like a shift in a tight-loose direction: pay less attention to teachers' training and other characteristics and instead focus on their results in the classroom. On the other hand, mandates that teacher evaluations include specific design elements may be overly prescriptive. Several states, for example, have gone beyond "Teacher Evaluation 2.0" and the federal RTTT and waiver guidelines and now require school districts to adopt teacher evaluations that employ a state-defined specific teacher evaluation system. Federal waiver criteria require only that states create guidelines for teacher evaluation systems and ensure local school districts implement systems that meet those guidelines, but states such as Delaware and South Carolina adopted a single statewide system required for all districts. It is one thing to stipulate that districts' teacher evaluation systems must include student achievement data, meaningful observations, and multiple differentiated levels of performance; it is another to mandate the tools used for observing teachers and analyzing performance data.

RIGID SYSTEMS RESTRICT FLEXIBILITY

States that mandate statewide teacher evaluation systems have good reason, as illustrated in "The Widget Effect," to be skeptical that districts, left to their own devices, will adopt or implement rigorous evaluation systems. Moreover, getting this more rigorous teacher evaluation right is a complicated business, as evidenced by the struggles of front-runner states like Tennessee and Delaware, and many districts lack the capacity or resources to do so without state support and guidance.

But policies that deny districts the freedom to be bad actors can also restrict their flexibility to innovate in ways that make these systems work better. If a school or district has already invested in a particular framework of quality instructional practice, requiring them to adopt a statewide rubric that is not fully aligned to that framework may be counterproductive.

Casting this tension in sharp relief is the juxtaposition—in both RTTT and ESEA waiver guidance—of teacher evaluation provisions with those intended to expand access to public charter schools and streamline state regulatory burden on schools. Charter schools are independent public schools of choice that, in many states, are granted broad flexibility from regulatory requirements in exchange for accountability. Charters often have more flexibility than traditional schools and districts in personnel matters, such as dismissing underperforming teachers. State teacher evaluation policies that mandate certain parameters could infringe on charters' historical freedom in personnel matters. Existing exemptions from state regulations may exempt charter schools from new evaluation requirements, but federal ESEA waiver requirements seem to discourage this practice.

The ESEA waiver guidance states that a state education agency "must develop and adopt guidelines for these systems" and that local education agencies (LEAs) "must develop and implement teacher and principal evaluation and support systems that are consistent with the SEA's guidelines."[20] Local education agencies typically are school districts, but in many states charter schools are also their own LEAs, so this waiver language appears to suggest that charter schools must also adopt evaluation systems consistent with state guidelines. In the District of Columbia, for example, the Office of the State Superintendent of Education initially prepared an ESEA waiver request stating that all LEAs in the district would adopt teacher evaluations meeting state education guidelines—even though 95 percent of the LEAs in the District are charter schools, and the District's charter school law gives the education superintendent no authority to mandate that they adopt such systems. In Florida, teacher unions decried a new evaluation law as an assault on due process. But, because the law applied to charter as well as traditional district schools, it actually subjected charters to more complicated evaluation and due process requirements than before.

The problem with these requirements is not simply that they interfere with charter autonomy. They could also jeopardize sophisticated human capital systems that some high-performing charter schools developed using their autonomy over personnel. These systems, which predate the current push for new systems of teacher evaluation, integrate teacher evaluation, development, and performance-based compensation with the school's instructional philosophy and culture in ways that may not fit into state requirements for more uniform evaluation systems.

POLITICAL DYNAMICS CREATE INCENTIVES FOR GREATER CONTROL

Policy makers and advocates who favor new teacher evaluation systems recognize that they are operating in a unique political moment, when a Democratic presidential administration and Republican governors and legislative majorities in many states favor substantial changes to current teacher evaluation policies. Further, unusual circumstances such as the RTTT contest and state demands for relief from ESEA requirements have provided this administration with unprecedented leverage to drive state policy changes, even in states with reluctant leadership. This unique—and clearly limited—political opportunity incents champions of teacher certification overhaul to design new policies that lock in as much of their agenda as possible before the window closes. Policy makers are working to mandate many key design features of teacher evaluation systems (see, for example, the detailed provisions of Florida's Senate Bill 736) rather than legislating broad parameters that leave space for district variation. As a result, policy makers tend to put key provisions in legislation rather than regulation—even when regulation may be a better vehicle for addressing many complex issues involved in teacher evaluation—because legislation is more difficult to change down the road.

While the political incentives are obvious, there is a real danger that, in seeking to lock in the most "rigorous" standards for teacher evaluation systems, policy makers and advocates may simply be locking in the current state-of-the-art teacher evaluation knowledge. Policy makers need to take action, but they also need to be willing to evolve—to learn from the results of the policies they put in place and to make adjustments as results demand. Legislating key design elements in an effort to protect them limits future policy makers' ability to adapt policies in response to the new knowledge that will inevitably emerge as teacher evaluation systems are implemented and studied, or as our education system itself evolves in other key respects.

EVALUATION IN AN EVOLVING SYSTEM

Teacher evaluation policies do not exist in a vacuum. Other forces are currently transforming our education system in ways that have implications for the design and use of teacher evaluations and that could create real challenges if policy makers do not take those implications into account.

Technological innovation, for example, is already beginning to reshape our understanding of what schooling looks like—and with it, the work teachers do. Blended learning models, such as Rocketship, Carpe Diem, and School of One, leverage technology to deliver education in new ways that may increase educational productivity and personalization to individual student needs. Blended learning models vary in design, approach, costs, and the extent to which technology enables teachers to be deployed in new ways. These models fundamentally change the way teachers do their jobs; teachers spend less time on traditional lecture and more time working with students one-on-one or in small groups, analyzing data to diagnose student needs, and crafting instructional experiences to meet them. Student groupings in these models are more fluid, and students receive instruction and tutoring from a variety of teachers as well as from technology-based modalities. As a result, it can be difficult or impossible in some of these models to attribute student learning gains in a subject to a particular teacher, which creates complications for teacher evaluation systems that rely on linking teachers to their students' academic results. Existing observational rubrics, such as those included in the Gates-funded Measures of Effective Teaching project and being adopted by states and districts, were not designed for the more personalized modalities in which blended learning educators often deliver instruction.

Nor is blended learning the only force increasing the number of teachers whose students do not have state test scores. Over the past decade, states and school districts have dramatically expanded the number of children they serve in early childhood and pre-K programs—a trend that is likely to continue once states and districts rebound from the recent recession. Early childhood students do not take state assessments, and because of the low adult-child ratios necessary in early childhood classrooms, preschool teachers often work in co-teaching settings that make it difficult to attribute students' progress to an individual teacher.

In other words, trends in education innovation will likely dramatically increase the number of teachers whose work does not directly map onto the state assessment performance of a specific, identifiable group. The greatest challenge facing most states currently seeking to implement new teacher evaluation systems is how to evaluate student achievement gains for teachers in grades and subjects not covered by NCLB's mandate to annually assess every student in grades 3–8 in math and English language arts. The experience of Tennessee, winner of $500 million in RTTT's first round and the birthplace of value-added measures, is a good example.

Tennessee has struggled to identify appropriate measures of student growth for the more than half of Tennessee teachers who work in nontested grades and subjects. Initially, these teachers' impact on student achievement was scored using school-wide value-added data in math and reading, a move Tennessee teachers and outside observers have criticized.[21] Delaware, which received $120 million during the first round of RTTT, has also struggled to identify "student growth measures" for grades and subjects not subject to state testing and, as a result, delayed implementation of teacher and leader evaluation systems based on those measures.[22]

Blended learning models decouple the link between an individual student's progress and an individual teacher, but this does not mean blended learning teachers cannot be held accountable for their impact on student learning. Teachers at the Florida Virtual School, for example, are paid only if their online students complete their courses. Because blended learning teachers work collaboratively in teams with shifting groups of students and constantly collect and assess data on students' progress, there is more transparency for their work than for more traditional teachers. The data analysis and collaborative teaching that occur in blended learning situations actually open the door for entirely new forms of teacher performance evaluation that are still tightly linked to impact on students but look very different from the 1.5 models.

Unless state policies provide for additional flexibility around teacher evaluation in blended learning and other innovative approaches to schooling, we will miss out on the opportunity to develop these new forms of evaluation. More troubling, teacher evaluation requirements could become a barrier to the expansion of blended learning models or to the development of new models combining in-person teaching with technology and other delivery mechanisms to personalize student learning experiences. Charter school authorizers may be unwilling to approve schools using new models if those schools cannot explain how they will comply with state teacher evaluation laws.

EVALUATING TEACHERS AS PROFESSIONALS?

Efforts to establish new teacher evaluation systems are often accompanied by heated disputes about their impact on the standing of the teaching profession. Advocates argue that holding teachers responsible for their performance will bring teaching more in line with norms in other fields. Advocates also maintain that new evaluations will raise the status of the profession by encouraging dismissal of poor teachers who give teaching a bad name and facilitating the implementation of performance-based compensation programs that increase salaries for the most effective teachers. Critics of new evaluation systems argue that mechanistic teacher evaluations based on test scores and rubrics are demeaning and neglect the nuanced art that goes into teachers' work. Both sides have a point.

New teacher evaluation systems are an attempt to affect attitudes on human capital in education. The current industrial-era model treats all workers as interchangeable parts; the goal is a more performance- and talent-sensitive orientation along the lines of law, medicine, and other professions. The title of "The Widget Effect" alludes to this. Gordon, Kane, and Staiger also argue that increased accountability for student achievement will ultimately improve the status of teaching and attract more skilled people to the field.[23]

Some features of 1.5 teacher evaluation systems, however, are very different from evaluation norms in other professions. Most professional fields, including business, medicine, and law, rely on a combination of data and managerial judgment for personnel decisions and subsequently hold managers accountable for those decisions. Methods that lack human discretion are rare. Indeed, far from eliminating subjective feedback from personnel evaluation, many firms have moved to adopt 360-degree feedback mechanisms in which employees receive feedback from managers, direct reports, peers, and clients. Others combine objective quantitative measures—such as dollars or clients brought into the firm—with more subjective performance indicators. 1.5 policies, in contrast, seek to minimize the role of managerial judgment by relying on "objective" value-added data, common rubrics, and third-party evaluators. In contrast to other fields, these systems seek to minimize opportunities for managers and educators to provide meaningful development feedback to their direct reports and peers.

There are clear tensions around using human judgment in teacher evaluations. As is often the case in education, politics and mistrust exacerbate the challenge of designing evaluation systems. The current emphasis on objective data and rubrics, as well as third-party evaluators, is in large part a response to the opposition of teacher unions and associations to past evaluation and performance pay initiatives that were viewed as giving principals too much managerial discretion. No one wants a system in which employees are at the whim of arbitrary managerial judgments, but some labor concerns reflect a pre-union, pre–civil rights era when employees lacked many of the protections against discrimination and arbitrary dismissal that exist today—and that will continue to exist regardless of changes in evaluation systems or policies. Moreover, the best protection against arbitrary or biased managerial judgment is not to eliminate that judgment altogether but to ensure that the managers themselves are also held accountable for performance.

In designing value-added systems, policy makers should consider whether the design elements they put in place move education away from or toward professional norms in similar fields.

For example, design decisions are currently driven in large part by concerns about whether evaluation systems can withstand legal challenges to dismissal of the worst teachers—a legitimate focus in systems that convey a property interest in continued employment on tenured teachers. But the result is that design elements that support professional improvement become secondary.

Human judgment is critical to making smart assessments of teacher performance and to using those assessments in ways that improve instruction. Given the limitations of our current value-added and observational rubric tools, evaluation systems that rely on them will almost certainly result in nonnegligible numbers of both Type I (false positive) and Type II (false negative) errors. That is not an argument against using these tools (our current system, in which more than 99 percent of teachers are rated satisfactory, yields few false positives but likely many false negatives) but an argument for providing space for human judgment to intervene when such errors seem obvious, along with the right incentives and capacity building to encourage sound managerial judgment.

By the same token, building evaluation and professional growth systems that develop teachers as professionals is impossible without providing space for human judgment and feedback apart from purely objective and impersonal mechanisms. New evaluation systems, particularly those including student growth data, are being billed as the panacea to public education's talent management problems. School cultures traditionally discourage candid conversations about performance, and school leaders fail to take responsibility for difficult personnel decisions. Well-designed teacher evaluation systems give principals a tool to enable these conversations, making them more accountable for having them and reducing some current barriers to dismissing low performers, but evaluations alone cannot transform a culture that is so resistant to frank discussions of performance. The culture and capacity for feedback become particularly important when we consider that the purpose of new evaluation systems is not just to dismiss low-performing teachers but to help all teachers improve their professional practice and performance.

Conclusion

Because there are real trade-offs and tensions in the design and use of teacher evaluation systems, we need flexible systems that can adapt to circumstances and changes over time. It is critical to transparently engage policy makers, educators, and the broader public in conversations about trade-offs rather than glossing over them. Such conversations can provide an opportunity for input about the priorities policy makers should take into account when designing teacher evaluation systems, and in the process can build public and educator understanding and trust in those systems. There are several key implications for policy makers to consider.

Be clear about the pain points. Policy makers need to be clear about the problems teacher evaluation systems intend to solve. Right now, teacher evaluations are too often marketed as an educational wonder drug without a clear plan for how evaluation results will translate into improved teaching or what system elements are necessary to foster effective teaching. Policy makers must be clear about the problems they are trying to address, their goals, and their theory of action, and they must make design choices and trade-offs that reflect that theory of action.

Do not treat processes and systems as a substitute for cultural change. Policy makers rely heavily on new teacher evaluation systems and the processes they mandate to improve teacher effectiveness, but teaching is ultimately a people business, and getting improvements in teacher effectiveness, whether through professional improvement or deselection, will require human judgment and interaction and deep cultural change within our educational system. Processes cannot do it alone! Teacher evaluation systems and processes can help facilitate this cultural shift by setting clear expectations, creating language and venues within a school to talk about performance, and empowering leaders to confront or dismiss low performers. Other elements, however, such as meaningful outcomes accountability, competitive pressure, and new approaches to training, are also needed to foster a culture that takes performance seriously.

Look at the entire ecosystem. Policy makers must pay attention to the ways in which teacher evaluation systems relate to other

components of the education ecosystem. How will new evaluation requirements affect the teacher labor market, principal training, and teacher preparation? Further, as policy changes increase
high-stakes individual accountability for teachers, in some cases
they simultaneously reduce school-level accountability, and the
direction of new state accountability systems under ESEA waiver
requests is not always well aligned with states' educator accountability proposals. This is unwise. Strong school-level accountability
is essential to effective teacher evaluations and must be aligned with
them. Well-designed and aligned school- and system-level accountability create the right incentives for school-level leaders; they can
reduce the need for excessive state control on teacher evaluations
and create space for more judgment.

Encourage and respect innovation. Education has a long history of
"one best system" thinking that leads to policies that freeze in amber
the current state of the art, curtailing innovation and rendering the
system unable to adapt to changing needs and challenges. It would
be a mistake to bring this "one best system" thinking to teacher
evaluations. A better model to emulate might be the approach taken
by law or other professional services firms where there are some
clear commonalities in operations, norms, and performance expectations, but evaluation and accountability metrics reflect diversity
in what is valued most. Similarly, policy makers must ensure that
evaluation requirements do not curtail existing autonomies. Charter schools, for instance, should be held accountable to their authorizers for their outcomes, rather than bound by new evaluation
requirements that curtail their autonomy in personnel matters.

Think carefully about waivers versus umbrellas. One potential
strategy to prevent new teacher evaluation systems from stifling
innovation is to enable innovative providers to gain an exemp-
tion to teacher evaluation requirements if they demonstrate strong
performance or well-designed alternative teacher evaluation and
development mechanisms. Relatively few states have built such
well-designed waivers into their teacher effectiveness legislation,
and those that have not would be well advised to do so. At the
same time, policy makers need to think carefully about whether it
is possible, and perhaps smarter in the long run, to design teacher

evaluation policies with a broad umbrella that can cover both traditional and innovative models. The answer to this question likely depends on one's assumptions about the potential scale of blended learning and other innovative models and the speed at which they will grow, as well as how different teaching arrangements in these models are likely to be from traditional schools.

Do not send legislation to do a regulation's job. In a rush to institutionalize, reformers have turned to laws to protect reforms. Laws are obviously more durable than regulations, and the legislative process can, although not always, build greater buy-in from stakeholders. But legislation can also lock in policies that should be tweaked or even overhauled. Because the old model of evaluation was so ubiquitous and we are only beginning to experiment with alternative models, there are many things we do not know, and implementation of different models is likely to yield considerable learning about what does and does not work in different contexts. What can and should be handled in legislation versus regulation varies with state context, but, in general, policy makers should try to avoid locking in legislation components of evaluation systems for which implementation is likely to provide important lessons about how to do things better.

Create innovation zones for pilots—and fund them. Within the overall context of federal and state policy, there must be room for school districts, consortia of school districts, or even entire states to try new approaches. Federal dollars from Title II of the ESEA and the Teacher Incentive Fund can support innovative projects to try alternative teacher evaluation methods that combine quantitative and qualitative methods or are designed specifically for new education delivery models. In keeping with its role in fostering research and innovation, the federal government should not simply require states to establish new teacher evaluation policies but should simultaneously provide waivers and investments to support state, local, and charter school innovations that meet certain standards for rigor and protection of civil rights.

Public education in the United States has for too long lacked a performance mind-set or a strategic orientation toward developing human capital. The current move toward new teacher evaluation systems represents significant progress to correct these shortcomings. That said, if advocates of 1.5 teacher evaluation rush too quickly to create new systems or do so without appropriate humility about what we do and do not know, there is a risk that they will end up replacing old broken systems with new ones that, while better, are equally inflexible or create barriers to innovation and reform. In other words, the nation's teacher evaluation spree could turn into a big headache. The best way to mitigate this risk is not to ignore it or brush it under the rug but to be honest and transparent about the trade-offs and tensions, the reality that new systems will not be perfect, and the need to learn as we move forward.

PART II

Elements of a New System

CHAPTER 2

Staffing Design

The Missing Key to Teacher Quality 2.0

BRYAN C. HASSEL, EMILY AYSCUE HASSEL,
AND SHARON KEBSCHULL BARRETT

F OR ALL THE CONTROVERSY that rages about teacher quality and
policies needed to improve it, combatants rarely engage in any
debate about one thing: the basic staffing design of America's public schools. While there are exceptions, schools follow a pattern
of staffing design that is familiar to all of us as parents, teachers, and, in the near or distant past, students. At the elementary
level, schools divide students into classrooms of, say, twenty or
twenty-five students, with a single teacher in charge of all of the
core subjects for a given classroom of students. At the secondary
level, teachers specialize by subject but, again, are assigned sole
responsibility for a set of classes within their disciplines. At both
levels, personnel with titles like "literacy coach" or "math facilitator" are not responsible for any particular classroom, supporting
willing classroom teachers as they do their work.

The standard model creates two large challenges for reformers
and for school or district administrators who want to dramatically
improve the quality of teaching in schools. First, the only way to get
traction in the teacher quality quest is to change the composition of
the teacher workforce. Since about 25 percent of teachers are what
we call "excellent teachers," delivering well over a year's worth of
growth and the higher-order thinking skills that students need to
close achievement gaps and leap ahead, then leaders' only hope is
to move that number from 25 percent upward. They can recruit and

select candidates more effectively. They can identify chronic low performers more quickly and dismiss them. They can do a better job with professional development for their teachers. And they can increase the rate of retention of their excellent teachers.

But when we created models in which schools succeed fantastically on all these fronts, it became clear that even significantly better recruiting, professional development, low performer dismissal, and high performer retention would not come close to putting an excellent teacher in every classroom. Specifically, if the nation succeeded in attracting fifty thousand more new teachers each year who ended up as effective as today's top 25 percent, tripled the dismissal rate of ineffective teachers, and doubled the retention rate of excellent teachers, even after five years the number of classrooms with excellent teachers in charge would rise from 25 percent to just 40 percent. Most students would still have less-than-excellent teachers.[1]

And that leads to the second challenge the current staffing model creates: schools and districts struggling to "succeed fantastically" in changing the composition of the teaching workforce. For example, one natural way to think about making the profession more attractive to high-potential candidates and high-performing teachers would be to increase their pay. Average teacher pay per hour has increased only 11 percent in the past forty years, as did teachers' work hours—effectively leaving pay flat.[2] But raising pay would be phenomenally expensive if staffing models remain constant. With 3.2 million teachers, raising pay across the board by just $1,000 would cost $3.2 billion annually. Boosting it by the tens of thousands likely needed to fundamentally change the recruiting and retention picture in our economy seems unthinkable in most any fiscal climate.

Another primary lever organizations use to attract and keep talent—career advancement opportunities—is also highly constrained by the one-teacher-one-classroom model. The only way to advance in most schools is to relinquish responsibility for students' learning by becoming an administrator or a supporter of classroom teachers. In contrast to most other professions that are replete with opportunities to advance by leading teams, specializing, or taking on more challenging assignments while still practicing one's craft, teaching is one of the few professions in which one must essentially keep doing the same job throughout a career or leave the job altogether.

A final lever that is difficult to pull in the standard model is professional development. In theory, the standard model could produce much better teaching quality if existing teachers received much-improved professional learning. But in a model where each teacher works largely solo, without much regular observation and feedback or the time or opportunity to see excellent peers in action, professional development is inherently constrained. The kind of job-embedded, daily professional learning that experts seem to agree is most effective in education—and that's common in other professions—is hard to come by in the one-teacher-one-classroom setting.

This situation leaves advocates for improving teaching quality with a fundamental unresolved dilemma. To boost teacher quality significantly within the existing model, reforms need to transform who enters teaching, who stays, and how professional learning happens on a daily basis. Otherwise, the vast majority of classrooms will continue to be led by teachers who do not produce the year-plus learning growth students need. But transforming who enters, who stays, and how professional learning happens is nearly impossible given the way schools are configured.

New Thinking about Staffing Design

This tough reality has prompted many practitioners, scholars, and other commentators to call for new ways of thinking about school staffing design. Frederick Hess has questioned the "people everywhere" approach schools and systems tend to take in the face of nearly every challenge in education and suggested ways of "unbundling" the teacher role to enable individuals to be more effective. The National Network of State Teachers of the Year has called for new "career continuums" for U.S. teachers that enable teachers to take on new roles over their careers. The National Education Association's Policy Statement on Digital Learning explained that "our traditional school models are not capable of meeting the needs of the 21st century student." Teach Plus's Boston Teacher Policy

Fellows developed the idea of Teacher Turnaround Teams, which sends a team of trained, excellent teachers into a struggling school to play leadership roles in the turnaround effort. Barnett Berry, CEO of the Center for Teaching Quality, and his collaborators have explored varieties of "teacherpreneurship," hybrid roles in which teachers can teach part time and perform other roles with the rest of their workdays. Researchers Jane Coggshall, Molly Lasagna, and Sabrina Laine call for "neo-differentiated staffing," which "unpacks and reassigns the many jobs of a teacher" so that "educators can focus on their strengths and function with greater effectiveness as teams."[3]

We have written about new models that "extend the reach" of excellent teachers to more students, for more pay, within available budgets.[4] Here, we focus on that set of ideas because they present a way to boost teaching quality by replacing the traditional school staffing model with something different: extended-reach teaching roles that increase pay sustainably, provide on-the-job development in teams, give great teachers clear accountability for more students and the authority to lead, and let schools become more selective about who teaches.[5] In this section we describe these designs and in the next section give three examples of district and charter schools putting the designs to work. In the final section we delve into some of the policy issues faced by leaders seeking to implement models like these, especially in district schools.

Models that enable excellent teachers to reach more students, for more pay, can be grouped into five categories:[6]

- *Multi-classroom leadership.* In multi-classroom leadership, teacher-leaders bring excellence to multiple classrooms by leading teams. Of course, some schools already have grade-level or department leaders, but rarely do these teachers have accountability for other teachers' student outcomes, authority to select and evaluate peers, and enhanced pay that is sustainably funded. With full accountability for all students in a pod of classrooms and explicit authority to lead teams, multi-classroom teacher-leaders have an enormous incentive to develop other teachers and help them discover and use their strengths. This kind of fully accountable mentoring—with the leader ultimately responsible for team outcomes—is very common in other professions but rare in teaching (though it has proved quite popular in pilot schools using these models).

- *Specialization.* At the elementary level, teachers specialize in their best subjects or subject pairs—math and science or language arts and social studies, for example. Meanwhile, paraprofessionals take care of students during lunch, recess, and transitions, developing their social and behavioral skills and completing noninstructional paperwork. Some elementary schools are already "departmentalized," but they typically employ the same number of teachers as they would under a conventional staffing model. Where a traditional grade level might have four teachers and one hundred students, a reconfigured grade level might have three teachers—one teaching everyone math and science and the other two each teaching literacy and social studies.

  At the secondary level, of course, teachers already specialize by subject. But they could specialize further within their disciplines in order to reach more students. Excellent writing teachers, for example, could teach writing to far more students if they did not have to spread their time across the whole language arts curriculum. Teachers could also specialize by role, focusing on large-group instruction, project supervision, or other aspects of the teaching job at which they excel, and teach more students than they would in the traditional model. With paraprofessionals doing administrative paperwork, supervising some of students' skill practice and independent project time, and performing some routine instructional tasks, both elementary and secondary teachers can free their time to reach more students, collaborate in teams, and focus on the most challenging elements of instruction.

- *Time-technology swaps.* In time-technology swaps, students spend a portion of time learning digitally—as little as an hour daily. This lets teachers teach more students, for higher pay, without reducing personalized, higher-order instructional time. If scheduled correctly, teachers gain planning and collaboration time, too. At the secondary level in particular, schools manage teachers' total student loads by making smart decisions about how many additional classes, and of what size, each teacher has. Some schools are increasing excellent teachers' reach while *reducing* the size of groups that teachers have at a given time. And in some versions of this approach, the very idea of the "classroom" is undone, with students working in ever-changing groups based on their current needs.[7]

- *Class-size changes.* One option is to allow willing excellent teachers to teach more students for more pay. How many more is a nuanced decision for the teacher and school and would depend on the students' ages and other needs. The averages of high-performing nations with larger class sizes would be one potential outside limit. Schools could move toward larger classes for all teachers while increasing hiring rigor and classroom-management skills, with increased paraprofessional support for teachers with large student loads. Or they could shift small numbers of students into classes of willing, consistently excellent teachers, which would give other teachers smaller classes, such as new teachers or others who, for whatever reason, would benefit from fewer students. Of course, many teachers already volunteer to take larger classes, but they don't earn extra pay for it, as they would in other professions. As we note later, sites implementing reach models to date have chosen other models that break free of this one-teacher-one-class model and enable more teamwork and on-the-job-development; class-size changes, however, require minimal scheduling and administrative change.

- *Remote teaching.* An excellent, in-person teacher may always be best, if one is available. But some schools have critical shortages of teachers in some subjects—higher-level math and languages are common—or shortages of *excellent* teachers in many subjects. Technology, such as webcams and interactive whiteboards, lets teachers teach students who live anywhere, from anywhere. This kind of live but not in-person interaction essentially warms up and personalizes the growing prevalence of purely online learning. With remote teaching, an excellent, accountable teacher ensures that each student is learning well, even if students are spending some of their time learning digitally with videos or software. No student should lack an excellent teacher just because of where he or she lives.

Each of these models can help schools address the first big challenge facing the traditional model: the unlikelihood of reaching all classrooms with excellent teachers. Even if (inevitably) only a fraction of a school's teachers are as strong as the top 25 percent of teachers, that fraction can potentially reach all the students in the school through these models. While in the traditional model the notion of "a great teacher in every classroom" is largely a bumper sticker–style aspiration, schools thinking creatively about "reach" may in fact be able to place a great teacher in charge of every student's learning—either directly or by leading a team and being accountable for all of the team's students' results.

The models also have the potential to address the other big challenge: the unlikelihood of making the profession dramatically more attractive to high-caliber candidates and performers. These models address all four elements that the conventional staffing model is hard-pressed to offer, thereby creating what we call an Opportunity Culture.

- *Dramatically higher, sustainable pay.* Each model is designed to produce some kind of savings. Generally, most of these savings come from one of two sources: (1) the use of paraprofessionals, who earn less than teachers, to carry out functions that teachers do not need to fulfill; and (2) the shift of nonclassroom specialists (literacy coaches, math facilitators, etc., though not special education or English language learner specialists) into higher-paid roles where they are accountable for a specific set of students—for example, by serving as multi-classroom leaders. The savings from these shifts make it possible to pay the teachers taking on these extended-reach roles substantially more within existing funding structures. Teachers instructing more students directly can earn 20–40 percent more; teachers leading multi-classroom pods can double their pay.[8] Teachers on teams led by excellent teachers could *all* earn more under these models, even when team leaders' pay increases more than 65 percent. And pay could be raised even further if districts reallocated spending from other functions to pay teachers more. Because the funding for the added pay comes from school-level savings, it can be sustained over time in a way that pay supplements funded by special grants or other temporary sources cannot. This means teachers can count on them, making them a more potent tool for recruitment and retention.

- *Enhanced career opportunities.* Each model also creates a path for teachers to advance in their careers without leaving classroom teaching and directly increases the number of students a teacher reaches each year. A multi-classroom leader, for example, could lead larger and larger pods of team members and students. As a teacher becomes more proficient at blending her instruction with digital learning, she could reach more students successfully. Specialists can reach increasing numbers of students directly or take on multi-classroom leadership to increase their reach further. And so on. A district or charter network using a combination of these models could offer teachers not just a route out of the classroom (as in the traditional model), release time for temporary leadership roles (often without extra pay), or a single "ladder" up, as we see in some districts trying to create new teacher roles, but instead a diverse range of ways to move ahead and earn more while remaining a teacher.[9]

- *Real opportunities for all teachers to develop on the job.* These models, especially multi-classroom leadership, also have the potential to improve on the often weak professional development typical in U.S. public schools. Professional learning is too often disconnected from daily practice, with teachers attending workshops or, increasingly, going online to seek help from peers teaching elsewhere. And within the traditional model, individual teachers are largely the only ones accountable for their own development. While they may have a coach or mentor, this person is likely someone who is available to help but who ultimately is not responsible for the teachers he coaches, much less their students. This setup stands in marked contrast to most other professional settings, where excellent performers advance by leading teams and adding paraprofessional support explicitly to save time. Organized into teams, professionals have powerful incentives to attend to one another's development, since their success hinges in large part on their teammates' capabilities. And the team leader feels that incentive most acutely; a well-developed team is a high-performing team. Multi-classroom leadership of teams could bring the same drive for development into the daily routines of K–12 classrooms.

* *Selectivity.* When models require fewer teachers to reach a given number of students, and when career advancement and pay opportunity are plentiful, schools can be more selective in their hiring. Like the world's top education systems, which draw entirely from the top 30 percent of their graduates, states and districts could become selective about who can teach.[10]

New Staffing Models in Practice

We profile three different efforts to put new staffing models into practice, two charter networks and a school district reform initiative.

ROCKETSHIP EDUCATION

Rocketship Education is a network of public charter elementary schools in San Jose, California, and Milwaukee, Wisconsin, with plans to expand to other states and serve at least twenty-five thousand students by 2017.

The network has shown strong results, becoming the top public school system in California for low-income elementary students, with 90 percent of its students coming from low-income homes. Eighty-two percent of its students scored "proficient" or "advanced" on the California Standards Test for math in 2011–2012, compared with 87 percent of students in California's high-income districts. About 90 percent of Rocketship's lowest-performing students move out of the bottom quartile within a year.

Founded in 2006, Rocketship was an early pioneer of two of the staffing innovations described above: using digital learning in a computer lab to provide students with personalized instruction while freeing teachers to be with other students and having teachers specialize in their best subjects. The network decided to adjust its structure in 2013–2014, using an open, flexible classroom space for its fourth and fifth graders only. Instead of reporting to a separate computer lab, students move within this classroom between digital learning and in-person instruction, based on their individual needs and the roles that specific excellent teachers are best suited to play. (At the time of this writing, student results under these changes were not available.)

In 2012–2013, most Rocketship students spent about half of their instructional time each day in traditional classrooms of 20–25 students focused on English language arts and social studies (other students participated in a pilot of the new model). They split the remainder of the day between learning math and science in traditional classes and going to a learning lab in groups of anywhere from 30 to 115 students for computer-based instruction, small-group learning, and independent reading time, overseen by "individualized learning specialists." These specialists were not certified teachers but tutors, lab monitors, and providers from community-based organizations. Rocketship schools, which run from 8:00 a.m. to 4:00 p.m., also offer afterschool tutoring for struggling students.

Several features of Rocketship's staffing approach are worth noting. First, it enables the schools to be significantly more selective in hiring. Where a traditional elementary school would have to hire about 4 teachers to reach 100 students, Rocketship generally has 3—2 for literacy/social studies and one for math/science—without increasing class size. A literacy and social studies teacher reaches about 50 students, twice the number of students reached by the typical elementary school teacher. A math and science teacher reaches about 100 students, four times the number reached by the typical teacher.

Second is the important role of individualized learning specialists working as tutors and lab monitors. They help students with basic skills to supplement their online instruction, freeing teachers' time to engage students in higher-order learning. Some Rocketship schools also get assistance from community organizations, such as Recess 101, which recruits and trains enrichment coordinators, or the YMCA, which provides afterschool help and homework support.

Finally, the model creates economic savings that, in large part, contribute to paying Rocketship's teachers more. Rocketship teachers earn 10–30 percent more than their peers in the local public school system. At Si Se Puede School, for example, the principal was able to offer the school's excellent third-year teachers salaries of about $70,000, which was nearly 30 percent higher than their peers in a neighboring district.

Hiring blended learning teachers requires finding candidates with leadership and teamwork competencies, strong planning skills, the ability to use the technology and its data well, and the ability to deliver personalized and enriched instruction. To develop those skills, Rocketship requires its principals and assistant principals to serve as coaches for teachers and to be accountable for the results of at least one grade level's teachers and students.

In the 2012–2013 school year, Rocketship piloted some changes to its learning lab structure. In a few classrooms in various grades, Rocketship tested a more open, flexible classroom space, rather than sending students down the hall to a lab. In blended learning parlance, this is known as shifting from a "rotation" to a "flex" model. In these pilot classes, schools removed some classroom and lab walls and installed sliding, partial glass walls, so that computers were within one large classroom with multiple teachers and classes of students.

Not only was the space flexible, but so were the teachers: now they specialized not just by subject but by role, whenever possible. For example, some teachers continued to specialize in one subject, while others specialized within a subject. Thus, a teacher who excelled in planning and leading differentiated, small-group reading instruction focused her instructional time on guided reading, while other teachers handled different aspects of literacy instruction. The pilot led to a decision to use the flexible, open-space model in all of Rocketship's fourth and fifth grade classes in 2013–2014.

For fourth and fifth graders, Rocketship saw several ways this flex model could change teachers' roles and free even more of Rocketship's teachers' time, among them:

- While one teacher works with 20 students for a full-group exercise, 30 students focus on projects with another teacher's supervision, and 15 students work in small groups with the third teacher's oversight. Meanwhile, 40 students work online while 15 others work independently, with an assistant monitoring both groups.
- Or, two teachers teach the same objective to different groups within one grade, using different approaches and amounts of time. At the same time, a third teacher and a tutor pull out small groups for intervention work.

Adam Nadeau, principal of Rocketship Mosaic, a K–5 San Jose school, puts it this way: "The essential question at the heart of all this is, Does every child need every lesson? [You need] the right kids in the right groups, in the right spaces."

TOUCHSTONE EDUCATION

In 2012, New Jersey charter management organization Touchstone Education opened its first school, Merit Preparatory Charter School of Newark with eighty-four sixth-graders, 90 percent of whom are low-income, with most entering several years behind grade level. The organization plans to build a network of schools serving grades 6–12 that will be staffed very differently from conventional schools in a couple of ways. First, "master teachers" in English language arts (ELA), math, and science will each extend their reach to as many as 240 students and lead teams of teachers. Although each content team will be responsible for the student outcomes of all students within that subject, the master teacher will have ultimate accountability for leading the team to strong student outcomes by developing team members and taking on the hardest teaching roles.

Second, students will spend significant time working with personalized online "playlists," which show each student what lessons, activities, and assignments—both in-person and online—they are to complete during the week. All students bring to class their personal MacBook Air laptops, provided by the school, and follow playlists that teachers adjust using student learning data to select each student's appropriate digital content and traditional learning activities. Students may start out with whole-class lessons to learn new material from the teacher, but they spend most of their class time following the playlist's guidance through personalized lessons, freeing teachers to reach more students and focus their instruction to meet students' needs. These lessons may include whole-group discussion, partner work on practice worksheets, small-group activities in seminar rooms with in-person teachers, or personalized online modules.

In 2012–2013, Merit Prep Newark started out with just a sixth grade, only a small start toward this broader vision. In reading and science, Merit Prep Newark showed strong early results: in March 2013 tests, students already demonstrated two years of growth in reading and 1.25 years of growth in science, based on the Northwest Evaluation Association's Measures of Academic Progress (MAP) assessment.

Its reading gains came out of an ELA program led by a master teacher, an excellent teacher who taught with and led a first-year teacher. In math, where Touchstone leaders were unable to hire a master teacher, Merit Prep's students had made three-fourths of a year of growth by March. "Traditional education looks a certain way," says master teacher Tiffany McAfee, who has taught ELA for about a decade. "The challenge is to change the way I think education should be—to revert back to my innocence."

MULTI-CLASSROOM LEADERSHIP. Touchstone's model calls for a master teacher leading the instruction of all students in a content area. In its first year, Merit Prep Newark had just one master teacher, McAfee; the school was unable to find a suitable candidate for math. She worked on a team with first-year Teach for America teacher Jonathan Wigfall, developing his skills.

In the school's first year, with just a sixth grade, McAfee and Wigfall had about twenty-seven students in a typical subject block; Touchstone kept the student-teacher ratio low to test the model and adjust it before extending teachers' reach in the second year. Students sat in groups of four based on skill level, all equipped with laptops using the Canvas platform, which allows teachers and students to share files. McAfee directed students through their playlists, worked one-on-one with students, and led whole-group instruction, while Wigfall supported her by rotating among the students, guiding, redirecting, and assisting them when they had questions.

Throughout each school day, McAfee also coached Wigfall; she said working with him and the school's other teachers proved especially rewarding. She and Wigfall spent significant planning time together throughout the week but mainly on Fridays, when they reviewed that week's data. They had the autonomy to change the curriculum or how they used class time based on week-to-week student results. Wigfall then created weekly assessments using questions pulled from item banks aligned to MAP assessments, while McAfee took the lead on creating instructional playlists for students.

In addition, she met weekly with the school's reading specialist to plan the daily, three-hour afternoon reading intervention time, during which the school most took advantage of the personalized instruction that blended learning models offer. In this block, McAfee, as the master teacher, led all the other teachers in the school, including the reading specialist and special education teacher, in working with students on literacy. Students and teachers started the block together, before students moved into groups that changed daily according to their learning needs, generally working online and in small groups. During this block, students also got pulled out for an hour of physical education each day.

In its first year, Merit Prep's math results showed Ben Rayer, Touchstone's founder and CEO and former president of Mastery Charter Schools, the immediate need for a multi-classroom leader there, too. Math was taught largely using the blended learning model and by a first-year teacher, who would work in a team the following year with two other much more experienced teachers.

USING TECHNOLOGY. Swapping a portion of teaching time for digital learning gives teachers the time to teach more students, focusing on higher-order thinking skills, as well as the chance to plan and collaborate with other teachers. In Touchstone's modified flex model, students sit in groups of four or five in an open "stadium" space, with glassed-in seminar rooms along the back. Student groups are flexibly assigned by level or mastery, and teachers place students into new groups every week based on formative assessment data. During the subject block, students may work in groups, in pairs, or individually on projects and assignments determined by the teacher. Merit Prep's students rotate among science, ELA, and math in fixed one-hundred-minute blocks. Science classes are held in a lab, while ELA and math classes are held simultaneously in the stadium.

OPPORTUNITIES FOR TEACHERS. Developing teachers along a career ladder with multiple opportunities, as Touchstone intends, provides appealing options for its current teachers:

- *Associate teacher.* Designed for new teachers, this role allows early-career teachers to support others on their team through tutoring, supervising online learning, grading, and administrative duties. Rather than only trying to find "superman or superwoman" candidates, Rayer says, he intends to hire high-potential new and solid teachers whom Touchstone's master teachers can develop toward excellence.
- *Teacher.* These teachers support their master teacher through direct instruction, interventions, and small-group activities. This role provides a spot for experienced people who want to teach but not lead others.
- *Master teacher.* Rayer sees this role as the key to retaining excellent teachers who want to keep teaching and also lead their peers, providing them with the development they need to manage other teachers. "They'll have to start taking on managerial responsibilities," he says. "You will never be a master teacher unless you embrace accountability for [your] content area— assigning yourself and [your team members] appropriately and doing what it takes to make sure your team is successful."

As Touchstone moves forward, its leaders intend to provide better professional development in using the technology effectively, especially given that blended learning teachers can find few external support networks. And McAfee looked forward to more development from Touchstone for her leadership skills, saying, "I don't want this just to be about new teachers. I want to be developed, too. I want it formally."

PROJECT L.I.F.T.

Charter networks like Rocketship and Touchstone have the chance to design and build more or less from scratch, developing and trying new models from the beginning. But with the vast majority of students nationally attending existing schools, it is also worth looking at examples of districts seeking to introduce new staffing models within that setting. One example is Project L.I.F.T., a public-private partnership to improve academics at historically low-performing, high-need schools in Charlotte, North Carolina. According to Denise Watts, zone superintendent and L.I.F.T. director, "If we didn't try something truly different to change education, many of my students were not going to graduate."

Four schools took on the challenge: Allenbrook Elementary, Ashley Park PreK–8, Ranson IB Middle School, and Thomasboro Academy. Each of the four schools created design teams composed of school leaders and excellent teachers to completely redesign their schools' staffing models. Working on their own to develop new plans as well as spending many hours in meetings sharing ideas and solving problems, the teams developed three-year transition plans that would get their schools to full implementation by fall 2015 and reach L.I.F.T.'s goals by 2016.

Creating models that stayed within budget while remaining flexible in response to changing allotments from the district proved difficult. However, this process of creating new staffing models and roles that would be sustainable, without the need for additional dollars or allotments, was a turning point for some teams. "The need for change and the need to have excellent teachers reach more kids was already a common ground," says Jessie Becker, assistant principal at Thomasboro Academy. "What made the initial buy-in truly happen was the crunching of the numbers, which showed that the dream could become a reality." Daniel Swartz, L.I.F.T.'s human capital strategies specialist, worked closely with the district to ensure that L.I.F.T. schools had the needed flexibility and district support to reallocate local funds to pay more for teachers in these new roles without increasing school budgets.

The schools chose to "exchange" some of their locally funded positions. In some schools, design teams working in coordination with Swartz swapped some teacher positions for paraprofessionals, who will handle noninstructional and less complex instructional supervision so that no learning value is lost. Some schools also converted academic facilitator positions, which were created as non-classroom specialists who support teachers, into multi-classroom leader positions, reinvesting in classroom instruction rather than out-of-classroom supports. As a result, all of the pay increases for advanced teaching positions are funded at the school level out of regular funding streams, not temporary grants. None of L.I.F.T.'s philanthropic grants will be needed to fund the pay increases in pilot schools.

Project L.I.F.T. recruited teachers for several new roles, with more pay for each. Specialized teachers at the elementary level could earn an added $4,600 in 2013–2014. Teachers reaching more students by enlisting paraprofessionals to oversee digital learning or other school work could earn an added $9,200. And multi-classroom leaders supervising teams of teachers could earn $16,000–23,000 extra, depending on the number of students reached and the number of teachers on the leader's team. Swartz says,

> The money starts making teaching become equal to other professions. This provides a way for them to provide for their families, not have to have a second job, and to see a career where [their] value is based off of your performance, not just how many years or how old [they]. And the pay is comparable to other leadership roles within education, like principalships. In a couple of cases, these roles kept people in the schools instead of pursuing positions outside of the classroom.

The following describes elements of how each school's approach will look by 2015.

At Allenbrook Elementary

- Multi-classroom leaders in K–3 will lead pods of three novice and/or developing teachers by co-teaching, observing, and developing team teachers and directly teaching groups of students.
- Teams of specialized teachers and teams of teachers led by a multi-classroom leader will get support from paraprofessionals who monitor students during noninstructional times and transitions, providing more teaching and planning time for teachers.

At Ashley Park

- Excellent blended learning teachers will extend their reach by teaching more students on a flex schedule, with lab monitors supporting them in digital labs.
- Multi-classroom leaders will lead small teams of novice and/or developing teachers, coteaching, observing, and developing them while also directly teaching groups of students, with support from learning coaches.

At Ranson IB Middle School

- In ELA, social studies, and science classes, multi-classroom leaders will instruct students directly and lead small teams of two novice or developing teachers and one paraprofessional.
- In math classes, excellent blended learning teachers will use blended learning rotations to extend their reach to more students and also work with a team of developing and novice teachers on their way to becoming blended learning teachers. A multi-classroom leader will lead all math teachers.

At Thomasboro Academy

- In grades K–2, multi-classroom leaders will lead and develop teams of teachers with support from teacher assistants.
- In grades 3–8, students will rotate not between digital instruction and in-person teaching but between paraprofessionals and excellent "expanded impact" teachers. Students will spend a

limited part of each day working with paraprofessionals on projects and basic knowledge and skills, enabling excellent teachers who specialize in one subject to extend their reach to not just one grade but two grades of students without increasing class size. Multi-classroom leaders will provide support to novice and developing teachers in these grades.

As of this writing, these schools were just beginning to implement these designs and could not yet examine any student achievement results. But based on the early interest of teachers, the district decided to expand its initiative, so that by the 2017–2018 school year almost half its schools will use these new models. And the pilot schools have seen their efforts pay off in other ways: Ranson started its first Opportunity Culture year with no vacancies in its math positions for the first time in recent memory, and the schools drew 708 applicants from twenty-four states for nineteen new positions in its 2013–2014 debut year. Candidates included current teachers—60 percent of whom had more than five years' teaching experience—as well as administrators, facilitators, coaches, and even staff in Charlotte-Mecklenburg's district office.

The district has identified critical competencies that candidates need for these new roles beyond those of a regular teacher, especially in leadership. It is working with partners to offer teachers in the new roles monthly sessions and one-on-one coaching related to these competencies, such as providing feedback to team members and leading team planning and development. The district also created a version of the standard teacher evaluation tool for multi-classroom leaders that rates them on both teaching *and* leadership and rolls the student learning results from an entire pod into the leader's evaluation results.

Policy Issues

Transitioning to new staffing models is partly a matter of imagination. As Hess points out in *Cage-Busting Leadership*, school and district leaders could do much more within existing policies to vary traditional staffing arrangements.

Yet there are real policy barriers to engaging in the kind of staffing redesign discussed here. The extent of these barriers depends on the context. Charter school organizations like Rocketship and Touchstone face the fewest because of their charter autonomy. Still, Rocketship uses a one-hundred-item checklist to vet the policy environment of states it is considering entering. District schools engaged in small-scale pilots face more constraints, but they often can obtain some leeway because they represent a small share of district schools. Policy barriers will become most restrictive when a district wants to redesign at a level of scale that goes beyond a few pilot schools.

The policy barriers that schools seeking to use new models like these confront fall into several important categories:[11]

Funding

- *Flexibility.* Too often, funding comes to districts in the form of set line items that require it to be spent in certain ways. Particularly troublesome for schools seeking to change staffing models are regulations that require schools to have a rigid number of teachers, teacher assistants, and other personnel based on their student enrollment. Schools in such a system may not use the savings from staffing model changes to pay teachers more, purchase technology, or employ different kinds of staff such as paraprofessionals. Below we discuss how Charlotte-Mecklenburg Schools has had to approach its staffing design work as a consequence.

- *Procurement.* For schools seeking to use digital learning to extend teacher reach, onerous procurement policies, textbook-use requirements, and multiyear vendor contracts make it difficult for schools to acquire hardware and software or to change vendors as needed.

People

- *Licensure.* For schools seeking to use "remote teaching," licensure policies can prevent excellent out-of-state teachers from reaching a state's students from afar.

- *Evaluation.* States and districts may simply lack teacher evaluation systems that meaningfully identify teachers whose reach should be extended. But even in places with new teacher evaluation systems, schools may face a mismatch between the new roles they are seeking to create and teacher evaluation systems that assume a one-teacher-one-classroom setup. For example, teacher evaluation systems may not be well-equipped to attribute an entire pod's student results to a multi-classroom leader. And they are almost certainly not designed to evaluate how well teachers are performing in new roles with different responsibilities.

- *Class size.* Strict across-the-board class-size limits can stand in the way of giving more students access to excellent teachers. While the schools we discuss in this chapter have been able to keep class sizes within limits, using other means to extend teacher reach, in other cases these constraints could block promising innovations. But under some states' policies, class size, at least at the elementary level, can mean the number of students for whom a teacher is accountable, not the number in a classroom at once. This places a limit on great teachers' reach, *even if* the number of students with a teacher at any given moment is reduced.

- *Seat time and "line of sight" rules.* Restrictions on the time students may spend with paraprofessionals and remote teachers, including literal "line of sight" requirements for students to be physically present with licensed teachers for certain activities or a set amount of time, can limit schools' ability to free the time of teachers to collaborate, plan, and learn together or to teach more students and free funding to boost teacher pay.

- *Salary schedules.* Many states and districts have salary scales that require teachers to be paid largely on the basis of experience and credentials. These scales do not reflect the role variation in new staffing models that encourage and enable teaching excellence. Moreover, after the first half-decade of teaching experience, most of the scales pay for things that do not improve student, or teaching peer, outcomes, according to research. But without better means of paying teachers more, these scales have stayed intact, and they are likely superior to reducing teacher pay overall. Pay for extended-reach roles can be a supplement to these scales. However, incorporating new pay scales that align with new career paths would make wide-scale implementation of paid career advancement via reach models more feasible for large organizations that thrive on clear rules.

- *Technology and data.* Schools seeking to use models involving age-appropriate digital learning can run into trouble if state and district policies do not enable access to broadband Internet and sufficient hardware to enable enough students to work digitally simultaneously. While nearly all public schools now have broadband access of some kind, not all have enough bandwidth or hardware to handle the increased use demanded by these models.

When districts are piloting new models in a few schools, they can often work around policy restrictions like these by requesting formal waivers or by being creative and resourceful in thinking of work-arounds. Two examples from the Project L.I.F.T. case above are illustrative. First, North Carolina's state funding system allocates positions to schools based on a complicated series of formulas linking different staff positions to different levels of student enrollment. Schools in the L.I.F.T. pilot, of course, wanted to change these allocations, reallocating savings either to create other positions or to supplement the pay of teachers taking on extended-reach roles. With some creative thinking, district officials were able to manage this primarily by funding positions at the school with locally generated tax dollars, which did not carry the same restrictions as the state funding. Then they could reallocate and use savings at will.

State funding, however, makes up a large proportion of the district's overall budget. It can only do so much with its local funding. What worked well for a small number of pilot schools (four) could be replicated to some degree. But district leaders would need state policy flexibility to offer higher-paid, extended-reach roles to teachers throughout the district.

A second example involves the district's teacher evaluation system. North Carolina's teacher evaluation rubric includes a measure of value-added based on the amount of growth a teacher's students achieved, known as Standard Six. For its multi-classroom leaders, Project L.I.F.T. was eager to define Standard Six in a way that held leaders responsible for all the students in their pods, including students who might be assigned formally to other teachers as their classroom teachers of record. While the state's system did allow teachers to share accountability for a student, it did so based on the percentage of a student's instructional time each teacher occupied—a mis-fit with a system in which the multi-classroom leader may affect students by spending time with them or by helping team members be more effective. While L.I.F.T. felt confident it could communicate to multi-classroom leaders that they are accountable for all students taught by their teams, in spite of the mismatch with the formal measurement system, that works only at a small scale. To work district-wide, the state's approach to Standard Six would need to bend to accommodate the new reality of multi-classroom leaders being fully accountable for whole pods of students served by a team of teachers they lead.

Conclusion

The effort to improve teacher quality in the United States will likely grind forward, making incremental gains over time. But to make the quantum leap that is possible, schools need to address a topic they've largely left on the table: school staffing design. While the examples discussed above are nascent and small in scale, they suggest that it is possible to redesign staffing models, achieve results from doing so, and increase the attractiveness of the profession at the same time. Policy makers can encourage more of this kind of activity by addressing some of the barriers that now inhibit attempts to rethink the one-teacher-one-classroom paradigm. And they can increase school and district leaders' *will* to try new approaches, using both existing and new inducements for schools and districts to reach all students with the outstanding learning that today only a portion of teachers generate.

CHAPTER 3

HR with a Purpose

Building Talent for Distinct Schools and Networks

BETHENY GROSS AND MICHAEL DeARMOND

E DUCATIONAL LEADERS at all levels of government are rethinking how public schools hire, develop, and reward teachers. In cities like Washington, DC, Pittsburgh, Denver, and elsewhere, district leaders are taking human resource (HR) systems that were long driven by compliance and regulatory concerns and transforming them to take a more strategic and performance-based approach to managing talent. At the state level, legislatures are adopting new evaluation systems designed, for the first time, to meaningfully differentiate teachers by effectiveness; currently, thirty-seven states have legislation or state board policies that establish new teacher evaluation systems or evaluation standards that prioritize teachers' impacts on student learning. Standing behind all of this activity—and often motivating it—is the Obama administration's reform agenda and its emphasis on "great teachers and leaders."

When reform-minded leaders, advocates, and researchers talk about these and other ambitious teacher policy initiatives, they tend to frame the policy problem in stark terms: given the importance of teachers to student learning, public education needs to do a better job of finding, rewarding, and retaining the best teachers and developing or dismissing the worst. To be sure, this focus on performance—and differences in performance—improves on personnel systems that, historically, were indifferent to how well teachers do in the classroom. At the same time, this find-more-great-teachers-and-remove-the-worst formulation of teacher policy ignores the fact that performance, job satisfaction, and retention don't just depend on the individual characteristics of a teacher. Teacher performance also depends on the relationship between the teacher and the school where she or he works.

As Tom Stritikus, dean of the College of Education at the University of Washington, notes, it is useful to think about teacher quality not simply as an abstracted attribute of individual teachers but also as the result of "someone, teaching something, to particular students, in a particular school." In other words, effective teaching is a joint product of teachers and the places in which they work and, importantly, the match between the two. So even as HR reformers continue to push public education away from compliance-driven human resource policies and toward performance-driven ones, they should ask not just how schools can hire and reward effective teachers but also how the next generation of talent management systems in education can help schools find and develop teachers who are a good match for their school. Finding good matches will only become more complex as schools increasingly use technology to redefine what it means to be a teacher in a classroom.

A good place to begin thinking about how a system can support good teacher-school matches is to start with what it takes for *mission-driven schools* to find, develop, and reward teachers who match their program and improvement strategy, rather than jumping directly to district- or state-level policy. Schools, after all, are the unit in the system where the match between teacher, kids, and school environment occurs and are arguably the core unit of improvement in public education.

In light of a more contextualized understanding of teacher quality, this chapter provides a quick look at how four very different schools manage talent in ways that fit their unique situation. Two of these schools are district schools and two are part of tightly knit charter school networks. In every case, the schools carry out a specific mission, be its own mission or one shared within the network. Whether urban or rural, traditional or charter, leaders in these schools and networks use the way they recruit, hire, develop, and retain teachers to build talent that fits their goals, approach, and values. They all approach HR with a purpose, but they do it in their own way. A high-poverty urban middle school in a diverse neighborhood is not necessarily looking for the same teaching approaches or cultural competencies as a rural high-poverty elementary school with a 100 percent Hispanic and English language learner (ELL) student population. The needs of a small charter network in the poorest corners of Philadelphia are not the same as those of a charter network in western Pennsylvania.

We provide a brief impression of school-level practices for ensuring teacher quality that recognize the importance of match between teachers and schools. These practices are purposeful and raise important questions for district- and state-level HR reforms. Above all, they call into question the underlying assumption that states and districts can best ensure teacher quality through a top-down alignment of policy and practice. There's little doubt that alignment and coherence are productive qualities in individual schools, but when it comes to managing talent, these same qualities may be less tenable the farther we go up the policy chain from schools to districts to states. As we suggest in the next section, our skepticism about system-wide HR management is grounded in ideas about how HR—the way organizations hire, develop, and retain talent—matters to organizational performance.

How Does HR Matter to Organizational Performance?

In the search for ways to ensure that all students have effective teachers, policy makers and researchers have rightly looked at HR systems as a point of leverage. There is ample evidence that traditional school district HR systems do not focus on effectiveness and, in many cases, make it harder for schools to get the teachers they need.[1] There is also evidence from the private sector that strong HR practices can promote firm performance.[2] But how, more specifically, does HR improve organizational performance? If we take a more contextualized view of teacher quality as being the product of the teacher and the place in which he or she works, what's the underlying logic that links HR to improved teacher quality, if it's not simply about sorting teachers according to their individual quality?

To begin, the best thinking on HR systems and their link to performance focuses on a *system* of HR practices. That is, rather than just looking for more effective evaluation practices or better recruitment practices, effective HR systems contribute to performance by creating a constellation of practices that work together to benefit the organization. For example, when hiring practices are looking for the same attributes and qualities that are assessed in the evaluation system and rewarded in the compensation system, the result is mutually reinforcing.

But not just any coordination and alignment will do. Coordinated HR systems help performance when they are organized to develop the skills, knowledge, and motivations that the organization needs to implement its particular strategy for improvement. When people talk about "strategic HR," they mean that the way organizations hire, develop, and retain employees is aligned with the organization's strategic goals.[3]

So why would an HR system that's aligned with strategy actually improve organizational performance? In the early 2000s, researchers David Bowen and Cheri Ostroff theorized that aligned and coherent HR systems shape organizational performance not only by identifying high-quality employees but also by creating environments in which every employee understands what it means to be a high-quality employee—and how to become one.[4] Bowen and Ostroff argue that how organizations recruit, hire, develop, and reward employees influence performance primarily by creating strong shared perceptions and expectations among employees about what it means to work in the organization and about the organization's goals. Strong HR systems consistently tell people what they are expected to do and why it is important and then provide help doing it. Employees in weak HR systems face an ambiguous environment in which lots of different behaviors and attitudes are possible. Unlike today's teacher quality debates, which focus almost exclusively on individual teachers, this understanding of HR and its influence on performance begins with a focus on the organization, its goals, and its strategy for achieving them.

This focus on organizational goals and strategy suggests the importance of what we call a *purposeful* HR system. A purposeful

HR system is one that ensures that schools obtain, develop, and retain teachers who match the school's particular improvement strategy and mission. Purposeful HR systems create visible, distinct, and consistent policies around recruitment and hiring, development and evaluation, and rewards and retention that define and communicate common expectations as to what it means to be a successful teacher in that particular school.

It is easy to see why district leaders—or even state leaders— might take intuitive ideas about coherence and alignment and try to apply them to a district-wide or statewide system. Of course, some districts (District of Columbia Public Schools, for example) made progress in using performance evaluations in human resource decisions.[5] But schools often differ dramatically in their culture and approach within districts and certainly within states. And, if you think ahead to a future in which schools might become even more differentiated through new uses of technology and blended learning models, the idea that district- or state-level policy can ensure effectiveness everywhere with a top-down, standardized vision of effective teaching and personnel management seems daunting and perhaps untenable.

Four Schools with Character

To provide an impression of how schools can use purposeful HR practices to support performance, we draw on the experiences of four schools/organizations that represent a mix of location and governance structures. The schools operate in Pennsylvania and Washington State. Both states include an interesting mix of labor markets (urban and rural), and since neither state had fully implemented the next wave of state-driven teacher evaluation reforms at the time we profiled the schools, the schools were free to develop their own best thinking about how to manage talent (see table 3.1). Within these states we purposefully selected schools that are successful with students who otherwise have few educational opportunities or accomplishments. These schools convey a distinct character—a sense of who they are, what they do, and how they do it. Whatever their mission, a purposeful HR system was an important part of helping leadership and faculty understand what their school hopes to accomplish and how to get there.

PENNSYLVANIA

MASTERY CHARTER SCHOOLS. Founded in 2001, the Mastery Public Schools Charter Management Organization (CMO) now runs ten schools in Philadelphia. The network of schools contains a mix of new charter start-ups and conversions of traditional schools from the School District of Philadelphia and serves grades K–12.

TABLE 3.1
Profiled schools and organizations

	Mastery Charter Schools	**Propel Charter Schools**	**Mercer Middle School**	**Adams Elementary School**
Organization	CMO with 10 schools serving Philadelphia	CMO with 8 schools serving western Pennsylvania	Traditional school in Seattle Public Schools	Traditional school in Yakima Public School District
Students served	Urban, low-income, African American student population	Low-income, rural student population	Urban, low-income, and minority students	Rural, low-income largely Latino English language learners
Student data 2010–2011				
Minority	96%	52%	96%	97%
English language learners	1%	0%	9%	61%
Free and reduced-price lunch	83%	78%	75%	97%

Note: Mastery Charter Schools currently runs ten schools; however, only nine are represented in the 2010–2011 data.

Sources: Data for Mastery Charter Schools and Propel Charter Schools are aggregated to the CMO level based on District Report Card 2011–2012 from the Commonwealth of Pennsylvania. Data for Mercer Middle School and Adams Elementary School are from the 2011–2012 Washington State Office of the Superintendent of Public Instruction School Report Card.

The Mastery network is highly integrated with a common mission and expectations across its campuses. Like many high-performing charter networks, Mastery schools at all levels embrace the "no excuses" model. Teachers implement a very specific model of curriculum and instruction that focuses on building a solid foundation of core skills. Mastery Charter School students are defying their inner-city impoverished backgrounds. The CMO reports that between 2007 and 2012 71 percent of its high school graduates enrolled in college.

PROPEL SCHOOLS. Propel Schools is also a CMO, founded in 2003, that runs eight schools in western Pennsylvania serving more than 2,000 students.[6] Propel's mission is to close the achievement gap, and it has developed a set of nonnegotiable "Promising Principles and Powerful Practices" that guide its work toward that end. Despite the fact that 77 percent of Propel's students are classified as economically disadvantaged (compared to 40 percent statewide), Propel's students are more likely to be at grade level in both reading and mathematics than the typical Pennsylvania public school student.

WASHINGTON STATE

MERCER MIDDLE SCHOOL. Almost ten years ago, principal Andhra Lutz decided that Mercer Middle School in Seattle would be the state's first high-poverty, high-performing middle school. With only 55 percent of seventh graders proficient in reading and only 33 proficient in math at the end of the 2003–2004 school year, the faculty had tremendous ground to make up. To transform the school, she began to reorient the culture toward greater kindness among adults and between adults and children, dramatically elevate expectations for students and from students, and sharpen instructional practices around mastery of core skills. Lutz placed attracting and hiring teachers who understood this vision for excellence and transitioning-out teachers who didn't share this vision at the center of her reform strategy. The efforts paid off. Now on its second principal since Lutz's departure in 2010, 77 percent of Mercer seventh graders scored proficient in reading, and 82 percent are proficient in math on recent state assessments. The school remains a high-poverty school with 75 percent eligible for free or reduced-price lunch.

ADAMS ELEMENTARY SCHOOL. **Adams Elementary** is a traditional public school located in the Yakima School District in eastern Washington State serving high-poverty Hispanic students, a majority of whom are nonnative English speakers and 29 percent of whom are classified as migrant students. Beginning in 2009, Adams used federal School Improvement Grants to extend its school day and fundamentally shift its professional culture and norms of teacher collaboration. In one year the school went from one of the lowest performing in the state to the middle of the pack: math scores, for example, improved at all three grade levels from 25 percent (third grade), 10 percent (fourth grade), and 33 percent (fifth grade) passing to 40 percent, 50 percent, and 43 percent, respectively.

Although these four schools serve different student populations in different ways, all of them leverage their HR systems to find teachers who fit into their school, to develop and evaluate teachers based on their match with the school's expectations, and to work creatively to ensure that excellent teachers can stay and fulfill their professional goals within the school.

How Do Schools Use Purposeful HR to Recruit and Hire Talent?

From the first time a job candidate interacts with Mercer, Mastery, Propel, and Adams, they are exposed to the commitments and expectations of what it means to teach in each school through the schools' recruitment and selection process. Even though all four schools served large shares of disadvantaged students and, in the case of the two rural schools (Propel and Adams), faced tight labor markets, each organization was purposeful and highly selective during the hiring process. As more than one leader said, hiring someone who doesn't match the school is hard on the faculty and hard on the students; it's much better to know what you want in a teacher and be selective about finding it.

These schools used their recruitment and hiring practices to surface information about both the candidate *and* the school to help both sides assess how well they matched with one another. Scholars who study human resource management refer to these types of recruitment and selection practices as "information rich." The goal is *not* to pass candidates through a series of high hurdles and hire whoever survives. Through formal and informal routines, the schools' selection practices are designed to provide candidates with ample opportunities to learn about the school, and vice versa.

For example, on the formal end of the spectrum, teacher candidates at Propel Charter Schools participate in a wide range of experiences designed to help the school learn about the candidate and the candidate about the school and, in the process, remind incumbents about the school's priorities and professional culture. CEO Jeremy Resnick described the hiring process this way: "[Candidates] come in after an initial interview . . . and do a demonstration lesson, always. They critique another teacher's teaching. Then the applicants, in teams of four, work together and we give them a problem to solve. Then they have a lengthy interview with a panel that may be four or five principals and some coaches."

Echoing a sentiment we have heard in many other schools with these rigorous selection practices, a Propel teacher said, "While most people would say, 'I don't feel like doing this [hiring process]. This is way too much,' it really intrigued me that they would spend that much time looking at their candidates." The rigor of the hiring process sent a message about the value Propel places on teaching quality but also on collaboration, problem solving, and participation. Another Propel teacher said, "I left that interview and I remember telling my husband: 'They know what kind of teacher I am, and if I don't get the job, I knew that I probably wouldn't have wanted it either because, you know, just that fit [wouldn't be there].'" Propel's list of "powerful practices" codifies these demanding hiring procedures into an organizational priority, asserting that a rigorous recruitment and hiring process is the first lever for building a strong teaching community.

In Yakima, Adams Elementary School's hiring process is far more constrained by district norms and policy than is Propel's process. And yet the school's leaders and staff also use the hiring process to send clear messages to job candidates about the school's expectations for teachers as well as to reinforce them among incumbents. As Principal Lee Maras explained, all job candidates met with their prospective grade-level teams so that current school staff could explain to the candidate how teachers at Adams work together through formal teams and to express the staff's commitment to doing "whatever it takes" to help students succeed, including working together before school, at lunch, and after school—even when they were not being paid. As Maras said, "We want people [candidates] to understand that we take a *systems* approach at Adams. They have to know, this [working at Adams] is not about doing their own thing."

On the less formal end of the spectrum, Mercer Middle School used interviews with candidates to see how they talked about children and their expectations for students. During the initial transformation, Lutz said she looked for candidates with "a deep-seated belief that all kids could learn and a sense of their own efficacy; someone who never blamed home or parents and who spent a minute looking up our data and said, 'You have amazing data and I want to work here.'" She also made it clear to candidates that Mercer had a school-wide approach to instruction that involved continuous support and feedback, including daily walk-throughs and an anything-it-takes attitude—a reality that Mercer's leaders used to ward off candidates the district had on contract but had not found placements for in the schools.

Like the other three schools, Mastery used the way it recruited and selected teachers to send clear messages about what the organization was trying to accomplish, how it would achieve that goal, and what it would mean to work in its classrooms.

How Do Purposeful HR Systems Develop and Evaluate Talent?

A lot of the discussion about the development and evaluation of teachers in education today focuses on specific dimensions of instructional practice embodied in a framework, such as Charlotte Danielson's Framework for Teaching. With its four domains and twenty-two components, it provides a common language in which principals and teachers can talk about instruction and other aspects of teaching.

Having a common language around instruction is incredibly useful for schools and professional growth. But so is having a common language and set of norms regarding a work culture that encompasses instruction as well as collegial expectations and commitments. (To be fair, the Danielson Framework includes a component on participating in professional community.) All four schools in this chapter spent considerable time using their development and evaluation routines to socialize staff not just on teaching practice but also around the school mission and expectations about how adults should work together to improve practice, interact with students (not just in the classroom), and achieve the mission. With remarkable consistency, the schools developed norms of professional exchange and feedback that were a regular part of teaching practice, turning teaching into a public activity instead of a private practice. Rather than engage with each other only around a formal evaluation schedule, leaders and colleagues in these schools used embedded development and evaluation to constantly work together to improve their practice.

As in many coherent schools, the principal, other leaders, and teachers were in each other's classrooms almost every day at Mercer Middle School. The leadership team's job was to use its presence in the classroom to send clear messages about how people were expected to teach and interact with students as well as to provide support for responding to those expectations and create a climate in which mutual observation and critique was the norm. For the school's leadership, this daily development activity *in the context of the school* was far more important than assessing individual performance for evaluation. As Lutz said about evaluation, "There is a certain level of teacher who is dangerous to kids [and should be evaluated out]. But there is a group of people in the middle who want to be good teachers, but too often we don't frontload the support piece and instead get into the evaluation mode." Rather than focus on dismissal as a key tool for managing talent, these schools focused on hiring and development.

At Adams Elementary, one of the pillars of Principal Lee Maras's transformation plan was to increase collaboration and openness among the teaching staff. In addition to the more public nature of teaching encouraged by the kind of cross-classroom observation seen across all four schools, Maras emphasized engaging teachers in developing plans to address the school's improvement priorities, something he says has been critical in developing teacher buy-in to school-wide initiatives. Asking teachers to work together to develop improvement priorities and plans helped Adams build "a culture of openness," Maras said. He considered his job to be ensuring that teacher-developed plans were used to inform organizational routines at Adams, including the topics for regular walk-throughs as well as more formal evaluations. For example, he used specific strategies to support its ELL students in all classrooms (e.g., using lots of starter sentences or stems or a particular way of assigning partner work called "precision partnering") that were developed by a staff committee and then incorporated into "look fors" during walk-throughs. The main structure for teacher collaboration at Adams were grade-level teams, but these teams also sent representatives to school-wide work teams and a leadership team, a level of participation that reinforced the common connection between teachers and the school's overall approach.

The broader point in these examples is that the school's purposeful approach to development and evaluation created a strong environment for productive work not only because they made teaching and instruction public practice but also because they reinforced the work norms and expectations for adult learning, reflection, improvement, and collaboration. It was clear what it would mean to teach students in the school and to work with other adults.

All of the leaders we spoke with talked far more about development than evaluation, emphasizing the importance of providing teachers with constant informal observation and feedback. In fact, across all four of the organizations, informal observation and feedback was so constant that by the time any formal evaluations came around they seemed like an afterthought. By then, teachers already knew where they stood, what improvements they needed, and the expected time frame for improvement. By being public, open, and ongoing, development and evaluation became a true continuous improvement process for teachers. Whereas popular teacher evaluation reforms today seem to layer on formal observations, sometimes to the point of crowding out informal evaluations, constant informal feedback may even lessen the importance of formal evaluations.

How Do Purposeful HR Systems Reward and Retain Talent?

Under a purposeful HR system, teachers who embrace and exemplify what it means to be a teacher in the school are retained, and the best of these teachers are rewarded—though not always financially. Dismissing teachers for low performance was not a top priority in the four schools. Contrary to recent calls to remediate teacher quality by dismissing the "lowest 5 percent" of teachers, dismissal may actually be very rare in schools with purposeful HR systems. Throughout Mercer's turnaround, Lutz never dismissed a tenured teacher. Instead, she focused on quality selection and enforcing a real probationary period for new teachers that ended only when she felt certain that the teacher could contribute to the staff over the long term.

A probationary period for new, untenured teachers is already in most teacher contracts. In Seattle, Lutz explained, converting a first-year teacher's contract to a continuing contract (out of the probationary period) was as simple as "checking a box on a form." Unlike many of her colleagues, however, she only converted a teacher to a continuing contract when she was certain the teacher would succeed in her school. The probationary period is a powerful mechanism built into the teacher contract to help principals manage their teacher quality, and few avail themselves of it.

Though a priority, keeping the best teachers in a school is often an uphill battle. Schools serving high-need student populations see relatively high teacher turnover. Even in Mastery Public Charter Schools, rated as one of Philadelphia's "Top Ten Places to Work" by Philly.com for four years running, CMO leaders worry about the toll the work takes on its teachers and the degree of turnover they see every year. They are thinking hard about how to make the career sustainable and rewarding for its best teachers.

Mastery, not required to follow traditional salary schedules that reward experience and professional development credits, restructured the teaching positions into four bands, moving teachers through these bands as they become more expert and effective with students. Mastery will also hire new teachers into higher bands based on the expertise they bring with them. Teachers are also eligible for an annual bonus based on performance. In reality, however, few schools, even charter schools without collectively bargained teacher contracts, restructure compensation like Mastery Charter Schools does.

More often charter and district leaders align leadership positions to reward teachers who best carry out the mission and work of the school. Charter networks like Mastery and Propel create career ladders for teachers, elevating them to master teachers, coaches, principals, or central CMO leadership positions. Other schools rely on more informal leadership opportunities. The principal of Adams Elementary explained that he has few formal or compensation rewards to offer teachers, but he can keep them engaged and energized with expanding leadership in informal and formal ways, for example, by asking teachers to lead grade-level teams or chair school-based committees tasked with addressing some pressing problem in the school.

HR with Purpose

All of these schools approach HR with a systemic vision and a purpose. They did not leave hiring to chance or rely on a formula for determining quality. Instead, they sent clear signals about what the school expected of teachers and provided supports and incentives to meet those expectations. But, importantly, the schools did not all have identical expectations. At Adams Elementary, teachers were expected to focus on meeting the needs of ELL students, commit to participating in school-wide committees, and research solutions to address problems identified by the schools' leaders. At Mercer Middle School, teachers were expected to become experts in a specific reading program, to take a no-excuses attitude toward achievement, and to open their teaching practice to one another and their supervisors. At Propel, teachers were expected to be fully committed to a social justice mission and use a core set of principles and practices to reach it. And at Mastery, teachers carried out a no-excuses model focused on developing solid core skills in their students. That each of these schools took a purposeful approach to HR but with slightly different purposes in mind raises questions about teacher policies at the district and state levels that, however well intentioned, may constrain school leaders' opportunities to take a purposeful approach to HR.

WHAT DOES PURPOSEFUL HR IMPLY FOR DISTRICTS AND STATES?

A purposeful approach to HR is grounded in a view of teacher quality that is far more contingent, situated, and varied than most conversations about teacher quality today. Recent debates about teacher quality tend to abstract teachers from the places in which they work and assess their quality either through a common instructional rubric (which presumably applies to all classrooms) or through value-added scores, which frame organizational and student differences primarily as confounding factors or nuisance variables.

A single approach to identifying, evaluating, and placing talent is unlikely to work for all schools. As schools continue to innovate with new technologies, the work of teachers and the work of schools will only become more diverse and different and place new demands on HR systems.[7] A school with a blended learning model, for example, will send very different messages about what it means to teach and work in the school than will a more traditional school or a school structured around a community-based curriculum.

Purposeful HR systems need to identify, place, develop, and retain teachers who are right for "this school doing this work with these kids." As Lee Maras from Adams Elementary argues, you hire and develop teachers who are working for *this* school's mission and approach. "Prima donna teachers," he said, "are the enemy of school improvement."

The notion that effective schools distinguish themselves from other schools is at odds with some of the underlying assumptions behind today's top-down HR reforms that focus on system-wide alignment around models of teaching and evaluation. Andhra Lutz said she "would never get all of those Charlotte Danielson domains" because that vision of instruction didn't speak to the work that she and her team were doing around reading and math. The new demands of teacher evaluation policies—multiple observations and pre- and post-conferences—are surely an improvement on traditional systems that provided neither meaningful evaluation nor feedback to teachers. But these same systems risk crowding out the kind of informal evaluation and development seen in purposeful school-level HR systems.

The Pennsylvania Department of Education's recent teacher evaluation regulations, for example, specify not only the four types of data that must inform all teacher evaluations but also the percentage of a teacher's rating that must be based on each type of data; for example, 15 percent of a classroom teacher's rating must be based on building-level data that includes at least seven measures specified by the state. In Washington State, principals must observe all third-year teachers three times for no less than ninety minutes total using one of three approved instructional frameworks. Some district-level systems can be even more prescriptive. Such requirements will surely improve practice in many schools, but in others they may make it more difficult for teachers and leaders to engage in ongoing cycles of assessment and feedback that identify and target the needs of individual teachers. Principals working under these systems may find they have less flexibility to prioritize working with teachers who need more help and must rely on expert teachers to provide additional instructional leadership.

If the experience of these schools suggests that top-down HR reforms might create problems for purposeful HR systems at the school level, what is the alternative? How can a district or state system support effective talent management in schools?

Facilitating Purposeful HR

Both the experience of these schools and our other work studying school-level HR suggests four broad principles for creating district and state HR systems that support and facilitate purposeful HR but don't attempt to directly *manage* it.

SUPPORT SCHOOL LEADERS TO MAXIMIZE THE TALENT LEVERS THEY HAVE. Districts can train and support leaders to be proactive managers of talent. This means helping leaders take advantage of the flexibility that often already exists in labor contracts but also, where necessary, negotiating provisions that provide school leaders with the flexibility they need to build a purposeful HR system that supports their school's approach to improvement.

Teacher contracts already offer principals some latitude to manage their talent and use it to the school's best advantage. Few principals, however, know the contents of the local collectively bargained teacher contract well enough to push for what they need. District offices too often never invoke potentially controversial provisions of the contract and may defer to the union leadership to interpret gray areas.

Rebuilding the staff at Mercer required Lutz to "know the contract inside and out" and use it to her best advantage, finding "wiggle room" even in a tight contract. For example, she used the fact that she could eliminate certain positions on budget reviews to remove members of the staff who undermined efforts to transform the school. She reassigned teachers to better serve her students and to make complacent teachers uncomfortable. Knowing the contract meant that she never took on a fight she could not win.

It is, of course, the principal's responsibility to learn the contract, but district leaders can help principals interpret the contract and familiarize them with the provisions most likely to impact their own talent management efforts. In addition, districts can enforce the full latitude in the contract and assertively back the principal's position when it comes to interpreting vague language.

Districts tend to shy away from union conflict, leaving potentially powerful levers provided by the contract unused. Lutz explained that at the time she started her turnaround efforts, Seattle's teacher contract had a reconstitution provision that gave the principal considerable leeway in rebuilding a staff. That provision, however, was never used. Districts also avoid conflict by deferring to the union's more conservative interpretation of gray areas in the contract over interpretations that would favor a principal who is trying to make change in her school. Here again, Lutz knew she would have to provide the district with her interpretation of any vague contract language, otherwise the district would call the union leadership for the interpretation.

Supporting principals might also mean seeking some changes in the contract. Two examples of counterproductive HR policy coming out of teacher contracts are hiring timelines that leave schools waiting until August to hire and displaced teacher provisions that allow weak teachers to bounce through a system, potentially disrupting the most earnest turnaround efforts. Traditional salary schedules can also constrain a school's ability to reward performance and respond to market demand. A recent Tennessee initiative provides an example of how a state might rethink compensation by soliciting proposals from districts to pilot compensation models that dispense with automatic pay increases with experience and education credits and move toward flexible pay bands that allow principals to be more responsive to both performance and market demand. Contract issues having to do with hiring timelines and compensation may be politically challenging, but they represent fundamental problems for principals working to staff high-need, hard-to-staff schools.

System leaders need to think of themselves as supporting their school leaders in building the staff and school programs that will serve students well. Occasionally, they will need to take on fights with the union to defend this work.

OVERSEE AND SUPPORT THE SYSTEM WITH HIGH-QUALITY DATA AND ANALYSIS ON TALENT. Districts and even states can play an important support role and provide a global check on equity and quality across the system by providing high-quality assessment, measurement, and analytic capacity. Assessment tools, the technical infrastructure to store and disseminate data to schools, and the analytic capacity for system-wide oversight are expensive and come with significant scale advantages. For example, New York City has recently released a series of scorecards for teacher preparation programs with information on the performance, retention, and supply of graduates. Such information may spark a response from colleges and universities, but it may also interest principals when they consider candidates from various programs. Tennessee is pursuing a similar statewide teacher preparation report card. Central administrations in districts and states may be best suited to providing the assessment and measurement function.

Assessment is an integral part of human resource management in schools with a strong talent focus. These schools, including those profiled here, make productive use of formative assessments to provide continuous feedback to their teachers and spot teachers that need help. The central administrations for Mastery and Propel administered formative and summative assessments, and Mercer made extensive use of the district's benchmark assessments.

Central administrations can also have an important role in overseeing the distribution of talent across the system. Research is clear that schools serving large numbers of low-income and minority students receive demonstrably fewer qualified applicants and end up with significantly more inexperienced and low-quality teachers.[8] Moreover, they face greater turnover as teachers leverage a few years of experience in a high-need school to find a position in a more affluent school. These labor market effects result in significant inequalities in the distribution of quality teachers and resources throughout the system.

Armed with information on the number of applicants for teaching positions, the distribution of teacher experience and quality, and teacher turnover rates in schools across the system, central leaders can better target their human resource support to schools. For example, districts might target compensation bonuses for hard-to-staff schools or provide these schools the benefit of a central recruiter that can help to identify teacher preparation programs that suit the school's mission.

AGGRESSIVELY CURATE AND CULTIVATE A PIPELINE OF TALENT TO YOUR CITY AND STATE. Districts and states can help ensure that cities have strong pipelines of talent, which may entail curating this talent through relationships with a teacher preparation programs. Building pipelines of talent can take a number of forms, from teacher residency programs, like the one in Boston, in which teacher-candidates work with a mentor teacher in a year-long residency while earning a master's degree, to more proactive agreements with traditional teacher preparation programs, to building relationships with alternative sources of talent, such as Teach for America. Districts can take advantage of their data and position to assess the sources of supply in their area and think more systematically about both the quality and diversity available. Likewise, states have an important role to play in accrediting and overseeing teacher preparation programs but also in making themselves and their regions attractive places for other talent providers as well.

District central offices or other groups outside of the school have a potential role to play providing strategic supports to principals and schools that leverage pipelines and other resources for improving human capital that can match a school's particular needs, as with "HR partner" positions in places like New York City and Denver. HR partners are central office or support network positions that act as HR consultants for school principals, providing schools with HR expertise and advice and brokering resources around talent as strategic support for principals in managing their teaching staff.

FOCUS ALSO ON PRINCIPAL TALENT. Finally, when it comes to hiring principals, districts can build similarly purposeful HR practices. If a district wants principals who can lead coherent schools, its selection, development, and retention practices should be designed to both signal those priorities and assess the candidate quality against them. In the same way that many schools find a sample lesson a valuable addition to the selection process for teachers (not just to get a sense of the teacher's instructional approach but also how he or she interacts with students), districts might consider asking principals to engage in work-like activities during their selection process (conducting a walk-through or debriefing with an actual teacher). If you view teacher quality as a matter of the match between teachers and mission-driven schools, then one of the most important levers for improving teacher quality may be investing in quality school leadership.

Conclusion

As a tool for improvement, HR systems may have their biggest impact when they are used to build a staff aimed at fulfilling a particular approach to improvement aimed at a particular goal. To the degree that one agrees with the assertion that schools are the core unit of improvement in public education, purposeful HR systems may be most successful at the school level or across small networks of schools. Above all, today's debates about teacher quality should do more to recognize that teachers and the work they do are not separate from the organizations in which they work, and, in fact, what we need from districts and states are systems that create a space for schools to be distinct and have character.

CHAPTER 4

Closing the Opportunity Gap

Preparing the Next Generation of Effective Teachers

BILLIE GASTIC

O VER THE NEXT SEVEN YEARS (2014–2020), more than 2.4 million new teachers—almost 350,000 teachers a year—will be hired by our public schools.[1] From day one, these teachers will need to be prepared to lead classrooms where all students can acquire the knowledge and critical thinking skills that they will need to be successful in college and beyond, such as those covered in the Common Core State Standards or Next Generation Science Standards.[2] Teachers are essential to student success, and educational attainment has never been more critical to the pursuit of individual liberty and economic independence.

Yet, the demand for effective teachers far exceeds the capacity of the current human capital pipeline. By and large, teacher education programs have fallen short of recruiting and preparing teachers who are ready for the challenges facing students in twenty-first-century schools.

Fortunately, teacher preparation is the focus of a swell of disruptive innovation, the examples of which shed light on how programs can evolve to improve their capacity to attract and develop teacher talent that advances student learning. These reforms, which I collectively refer to as *Teacher Prep 2.0*, put students first and are unrelenting in their commitment to making sure that all children have access to educators who can teach, inspire creativity and curiosity, and lead by example.[3] Teacher Prep 2.0 programs are anchored by purposeful linkages between clinical experiences, classroom- and/

or Web-based seminars, and guided practice with experienced educators, through which teachers learn both how to teach and how to understand their role in the lives of their students. These programs also empower teachers to set high expectations, facilitated by the use of formative and summative assessments and targeted and responsive academic support.

I currently work with one such Teacher Prep 2.0 institution, Relay Graduate School of Education (GSE), as its director of research. In this role I manage institutional research activities and external partnerships and oversee institutional data collection, analysis, and reporting. I also lead a team of research faculty and staff on projects related to teacher and leader development and the measurement of teacher and leader effectiveness. After spending the early part of my career in traditional academe, I was motivated to join Relay GSE because of its mission and its strong belief that schools of education, and the research emerging from them, should be in service of the needs of students, teachers, and schools.

Reforming Teacher Preparation

For years, many teacher preparation programs have struggled with how to meet the needs of teachers, especially teachers aspiring to work in high-need schools, where teaching has the potential to make the biggest impact. Popular accounts of teachers ill-equipped for the challenges of the classroom abound. *Education Week*'s coverage of teacher preparation is packed with commentaries from young teachers describing how unprepared they felt for their first days as a classroom teacher. At Teachers College, Columbia University, in the fall of 2009, U.S. Secretary of Education Arne Duncan asserted that there was no evidence to show that schools of education had moved the needle on student achievement, saying, "By almost any standard, many if not most of the nation's 1,450 schools, colleges, and departments of education are doing a mediocre job of preparing teachers for the realities of the modern classroom. America's university-based teacher preparation programs need revolutionary change—not evolutionary tinkering."[4] Months later, at a research summit in Washington, DC, Katherine Merseth, director of Harvard University's Teacher Education Program, echoed Secretary Duncan's sentiments, proclaiming that "the dirty little secret about schools of education is that they have been the cash cows of universities for many, many years, and it's time to say, 'Show us what you can do, or get out of the business.'"[5]

Many teacher preparation programs are hamstrung by low selectivity, low academic expectations and rigor, incoherent or haphazard curricula, and a dearth of clinical practice.[6] The National Council on Teacher Quality has vociferously critiqued many teacher education programs for their light touch on practical domains, like lesson planning, instruction, and assessment.[7] Not surprisingly given the state of affairs, evidence suggests that teachers' effectiveness is largely independent of the preparation they receive. For example, while Steven Rivkin, Eric Hanushek, and John Kain underscore the important effect that teachers have on their students' learning in reading and math in their analysis of Texas educational data, they failed to find evidence that having a graduate degree explained any of the differences in teachers' effectiveness.[8]

What's more, a single institutional type (that is, public, state-subsidized colleges and universities) are monopolizing the supply of teachers and dictating the quality of their preparation. For example, according to its Web site, Southern Connecticut State University prepares the largest number of graduates for teaching positions in the state. This leaves K–12 schools dissatisfied with the caliber of the teachers that complete these local programs out of luck.

Early reform efforts to improve teacher quality disproportionally relied on selection. Alternative routes to certification are one example of this. In addition to being a way to recruit individuals with subject-area expertise, especially in math and science, alternative certification serves to increase the pool of teachers with strong academic credentials. Empirical research points to a consensus that a teacher's record of academic achievement is one of the few consistently significant predictors of their effectiveness in the classroom.[9] As professional opportunities for women and minorities increased in American society in the second half of the twentieth century, the academic credentials of teachers declined. Sadly, the situation is only worsening. For example, in 1971, 24 percent of teachers scored in the top decile of their high school achievement test; today, only 11 percent score in the top decile.[10] On average, teachers also tend to have lower SAT scores than others taking the exam.[11] However, the ensuing years have underscored the limitations of the selection approach. While campaigns to attract recent college graduates and midcareer professionals to teaching who would not have otherwise considered the profession have been successful (for example, Teach for America, TNTP), the sizes of those cohorts are insufficient to meet the demand for effective teachers. Alternative routes to teacher certification, while expanding, currently make up only a third of teacher preparation programs.[12]

Current efforts to reform teacher education have gained momentum. We have seen encouraging efforts supporting transparency about the quality of teacher preparation programs, such as those led by state systems (such as Louisiana), researchers, and the National Council on Teacher Quality.[13] Efforts like these help facilitate differentiation in the market, introducing long-needed information that teachers can use to make informed decisions about available programs. Increasing the availability and quality of data on the performance of program completers may promote an airing out of the teacher preparation sector, empowering teacher candidates to distinguish the rancid from the sublime and the mediocre from the solidly average.

The selection criteria for the U.S. Department of Education's Race to the Top (RTTT) fund's teacher and school leader reform plans require that states treat measures of student growth as a significant factor when determining teacher and leader effectiveness. RTTT also asked states to develop "ambitious yet achievable" goals to link student achievement data to teachers and principals and to the in-state preparation programs from which they earned their credentials. Since these data are also to be made public, RTTT has ushered in rigorous and promising accountability mechanisms for teacher and principal preparation programs. With respect to teacher preparation, RTTT's goal is to promote and expand programs and pathways that are successful at producing "highly effective teachers," defined as those able to produce gains in student performance on statewide standardized assessments or other rigorous measures of student achievement that allow for cross-classroom comparisons.[14] The majority of state RTTT applications included plans to track outcomes that would help hold teacher preparation programs accountable.[15] Teacher preparation program accreditors have also pushed for reform. In 2010, the National Council for the Accreditation of Teacher Education (NCATE) argued that teacher preparation programs must be subject to more rigorous accountability.[16] In 2013, the Council for the Accreditation of Educator Preparation (CAEP), NCATE, and the Teacher Education Accreditation Council (TEAC) moved boldly to compel teacher education programs to raise their standards. One example of this is CAEP's revision of its accreditation criteria to require that students, on average, hold a 3.0 grade point average.[17] CAEP is also proposing to make accreditation dependent on how well a program addresses the needs of schools and whether program completers are effective in their practice.

Emergence of Teacher Preparation 2.0

Teacher Prep 2.0 programs are designed with a clear vision of what effective teaching is and how it can be developed over time. Central to that endeavor are embedded and authentic clinical experiences paired with smart uses of video and online technologies to accelerate learning and facilitate self-pacing for adult learners. They are also not satisfied to rely solely on "gut" and instead use empirical and experiential data to drive curricular redesigns and program decision making.

Emboldened by the national urgency to cultivate teacher talent, new and reimagined schools of education and independent teacher preparation programs have entered the field, advancing their visions of what it takes to be an effective teacher. In the past five years alone, we have seen a number of examples of these, such as High Tech High (HTH) Graduate School of Education (which opened in 2007), Relay GSE (launched as Teacher U at Hunter College in 2008 and founded by leaders of Uncommon Schools, Knowledge Is Power Program (KIPP), and Achievement First), and the Sposato Graduate School of Education (founded by MATCH Education and approved in 2012 by the Massachusetts Board of Higher

Education). Such Teacher Prep 2.0 institutions play a vital role in ensuring that the next generation of teachers will be able to perform their duties well.[18] They do this by matching competitive selection models with rigorous, clinical preparation, focusing equally on recruiting new talent and producing proficient instructors. Their actions contribute to a long and proud history of local school and community involvement in teacher preparation.[19] Decentralized, diffused teacher preparation is powerfully positioned to meet and respond to locally defined educational needs that, knitted together, forecast the nation's well-being.

Among these new teacher educators are school leaders who have been frustrated by the unpredictable skills of teacher candidates graduating from incumbent institutions. Not all schools are the same, and there are different constellations of talent required to perform one's duties well, depending on the teaching and learning context, configuration, and approach. For example, in chapter 3 in this volume, Betheny Gross and Michael DeArmond describe how many charter schools have approached the work of identifying candidates whose talents and interests align with the needs and expectations of their schools. That alignment of skill and mind-set is essential for teacher success, effective collaboration with instructional peers and school leaders, and student learning.

Together, Teacher Prep 2.0 providers have also sparked a revival of attention to the fundamental elements of effective teaching and have invigorated a discussion about how to elevate the rigor and quality of teacher preparation. They are unapologetic about putting student academic growth and achievement front and center. For instance, the Sposato Graduate School of Education offers a Master of Effective Teaching degree (not a Master of Arts in Teaching) and requires that its graduate students demonstrate success as teachers via impartial external observers, student achievement gains (when available), student surveys, and principal evaluations.

These programs are deliberately anchored in best practices and insights drawn from classroom and school experience and educational research. These reformers have designed modern programs that are grounded in content, pedagogy, and clinical practice. At UTeach at the University of Texas at Austin, for example, teachers seeking certification are immersed in the theory behind inquiry-based math and science instruction but are also given regular and repeated opportunities to design and get feedback on the planning and execution of their lessons, given the guiding framework of the 5E Learning Cycle model (i.e., engagement, exploration, explanation, elaboration, and evaluation).

Characteristics of Teacher Prep 2.0

This emerging community of teacher educators is characterized by its distinctive features. First, these stewards of Teacher Prep 2.0 are mission-driven and have designed programs intentionally, with articulated theories of action that describe the practical, empirical, and conceptual underpinnings of their programs. Second, they hold themselves and their students accountable for their competency and performance. Their organizational and institutional philosophies act as a guide for purposeful and ongoing reflection about, and evaluation of, program quality and efficacy, fueling cycles of research and development to identify strengths and areas for improvement. Third, Teacher Prep 2.0 programs emphasize the importance of clinical practice in schools. Finally, these teacher educators integrate online and video technology to enhance and extend the reach of their instruction, feedback, and resources.

INTENTIONAL DESIGN

Preparation programs that embody the Teacher Prep 2.0 framework adopt concrete theories of action. The hallmarks of Teacher Prep 2.0 are its shared embrace of student achievement as the essential outcome of effective teaching and recognition of clinical practice as an indisputable element in the process by which teachers improve. However, there is no single stultifying framework to impede the ability of Teacher Prep 2.0 providers to elaborate and customize their programs to meet the needs of the teachers and schools with whom they work. Nevertheless, within a given program, faculty and staff share a common vision of what teachers need to know and know how to do and what methods are best suited to supporting teacher development in those areas. This mission alignment ensures the fidelity of implementation of their program design, which is essential for success.

Essential to the clinical focus of Teacher Prep 2.0 is a collective respect for the contribution that experienced and effective teachers can make to preparing new teachers. In traditional teacher preparation, these individuals are typically sidelined as "clinical" faculty, while Teacher Prep 2.0 programs give these talented individuals more prominent roles and responsibilities. Their faculty includes experienced educators who have demonstrated teaching success with high-need K–12 students and adult learners. As former or current teachers themselves, these instructors are able to model effective teaching techniques and strategies and work with small groups of teachers to provide the kinds of instruction, mentorship, and guidance that have been positively associated with the success of developing teachers.[20]

For example, at Relay GSE, faculty model effective instruction by designing session plans that follow Madeline Hunter's elements of effective lesson planning (for example, using an opening "hook," clearly stating the purpose of the session, incorporating independent and guided practice, checking for understanding).[21] These instructors also use this group time to demonstrate specific K–12 teaching strategies, give teachers the opportunity to practice, and give and receive feedback on their efforts.

Teacher Prep 2.0 efforts mirror growing trends in K–12 schools themselves to incorporate character and moral development into their curriculum. In his book *Character Compass*, Scott Seider presents three case studies of schools in the Boston metropolitan area—Boston Prep, Roxbury Prep, and Academy of the Pacific Rim—and describes how each approaches its commitment to building the moral, performance, and civic character of its students. This character curriculum was also the topic of Paul Tough's *How Children Succeed: Grit, Curiosity, and the Hidden Power of Character*. Two of the leaders of schools profiled by Tough, Dave Levin of KIPP and Dominic Randolph of Riverdale Country School, partnered with University of Pennsylvania professor and character scholar Angela Duckworth to found Character Lab. Awarded an initial investment by NewSchools Venture Fund, Character Lab aims to support and disseminate specific teacher-led interventions that evidence suggests will have a profound impact on youths' character formation and, by extension, their life trajectories.

ACCOUNTABILITY

Second, Teacher Prep 2.0 programs are introspective and support evaluation cycles to learn about the quality of their programs and inform decision making. These programs learn from what is going well, make necessary changes as they go, and capitalize on the experience that they are gaining to improve their programs. Surveys are used to gather data on teachers' attitudes about what they are learning, the merits of the modes of instruction and assessment, and how supported they feel in their program. Teacher performance data on course assessments and classroom observation protocols are also used to identify teachers' strengths and areas of growth to help pinpoint areas in need of additional instruction. Finally, these programs collect data on teachers' effectiveness to ensure that the skills teachers are learning as part of their program are meaningfully contributing to their ability to raise K–12 student achievement. By doing so, they model the data-driven practices that effective teachers and schools implement, such as those that are the focus of the teacher data team trainings the Wallace Foundation is supporting in districts across the country. In these training programs, school leaders and instructional staff learn how to interpret data to understand the individual and collective learning needs of the students in their schools and how to devise data-driven action plans to improve student achievement.[22] Workshops also provide advice on how to build internal capacity for this analytical work and how to identify and actualize opportunities to bring subject- and/or grade-based teams together to discuss student progress and collaborate on determining and carrying out the appropriate interventions.

Its data-driven approach makes Teacher Prep 2.0 nimble and responsive to the contemporary circumstances and conditions of K–12 education. Unlike traditional teacher education programs, which have been stymied by their reluctance or inability to change, Teacher Prep 2.0 understands that its adaptability, undergirded by its cycles of research and development, is one of its competitive advantages. For example, at Relay GSE, curricular revision is guided by a review of graduate students' program performance, including evidence of their K–12 students' learning gains. These discussions yield insight about where future iterations of the curriculum can be expanded or resequenced or around which topics or skills teachers need more support, and when.

CLINICAL PRACTICE AT THE CORE

Teacher effectiveness is not a function of experience in and of itself; instead, it is the result of time well spent on disciplined and purposeful practice.[23] Deborah Ball and David Cohen did not mince words when, in 1999, they said that asking teachers to learn how to teach without spending time in a classroom is like expecting someone to learn to swim on the sidewalk. Early career teachers have been found to be particularly responsive to practice. Data on the NYC Teaching Fellows showed how teachers enrolled in clinically rich programs, specifically those that focused "more on the work of the classroom" and offered "opportunities for teachers to study what they will be doing as first-year teachers," saw significant improvements in their effectiveness compared to other first-year teachers.[24]

Even still, and despite research that has shown the importance of well-coordinated and well-supervised clinical experiences, in 2008–2009, only half of students enrolled in teacher preparation programs took part in a clinical experience at all.[25] Furthermore, while most states require between ten and fourteen weeks of student teaching, most programs do not provide information about what this critical component of teacher preparation should look like or what the role and requirements for mentors should be.[26]

Teacher Prep 2.0 programs are rooted in significant clinical practice, whether working with pre- or in-service teachers. Such programs partner with K–12 schools for clinical placements and faculty expertise. Because of this, these teacher educators are not siloed; instead, they cultivate cross-cutting partnerships and coalitions for change. In the United States, Urban Teacher Residency United works with more than a dozen partners to promote a residency model that melds selective recruitment with clinical placements and graduate-level courses.

There are many exciting and specific examples of Teacher Prep 2.0 residency programs and initiatives around the country, many of which have received support from the U.S. Department of Education through its Teacher Quality Partnership program. The Chicago Public Schools' Academy for Urban School Leadership's Teacher Residency is a year-long program during which residents work in classrooms under the guidance of mentor teachers while earning a graduate degree from a local university partner. Serving the same metropolitan area, the University of Chicago's Urban Teacher Education Program is a five-year program that offers a gradual release to teaching beginning with observations, tutoring, field experiences via a rotation of schools, and a year-long student teaching experience in the fifth year.

Teacher residencies have introduced many young people to teaching, with inducements such as tuition incentives and loan forgiveness. In Washington, DC, KIPP partnered with a local charter school to found the highly selective Capital Teaching Residency which, in 2013, accepted 8 percent of applicants. Teaching Fellows programs in cities across the country have recruited and prepared thousands of new teachers to serve in high-need schools. At Hunter College–CUNY, where David Steiner helped incubate Teacher U (which became Relay GSE), the New Visions–Hunter College Urban Teacher Residency (UTR) program pairs teachers seeking positions in special education and English language arts with experienced mentor teachers in their subject. Over the past four years, all UTR graduates have found teaching positions in high-need schools in New York City.

Several teacher residency models blend preservice preparation and in-service instruction with a multiyear commitment to teach in local high-need schools. For example, Boston Teacher Residency (BTR) pairs a one-year preparation component with a three-year minimum requirement to teach in the Boston Public Schools (BPS). During their time with BTR, teachers also earn a master's degree in education from the University of Massachusetts Boston. According to BTR's Web site, "While UMass grants the degree, BTR hires its own faculty and designs courses tailored to BPS' curricular and instructional goals and activities. BTR courses and seminars are taught by experts from schools, universities and local community agencies who have demonstrated expertise in bridging theory and practice."[27]

Aspire Public Schools, a recipient of the U.S. Department of Education's Investing in Innovation Fund (i3) competition, runs thirty-seven schools across California and Memphis, Tennessee, and the four-year Aspire Teaching Residency. Residents work toward certification, a master's degree in curriculum and instruction from University of the Pacific, and, in their first year, work in a classroom four days a week, where they learn from an effective and trained mentor teacher.

In Arizona, iTeachAZ, a program of Arizona State University's Mary Lou Fulton College of Education, doubles the time that most preservice teachers spend in clinical practice. Teacher candidates are responsible for an academic course load while also learning from co-teaching in a classroom of a partner school. ITeachAZ also emphasizes the importance of student growth; it describes "the ability to assess and respond to the needs of preK–12 students and increase student achievement is the ultimate goal of teaching and iTeachAZ." The program also offers a stipend to qualified candidates in exchange for making a commitment to teach in a partner district for three years after the intensive year-long residency.

In Texas, the UTeach Natural Sciences program blends two phases of lectures and seminars on inquiry approaches to teaching and inquiry-based lesson design with student teaching for prospective teachers of math, science, or computer science. Also in Texas, the YES Prep Teaching Excellence program is a one-year teacher development and certification program that features induction, instructional and data-driven coaching, and professional development courses. The program aims to increase first-year teachers' effectiveness and student achievement and promote teacher engagement.[28]

Teacher Prep 2.0 models push us to think outside the box to embrace the possibilities of integrated and embedded teaching experiences that cultivate teaching talent. To be connected to, and embedded in, clinical practice also means helping to convene and facilitate a professional community that defines and discusses how to cultivate the core skills of teaching. This common vocabulary, such as that provided by Doug Lemov's *Teach Like a Champion* and Robert J. Marzano and John L. Brown's *Handbook for the Art and Science of Teaching*, help create the conditions for open communication.[29] Additionally, TeachingWorks, an initiative of the University of Michigan's School of Education, is an example of how teacher educators can promote a professional community that collaborates and shares lessons learned from working with teachers and schools with the shared aim of improving each other's ability to meet the emerging needs of the field and support student learning. TeachingWorks has identified nineteen "high-leverage practices" that, when performed well, "increase the likelihood that teaching will be effective for student learning." They include leading a whole-class discussion, setting up and managing small group work, designing a sequence of lessons toward a specific learning goal, and setting long- and short-term learning goals for students.[30]

USE OF TECHNOLOGY

To deliver instruction that is maximally accessible, rigorous, and differentiated, Teacher Prep 2.0 programs purposefully integrate technology into their curriculum. Video is emerging as a way for next-generation teachers to provide authentic, credible, and contextual evidence to demonstrate their skill before entering the classroom.[31] Teacher Prep 2.0 programs are moving to embrace performance assessments, such as edTPA, which require that teachers, both preservice and in-service, demonstrate their readiness not only through paper-and-pencil exams but also via performance evaluations covering planning, instruction, and assessment.[32] For example, teachers may be asked to showcase their abilities via digital video recorded in their K–12 classrooms or with authentic artifacts of instruction, such as a lesson plan and associated student work.

Next-generation programs also use technology to supplement in-person classroom observations with video-based observations, increasing the amount of direct feedback that teachers receive. The use of video has been shown to yield improvements in teacher practice because it enhances what teachers are able to observe about what is happening in their classrooms.[33] Video allows for the precise capture of particular pedagogical strategies and techniques, enabling teachers to isolate these actions for clear viewing, reflection, and analysis. Watching classroom footage opens the door to productive discussions that gradually focus less on teacher behavior and more on student academic engagement and behavior.[34] Teachers' ability to assess aspects of teaching based on watching a video of actual classroom instruction that is not their own has also been shown to be a reliable and valid measure of teacher knowledge. For example, in math, Nicole Kersting and colleagues at the University of Arizona's College of Education found that teachers' assessments of video were positively correlated with other measures of teacher knowledge and effectiveness.[35]

Interactive video review, where coaches can look in on teachers and give feedback on real teaching, fosters reflective practice and collaborative learning and supports the development of a language of pedagogy, thus increasing teachers' professional knowledge.[36] Educational technology firms such as Bloomboard, Edthena, SmarterCookie, and Teachscape, among others, are helping encourage the adoption of teacher video by designing flexible online platforms where teachers can upload video for review and feedback and engage with those advisers about specific ways to improve their teaching.

Video also facilitates peer review, which is valuable for both the focal teacher as well as those offering feedback. At first, teachers need to be guided through peer review sessions where their colleagues review, and provide constructive feedback on, demonstrations of teaching practice. In time, this reflection can be self-guided, after teachers learn how to watch themselves and others teach, identify opportunities for incremental improvement, and recognize that they can improve how they perform in the classroom. Video also creates opportunities for teachers to see and learn from diverse teaching situations and environments they would not otherwise have access to.[37] To make this possible for its students, Relay GSE has augmented its traditional library holdings with an online video library, a catalog of video clips of teaching moments that teachers can search by subject, grade level, or skill. These videos allow teachers to virtually visit, and learn from, hundreds of other teachers and their classrooms.

Moving Forward

The next decade will see the proliferation of Teacher Prep 2.0 models as the benefits of their collective approach to teacher education become better known and more widely recognized. As educators, Teacher Prep 2.0 programs model how teachers can commit themselves to continuous improvement so that they are responsive to, and hold themselves accountable for, their students' learning.

As they continue to grow, Teacher Prep 2.0 programs will grapple with several pivotal and perhaps uncomfortable issues that all programs must address in order to assess their capacity to contribute to efforts to innovate teacher education.

TEACHER PREP: ACADEMIC OR PROFESSIONAL EDUCATION?

Teacher education is caught between an applied academic discipline grounded in theory and a sense of urgency and an enterprise of professional education whose methods rely heavily on simulation, apprenticeship, and clinical immersion. Added to this mix, of course, are the liberal arts and pure sciences, in which teachers are now (more than ever before) expected to demonstrate their content knowledge.

Instead of benefiting from synergies between these rich fields, teacher education is stranded in the gulf between them: it is too interdisciplinary and multimethod to be legitimated as a proper and distinct academic discipline; its clinical components are often too shallow, inconsistent or infrequent to constitute rigorous clinical practice; and it is too often beleaguered by institutional demands to enroll students with tenuous foundations in the subjects that they seek to teach.

Unfortunately, for those programs that are housed within traditional institutions of higher education, prevailing politics can encumber valiant efforts to innovate and stretch beyond the antiquated models of recruiting, retaining, and rewarding faculty talent and to break free of the distractions of self-serving existential crises.[38] Another obstacle is the general persistent failure of schools of education to value or incentivize the practical application of research, unlike other fields such as the biological sciences, engineering, and economics.[39]

Despite this general cultural cocktail of entrenchment, there are pockets of hope within higher education. Traditional institutions are demonstrating how Teacher Prep 2.0 is not limited to those efforts that are able to design programs from scratch without structural encumbrances. Existing programs can adopt Teacher Prep 2.0 strategies by making incremental changes to their curricula and pedagogy. They can also ask themselves how their theory of action is manifest in their program design, course offerings, and culminating experiences. Leaders such as Deborah Ball (dean of the School of Education at the University of Michigan), David Steiner (dean of the School of Education at Hunter College–CUNY and former commissioner of education for New York State), and Tom Stritikus (dean of the College of Education at the University of Washington and former Teach for America corps member) are but a few examples of university-based scholars who are informed by, and engaged in, shaping the Teacher Prep 2.0 movement.

FACULTY EXPECTATIONS

Rethinking teacher education and introducing new models of supporting early-stage teachers has implications for faculty staffing models. As programs develop and integrate enhanced Teacher Prep 2.0 approaches to prepare teachers for their work, they must also plan for the pursuant challenges of managing the mismatch between current faculty expertise and what is needed. Without flexibility to recruit talent that is best suited for the demands of the work and to assign responsibilities on the basis of expertise and engagement instead of tenure, rank, and job classification, new programs will never have an opportunity to germinate and flower.

New faculty roles and responsibilities entail the development of new—or adapted—standards and practices for faculty hiring, retention, and promotion. While many of the core competencies expected of teacher educators will remain unchanged, some will be new. Teacher Prep 2.0 aims for an optimal compositional mix of skill, expertise, experience, motivation, and alignment with the teaching philosophy. Programs will need to determine what these new expectations mean for how faculty qualifications are determined, how scholarship is defined, and how teacher educators' professional duties are described and understood.[40] These human capital considerations are the foundation to attracting, cultivating, and recognizing the diverse talent on which Teacher Prep 2.0 depends.

PREPARING TEACHERS FOR NEW INSTRUCTIONAL MODELS

A competitive advantage of Teacher Prep 2.0 is that it leans on the lessons of the past, responds to today's pressing needs of schools and teachers, and works toward a future where effective teaching transcends context. Teacher Prep 2.0 prepares teachers to understand how to adapt and translate the principles that they have learned to inform, benefit, and contribute to educational innovations and opportunities that emerge over the course of their careers.

There is a special opportunity for Teacher Prep 2.0 programs to more proactively feature courses and structure opportunities for teachers to gain firsthand experience applying what they have learned about effective instruction to emerging schooling models. These include learning communities that integrate online education, such as School of One and Florida Virtual Schools, and models that otherwise disrupt the configuration of modern-day classrooms. The steady increase in popularity of these modalities is predictable, given the sizable investments that are being made in educational technology and the enthusiasm about their use. These formats introduce flexibility that all schools can take advantage of as they try to balance fiscal constraints with the advent of more rigorous academic expectations and the demand for individualized and customizable attention based on students' learning needs and styles. These technologies enable schools to better provide differentiated instruction and deeper enrichment to students across the performance spectrum.

These new school models need a pipeline of teachers and leaders, and the opportunity is ripe for Teacher Prep 2.0 to incorporate opportunities for their teacher candidates to demonstrate their ability to translate their instructional skill and content knowledge in these formats. Working across modalities, coupled with opportunities for more intensive immersion, would serve as valuable exercises to increase teachers' decision-making and critical thinking skills as they join the cadre of educators who can think deeply about how the expanding set of instructional possibilities can be best marshaled to activate students' curiosity, support their learning, and prepare them for lifelong learning. The fullest potential of these new school models will be more quickly realized if they are tested and pushed to their limits by skillful teachers who believe in their potential to revolutionize how the world's children learn.

Conclusion

Teacher Prep 2.0 is a collective call to action, reflection, and collaboration. In time, all those involved in shaping the early careers of novice teachers will share a language, set of standards, rubrics, and professional expectations so that teachers are well-positioned to master a highly complex and ambitious job with the help of a network of consistent supports in their schools and communities. Those programs that fail to join this learning community will soon reveal their obsolescence and find themselves struggling to justify their existence. Demand will shift to more relevant, affordable, and flexible programs where teachers are held to high professional standards of knowledge and skill under the advisement of strong instructors and coaches who are committed to improving a teacher's effectiveness.

Teacher Prep 2.0 models' momentum will grow as existing programs loosen their grip on outdated approaches to teacher development and welcome new teacher educators into the field.[41] The Teacher Prep 2.0 movement embraces pedagogical diversity, and providers have been thoughtful and deliberate about their program design and partnerships. Their efforts reflect a shared goal of preparing teachers who will lead their students to learning gains, inspire them to be engaged and caring citizens, and instill in our nation's children an appreciation for curiosity and knowledge and an appetite for hard work.

CHAPTER 5

Professionalization 2.0

The Case for Plural Professionalization in Education

JAL MEHTA AND STEVEN TELES

E DUCATIONAL PROFESSIONALIZATION has long been a powerful, if highly contested, idea. Since the field's modern founding at the beginning of the twentieth century, advocates have argued for greater professionalism. If only education could establish a real knowledge base to guide practice, develop training in that knowledge, and establish stringent licensure requirements which would ensure that credentialed teachers possessed that knowledge, these reformers have argued, we could eliminate educational quackery in the way that the Flexner report eliminated medical quackery. This idea is as old as the Progressive Era and as recent as American Federation of Teachers president Randi Weingarten's 2012 call for a "bar exam" for teaching. Proponents have repeatedly hoped that such a professionalizing process would not only improve the consistency of practice but also win the field the kind of status, respect, and pay that characterize more established professions like law and medicine.

At the same time, the notion of education professionalization has had its skeptics. These critics have long questioned whether education can ever be a profession on a par with law and medicine, given the sheer number of teachers in the field, its comparatively low pay, and the lack of unity about values and the weakness of its knowledge base. They also point to past efforts to professionalize as a cautionary tale: despite a century of efforts to develop knowledge, reform training, and increase licensing requirements, there is no sign that the field has either improved the consistency of its practice or achieved the status of more powerful professions.

In more recent years, a group of reformers has argued that pro- fessionalization is not only unworkable but also undesirable. From this point of view, the kind of faux professionalization that prevails in education is the worst of both worlds—it gives monopoly control to a group that has no track record of success and no knowledge base on which to claim its authority. These critics argue that profession- alization limits educational diversity, prevents innovation, forces a unity of values on a field that is deeply pluralistic, and restricts entry for potentially good teaching candidates and school provid- ers who do not meet the requirements of the would-be profession.

Both sides in this argument have a point, yet both sides are also missing the point. Proponents are right that the relatively under- developed professional structures in teaching are a key obstacle to durable improvement in the quality of instruction; it is hard to imagine improvement in practice at scale without a more profes- sionalized system. But critics are right that medicine may not be the best model for a public field with modest pay, an uncertain knowledge base, and widely divergent ends. They are also right that educational professionalization needs to embrace change. In a period of skepticism about expert control and of lackluster educa- tional results, the field needs a way to embrace new ideas, school models, and approaches to school improvement.

To make major improvements in teaching, we need to under- stand that professions come in many forms and that they need not possess the monopoly structure of law and medicine to effectively shape practice and generate cumulative, productive knowledge. The peculiarities of education lead us to suggest the idea of *plural profes- sionalism*—professionalism without monopoly.

Plural professionalism is not pie in the sky. There are other professions, such as architecture, psychology and psychiatry, the arts, and the academic disciplines, that combine a high level of expert knowledge, specialized and internally controlled train- ing, and insulation from extraprofessional control with, at least in part, a pluralistic rather than a monopolistic structure. And there are already elements of plural professionalism bubbling up in the educational field, experiments that, if taken to scale, could create a new teaching profession, one simultaneously more professional and more diverse than the one we have today. While we do not claim that plural professionalization would magically enhance the status of teachers to be on par with other leading fields, we do think that it has the potential to develop the kind of knowledge, training, and consistency of quality practice that education desperately needs. We hope that, over time, such improved practice might gradually win its practitioners the autonomy, respect, status, and pay that they have long sought.

Defining Professionalism

Professions have traditionally been defined as fields that possess the following traits:

- A well-developed knowledge base that practitioners are required to possess
- Control by the profession of licensing providers of training and certifying practitioners to ensure that entering members meet its standard of quality
- Common norms and standards of practice which ensure that practitioners continue to meet the standards of the field (for example, hospital rounds in medicine or peer review in higher education)
- A moral code that expresses the field's commitment to the common good.

The traditional justification for the state's granting professions the right to exclusively license practitioners (such as letting the American Medical Association or the American Bar Association license doctors or lawyers) is that the potential costs to clients of an unregulated market are high, and thus professional licensing to enforce standards is an efficient way to ensure competent practice in a field.[1]

From this perspective, teaching, like other feminized fields, such as nursing and social work, is an aspiring or "semi" profession. Training is relatively short, compared to that in more established professions, and is reported by many teachers to be of limited use in guiding actual practice. In part due to skepticism about the efficacy of traditional preparation programs, alternative certification programs, which put people into school with almost no training, have grown significantly in recent years. Emergency credentials allow teachers to teach before receiving a full teaching license. And teacher licensing exams, compared to their counterparts in law, medicine, and engineering, cover much less knowledge and reflect a much lower standard. Teaching has some of the accoutrements of professionalization, but it is not a fully professionalized field.[2]

Professionalization can also be seen as an expression of cultural power over a domain. As Andrew Abbott has argued, professions are characterized by their ability to take jurisdictional control over their arena—to convince other actors that they, and only they, can be responsible for doing the work in their area.[3] The strongest professions, like medicine and law, have been able to convince the public that their work is grounded in an extensive knowledge base that they exclusively possess, a claim which has helped shape their treatment by the state and make them attractive to prospective entrants. Education has always been a troubled field with respect to claiming this kind of professional power. As a public field from its inception, it has always been under the thumb of the state, which has limited its ability to develop the professional control that characterizes law and medicine. It does not have an extensive knowledge base that guides practice or a technical vocabulary that organizes its work. It suffers from the fact that everyone has been to school, and thus everyone thinks he knows what good education looks like and how it should be produced. It is also a highly feminized field, with relatively low status and pay. For all of these reasons, education has been frequently subject to the whims of the state and has not achieved the kind of professional power and autonomy that we see in other fields.

The Case for Professionalization

The case for greater professionalization of teaching is powerful and long-standing. It rests on problems in the quality of classroom instruction and the relatively haphazard quality of teaching training, professional development, and feedback from practice to knowledge creation. Proponents argue that to achieve significant improvement, teaching must become competitive with other occupations, not just by increasing salaries but also by altering the social prestige and control of the workplace that attract talented people.

The most powerful argument for greater professionalization of teaching is the wide inconsistency of practice in the field. The Bill & Melinda Gates Foundation reports that in their largest ever video study of American classroom practice more than 60 percent of classrooms were competently managed, but only one in five featured ambitious instruction that asked students to reason and to answer open-ended questions.[4] These patterns in how teachers teach are, of course, reflected in what students can do. Results on the National Assessment of Educational Progress regularly show that two-thirds or more of American students of all ages have mastered basic skills like reading and recalling information, but that only one-third can do work that involves application or analysis.

The inconsistency of teacher practice is not surprising, given the nonsystem through which teachers enter the profession. The United States lacks a professional system for producing quality teaching. Teacher training is conducted by more than 1,300 institutions of widely varying quality; there are fierce debates over what sort of knowledge is relevant for teaching but little codified knowledge of the kind that supports work in other fields. Particularly in high-poverty schools, many teachers are teaching in areas outside their area of substantive knowledge. There are many skilled teachers in the United States, but most of these have "picked it up" on their own—through watching good teachers when they were themselves in school, through trial and error, and through the advice of fellow teachers.

Compare this nonsystem to the way in which more mature professions work. Professions assure quality control by developing knowledge to guide the work in their fields, training people in that knowledge, licensing them only when they have demonstrated competence in that knowledge base, and then developing ongoing standards that guide the work in the field. We hire dentists to examine teeth, lawyers to draw up probate contracts, and pilots to fly planes because there are established ways to successfully do these things that are enforced by members of the field. If serious reform requires establishing quality practice across fifty states, 15,000 districts, and 100,000 schools, the cross-cutting power of professionalization is a very attractive lever.

There is also some preliminary evidence that countries at the top of the Program for International Student Assessments (PISA) rankings use a more professional approach. A McKinsey & Company study from 2007 found that top-scoring countries generally draw their teachers from the top third of the prospective teacher pool, in contrast to the bottom 60 percent in the United States.[5] Training is also much more extensive and more frequently paid for by the state. This emphasis on selection and training on the front end lessens the need for the extensive testing on the back end, which is what we see in the United States. Teaching in such a context is also a much more desirable job (the most preferred career option for fifteen-year-olds in Finland, for example), which creates the strong pool of potential applicants that the professional approach requires.[6]

Finally, the professional approach is right to suggest that giving the field power over the core processes of knowledge development, training, professional development, and management of schools is critical both for developing skilled practice and for generating enough autonomy from the state to make teaching a desirable career. Professions are regulated by the state to ensure that they serve the public interest, but states are generally not good (in any field) at developing the kind of complex processes needed to generate quality practice. And a system in which teachers themselves had more say in the development of knowledge and standards of practice could better link research with day-to-day work in the classroom, while also engendering less resistance by teachers to efforts to make their behavior more uniform. Thus, professionalization has many virtues which should be capitalized on in a system that seeks to produce consistent quality practice at scale.

Challenges to Professionalization

The argument for making teaching more like other prestigious professions is powerful, but not unassailable. The great waves of professionalization in fields like medicine and law crested in an era in which faith in experts was exceptionally high, an era that today seems like another world. The power that those fields have over their own practice continues to be exceptionally strong, but it is hard to imagine that a field in which only 19 percent of Americans say they have a high or very high degree of trust would obtain the control over practice that lawyers have if they had to build it from scratch today. While high-profile scandals and the growing reach of the market have certainly put a dent in many professions, they have also been damaged by the increasing currency of broader critiques of the professional ideal. Conservatives in particular have argued that while professions claim that their power is necessary in order to protect the consumer, in practice the power of experts is simply a back door for the profession and the state to collude in promoting their own interests and in shrinking the scope of the market and civil society.[7] And both those on the Left and Right have attacked professions as self-interested devices to drive up prices and reduce consumer options by limiting market entry.

Another set of concerns emerges from what critics take to be the peculiar character of teaching as a field, rather than the nature of professionalism. The argument for professional control is strongest where the costs of substandard care are acute, immediate, and irreversible. Bad doctors can lead their patients to die on the operating table, and poor lawyers can cause their clients to go to jail or face financial ruin. While the long-term costs of poor teaching are certainly significant, they are not of the sort that critics believe can justify the risks associated with provider control of market entry.

Just as significant, education displays fundamental differences of opinion about what the goal of expert treatment ought to be—that is, what constitutes an educated person. Contrast this with medicine, where maximum longevity is a widely accepted goal. In a developed, pluralistic, liberal democratic state, education needs to accept a diversity of educational ends. Less normatively, but with roughly the same effect, the United States has sufficient diversity that it may be impossible to get political agreement to impose all but the most anodyne of educational ends. Thus, allowing different communities to define those ends is the only way to prevent watered-down, lowest-common-denominator schooling. The lack of social consensus on ends, therefore, means that there is insufficient grounding for a professional claim to advance broadly accepted goals.

Critics also point to the absence of the knowledge base that exists in other fields. With a couple of signal exceptions (such as early reading), the field has not developed a knowledge base that would legitimate the establishment of a canon of accepted practices, training teachers in them, and clearing out those who fail to conform to them. Of course, many fields in the past, the medical profession above all, established professional control in advance of having a comprehensive set of demonstrably efficacious techniques.[8] But at least the medical profession had a widely legitimate basis on which it could promise the discovery of more effective techniques and, over time, has created a progressively accumulating knowledge base that has delivered on that promise. Given that a century's worth of educational research has not, in most cases, led to a consensus on effective educational practices, either we need a different model of research or there is no consensus to be had. And with millions of teachers out in the field, the challenge of corralling them all to consent to a collective understanding of the job is much harder than with occupations like law and medicine.

These are serious criticisms, and even those—like us—who think the case for some form of professionalization is strong need to develop an approach to improving teaching that takes these critiques into account rather than dismissing them. Professionalization faces significant headwinds, and the peculiarities of teaching show the limits of overreliance on the medical model of professionalism. Thankfully, there is not a single model of what a profession is or should be. And in that diversity of models of professionalization we believe there is hope for finding a way forward that may achieve much of what advocates of making teaching a profession want while avoiding the problems and pathologies identified by their critics.

A Synthetic Alternative: Plural Professionalization

Professionalizing education is a huge project. It would require changes in status, pay, training, and the way in which the field is treated by external actors. A full treatment of those issues is beyond the scope of this essay.[9] But critical to a profession is generating mechanisms to develop knowledge, training people in that knowledge, certifying them, and getting that knowledge into use. A would-be profession today also needs to accommodate the dynamism of technological change and innovation. We believe it is possible for education to become more professionalized, in the sense of being characterized by consistent skilled practice, while adapting itself both to the special challenges of American pluralism and to education's idiosyncratic features.

The answer might be in plural professionalization. The primary virtue of professionalization—assuring core competency grounded in accumulating knowledge—does not need to be tied to the idea that there is one standard knowledge base or accrediting body through which everything flows. Rather, we take our cue from fields like psychology, architecture, higher education, and the arts, in which individual practitioners work within traditions or schools that govern and shape practice but also in which, across a given field, there is a pluralism of different approaches.

Consider the field of psychology. Psychology has many similarities to education—heterogeneous human clients whose cooperation is essential for successful outcomes; frequent disagreement over how successful outcomes should be defined; and the need for licensed practitioners to competently deliver critical services despite these challenges. Within psychology, a range of different approaches has developed over time, including cognitive-behavioral therapy, psychoanalysis, and many others. The differences in approach do not impede the field, within its various traditions, from developing knowledge and technique over time. Within each of its strands there is an evolved sense of what good practice should look like, which then lays the foundation for training in that particular subset of the field.

The arts provide another good example. In visual art, dance, theater, and classical music there are highly divergent visions of what it means to do "good work." But that doesn't mean anything goes. To the contrary, there are exacting standards for how to play Bach or perform a turnout in ballet. Again, the organizing unit is the school or tradition. For example, some classical musicians insist on the use of period instruments and a commitment to performance traditions in place when was the music was composed, while others are attracted to what they see as the greater range and power of modern instruments and the performance possibilities they open up. These decisions imply choices about technique and about antecedents, which serve as the departure points for new work. And, of course, styles are not sequestered from one another. Artists bridge traditions and develop new ones. The arts are not a profession in the sense of requiring formal licensing from the state, but they show how very high levels of practice can accumulate across a diversity of traditions and schools.

The academic disciplines are another good analogue. Here, the core organizing units are the disciplines, which in a broad sense maintain similar standards in the awarding of the PhD but are highly heterogeneous in their judgments of what counts as good work. This pluralism allows disciplines and subfields of scholarship to develop in very different ways without having to resolve underlying disagreements about values, methods, epistemology, and other issues. Again, as in other fields, sometimes subfields that had considered themselves distinct come together in unpredictable ways to create new disciplines or fields (biochemistry). Developing knowledge within distinct traditions does not eliminate the possibility of cross-pollination; in fact, it can enhance it by creating separate but related strands that then can both critique and reinforce one another.

There are also hybrid examples, which combine common knowledge that everyone in the field has to know with particular knowledge that develops in schools or traditions. Architecture is a good example. All architects have to pass licensing exams which ensure that they share the scientific knowledge that underlies the engineering of structurally sound buildings. But as they design, individuals choose among the variety of architectural traditions and styles that culture and history have made available to them. Psychiatry, because of its ties to medicine, is also a hybrid example: all psychiatrists have to attend medical school and pass common boards in both general medicine and psychiatry, but some then pursue additional training in one or other of the many various approaches.

Why Education Is a Good Candidate for Plural Professionalization

There are four key reasons why these pluralized fields provide the right analogue for the teaching profession. First, education is inherently a highly pluralistic field in terms of both means and ends. Second, enabling this kind of pluralism would link science and craft, as well as training and practice, within traditions in ways that are more likely to be effective than a one-size-fits-all approach. Third, the most successful models that exist in American education already take this form. Fourth, attempts to establish uniform professionalism have not worked well because they have tried to paper over the pluralism of the field in lowest-common-denominator compromises that are the antipathy of good educational practice.

Our starting point is that education is a highly pluralistic field in its means and ends. The purposes of education are highly contested. Schools are intended to fulfill economic, civic, social, moral, and other functions, and Americans disagree on their relative importance. Some see schooling as inherently conservative, a way of transmitting the wisdom and values of previous generations to the next; others see it as a fundamentally progressive force, one that should empower the next generation to reshape the world according to ideals of justice and progress. Some think that students should learn through individual academic disciplines; others think that they should be taught to work across them or to understand the epistemology that underpins them. And, of course, there are major disagreements over whether students should be taught the Western canon or be exposed to a multicultural curriculum. None of these questions has a right answer, nor are any of them likely to be resolved. Across more than 300 million people in a highly diverse nation, citizens can and will continue to disagree about such fundamentals.

Education is also pluralistic in its modes. Teaching and learning can be accomplished through lectures, projects, labs, Socratic seminars, Harkness tables, and case studies, among many other approaches. Disciplines and fields also have methods that have been found to be well-suited to their aims. Business schools use case studies, archaeologists invite students along on digs, physicists and biologists work in labs, and architects work in design studios. Often these means are linked to presumed ends: small seminars are critical for a liberal arts education; projects are favored for those who want students to discover as opposed to only receive knowledge; business school cases help professional students think through practical dilemmas they are likely to confront.

Such diversity in terms of both means and ends is not a problem to be overcome but a predictable outgrowth of the diversity of human experience. Education is not one thing; it is many things. Embracing this pluralism allows education to travel down its many tributaries, assuming the forms that are most natural for its ends.

A system organized around a pluralism of approaches would be more likely to produce consistently good practice because it would embrace rather than avoid the necessary intersection of values and techniques that comprise good education. However, our current system, when it has sought coherence, started from the least objectionable set of ends (basic literacy and numeracy) and then used the methods of science to arrive at the means most likely to achieve those ends. This kind of technical rationality has a number of problems: (1) the ends are limited when it comes to good education; (2) given the complexities of classroom teaching, it is very difficult to develop an intervention and expect it to be robust enough to guide teachers across the many contingencies she may face; and (3) in practice, teachers frequently ignore research, especially research that is philosophically incompatible with their views of how to teach.[10] This is especially the case when teachers believe that what is demanded of them one year will shift—perhaps radically— the next.[11]

In contrast, decades of research on effective traditional public schools, parochial schools, and now successful charter schools have repeatedly identified the importance of developing a clear mission and pedagogical approach based on a set of values about what good education looks like, as well as what kind of people the school is trying to produce.[12] This mission grounds the work of these schools—engendering commitment from faculty, students, and parents—and provides a standard to guide educational decision making. These are schools in which the people who run them possess *conviction*—a clear view of what is worth learning and why and what pedagogical activities might achieve these ends. Of course, they differ widely in those convictions, from the strict traditionalism of most Catholic schools to the optimistic progressivism of Deborah Meier, but they each have a clear sense of what they are about. Just as important, a clearly stated educational philosophy operates as a compact between teachers and education leaders, making clear to teachers that if they invest in mastering a set of practices, their supervisors will not scrap these practices just a few years later.

The challenge to date, however, has been that these "effective" schools have tended to rise and fall with their leaders. The question is how they might operate more consistently over time and at much greater scale. Our hope is that plural professionalism might provide the means by which we could move from individual schools with distinctive missions to a field that is more organized around distinct traditions.

What would it mean to organize around schools or traditions? Consider five examples—Montessori, International Baccalaureate (IB), no excuses, classical education, and blended learning. Freed of the need to achieve consensus, each of these approaches takes a strong stance on the nature of a good education, on how to balance breadth and depth, and on how students will demonstrate their learning. Teachers, students, and parents choose approaches that are consistent with their values, removing the problem of philosophical incompatibility. Within each of these approaches is not a single intervention but, rather, a dense body of *stuff*—teacher training, norms, materials, assessments, and a thriving community of people who have taught within this tradition—which, taken together, creates greater consistency across different classrooms.[13] The paradigm here is a mix of science and craft, as those working within a tradition are expected to share certain assumptions, work with certain materials, and use certain techniques, which mark them as professional members of the clan.

The strength of this approach is the creation of vertically integrated systems that would link the various levers which guide practice into coherent streams. Each of these networks would train practitioners, organize schools, generate curricula, develop assessments, and create mechanisms of accountability aligned and anchored in a strong vision of good instruction. We can see this in the IB program: teachers are trained and certified by IB; IB assessments serve as the anchor for lesson planning and the development of a curricular scope and sequence; and externally administered exams provide accountability for students and schools alike. Individual teachers have considerable flexibility in developing specific lessons and teaching particular classes, but they do so within a framework that provides a clear conception of what a good education is and how it can be realized.

The result for individual practitioners would be a much more coherent process of developing skill and expertise. One becomes "expert" from 10,000 hours of practice, yes, but research suggests that all practice is not created equal. Practice works only when it is situated within clear expectations that are embraced by the practitioner and that are accompanied by targeted feedback measured against those expectations. In a system organized around multiple traditions of good education, the result is that new practitioners know what they are aiming for and can get better as they move closer to a shared standard.

At the level of the field, this kind of pluralism could accelerate the accumulation of knowledge by enabling technical sophistication about how to make each of these traditions work. The pattern in American education has been to lurch wildly between antithetical extremes—one decade is about "back to basics," the next about "higher-order thinking," and then back again. These kinds of fights, while providing fodder for op-ed pages, do nothing to advance the specific, technical types of knowledge that help teachers improve their practice. Since educational traditions take a stand about what is taught and how, they enable professional discussion among relatively like-minded people. Freed of the need to debate first principles, these smaller, more compatible communities can more tightly focus on what scaffolds are needed to help students undertake a historical investigation or how best to help students master "core knowledge."

Research suggests that teachers already do this on an individual basis. Rather than looking to a unitary body of science for guidance, they consult philosophically aligned teachers, seeking to scavenge materials, activities, assignments, and other teaching materials that will help them solve practical problems in their classrooms.[14] By moving this process up to the level of the tradition, we can enable individual teachers to learn what like-minded colleagues are doing and, as a field, allow knowledge to accumulate within each of these approaches. There are better and worse ways to run a project, organize small groups, or deliver a lecture; to be an expert in a tradition would mean knowing the best approaches. What we need are mechanisms that enable these traditions to develop, capture, and share knowledge and make that knowledge part of the training of new practitioners.

Plural professionalism also has the advantage of more closely tying practice to knowledge production. Currently we have institutions, like schools of education and other research institutes, that are fairly distant from practice and are not focused on the needs of the field. Instead of a horizontal model—with a layer of research/theory/training separated from a layer of practice—we would have a vertically integrated model in which different traditions developed practices and trained their practitioners in those modes. We are beginning to see this already. As Billie Gastic describes in chapter 4, "no-excuses" schools like KIPP, Achievement First, and Uncommon Schools have partnered with Hunter College to create the Relay Graduate School of Education, which trains its practitioners in the management skills one needs in no-excuses schools. Conversely, High Tech High, a project-based network of schools in San Diego, has created a graduate school of education to train teachers in interdisciplinary, project-based methods. Both of these models are heavily driven by the needs of practice and, in fact, were started out of the realization that education schools were not producing teachers with the particular types of skills needed in their classrooms. The outcome of these new models, from the perspective of the potential teacher, is a coherent experience. From her beginning days of teacher training through to becoming an expert teacher, she is working within one conception of what good education looks like, a coherence that enables her to accumulate knowledge, skill, and technique within that tradition.

Of course, there may be some knowledge about teaching and learning that is more universal or broadly shared. If there is a growing knowledge base about early literacy, the importance of noncognitive skills, or how people learn, students in all of these traditions should learn it. But, even here, the traditions are important as each, in its own way, incorporates new knowledge into its distinct community and value system.

Plural Professionalization in Practice: The Teacher's Eye View

What would plural professionalism look like in practice? Compare the experience of a hypothetical teacher, Pam, in today's system to what her experience would be in a pluralistic system of the future.

In today's model, Pam graduates from college in the spring of 2014 with a major in biology and a desire to help children, so she decides to become a teacher. She applies to education schools chosen primarily by geographic proximity, is accepted to one, and picks the one with the lowest tuition. She attends school there for a year and learns a hodgepodge of material, including Vygotsky, Dewey, adolescent development, the achievement gap, and the importance of helping students become active thinkers and learners. She does some student teaching in a nearby suburban school, drawing mainly on what she remembers from her own tenth grade biology class, but receives little feedback from her university supervisor, who himself has not taught in many years.

The next year she starts her full-time teaching in an urban school nearby. She finds she is radically underprepared for what confronts her. The students won't pay attention to her directions, and some of them are years behind grade level. Her first year is miserable. Over the summer before the second year she asks a couple of veteran teachers for advice, and they suggest a set of behavior-management routines to achieve order in her classroom. She tries these, and, over the second and the third years, she is able to achieve a level of stability in her classroom. Her kids are mostly doing worksheets in biology (so much for Dewey!), but at least they are doing some work.

Now imagine instead Pam's experience in a plural professionalism system. On graduating from college, she looks at the local options for teacher preparation and identifies five broad approaches available to her: classical education, IB, project-based, no-excuses, and a new network of blended learning schools. Excited by her work in a lab in college, she elects the project-based option. There she learns the ways in which a project-based approach fits into the broader landscape of educational choices, and she recognizes that as a method it values depth over breadth. She then begins an extensive apprenticeship in project-based teaching. She watches many videos of expert teachers running projects and develops a series of project-based lessons as part of her unit on lesson planning. She learns how to incorporate mini-lectures and other more traditional teaching techniques into units that feature projects but are not exclusively organized around them. Her student teaching takes place at a local school that is project based and that is also run by her teacher training institution, creating continuity between her classwork and her initial entry into the profession.

When she begins teaching full time the following year, she looks for another project-based school that is part of the same network. There things look familiar from her student teaching—the same conceptions of what good work looks like, the same teaching philosophy, and the same expectations about how to scaffold projects. The school also provides explicit guidance on how to solve the most common problems associated with project-based teaching. She works with other teachers on how to implement projects while also providing her students with the background and contextual information they need in order to develop their understanding of biology. Parents and students explicitly choose the school because they are attracted to its philosophy and tradition. Pam has a highly successful first two years that grow coherently out of her teacher training program.

In her third year, Pam's school is visited by an accreditation team that is steeped in project-based methodology. Accountability through this kind of accreditation frees the school from the need to do the broad but not deep testing that has bedeviled project-based schools in the past. The accreditation team offers detailed feedback on what the school is and is not doing well in a way that is consistent with the school's goals; in particular, it draws on the work of leading schools in the network to suggest ways to integrate technology and to deepen instruction. The school comes out of the accreditation visit energized and with a number of new ideas about how to extend its already ambitious practice.

Plural Professionalization in Policy

The vision of a pluralized teaching profession that would give Pam this kind of experience is an attractive one. It holds the potential to attract a good number of motivated, idealistic young people who are turned off by the thinner and more uniform face of the teaching profession today. And, in many ways, it represents the "hidden potential" in changes already afoot in the sector. But it is far from obvious how policy can help us get to that more attractive world. Since the prevailing winds are, to a degree, behind plural professionalism, the key for policy reform is treading carefully, focusing on removing the obstacles, and providing resources and encouragement to those willing to push plural professional experiments. While we imagine that, in the long run, there may be ways in which all of education could become more pluralized, in the short run we focus on concrete policy steps that might enable those actors already inclined to move in this direction to broaden their reach.

The basic principle here is that the role of the state should move to licensing networks rather than licensing individual teachers. One could begin by keeping all of the existing apparatus of state regulation—rules governing the degrees teachers need to have, state testing of students, choice of curricula, etc.—but allowing waivers for vertically integrated networks of practice if they can demonstrate their own rigorous, internally imposed standards. To a degree, portfolio districts offer a model for accountability since the central authority is held responsible for ensuring that schools meet the standards districts have established for themselves. The same approach could be applied more broadly to networks of practice in a world of plural professionalism, with an accrediting body ceding authority to those that incorporate the full range of professional functions and that meet specified outcome standards. As those networks grow and new ones develop, the one-size-fits-all rules and regulations would not necessarily have to be eliminated, but they would gradually become less important. And the opportunity to opt out of state regulation would provide strong incentives for new networks to develop and for smaller groups of schools to align with others that share their values and pedagogical approach. We think it would be particularly promising if leading traditional providers that have a defined point of view (like Bank Street College of Education, for example) decided to form such networks, along with the new entrants that have become prominent in recent years.

Particularly important in moving toward this world is a shift in the mechanism of accountability. Today's insistence that all schools be measured by the same standards is a critical impediment to plural professionalism. Holding teachers and schools accountable to one set of tests inevitably focuses attention on those assessments. The result for teachers and schools is to force them to pay attention to multiple masters in ways that inevitably lead to incoherent education (projects one day, test prep the next). Rather, as is already the case with private schools and universities, accountability should be done through accrediting teams that share the basic values of the schools they are assessing. The role of the government should be to certify these vertically aligned networks, which would need to show that they have robust processes of accreditation in place.

In the model we are proposing, the existing network of regulations and standards does not disappear. For example, nothing we are saying here would impede the rollout of the Common Core State Standards or assessments based on them. They would still apply to all parts of the educational system outside of certified professional networks, and they would provide a baseline against which those networks would have to justify their curriculum and assessments to accrediting authorities. But in the world we are describing, students within these networked schools would be trained to quite divergent measures of what constitutes an educated person, and thus tests in one network would be incommensurate with those in others. This is a feature rather than a bug. The more educational terrain covered by these networks, the less "common" assessments based on Common Core would become. But that only suggests the need to move toward universally applicable measures of outcomes based on long-term measures of success rather than universal testing—measures like college admission and completion, future employment, or involvement with the criminal justice system.

To be certified in the way we are recommending, vertically integrated education networks would need to develop institutions that cover many functions currently filled by different institutions across the sector. They would need to develop their own teacher training institutions (which would not be primarily MEd machines but networks of graduate schools to which teachers would continually return throughout their careers), their own research shops (through which federal research might increasingly flow), their own curriculum and assessment tools, their own teacher accreditation systems and network-wide processes for removal. Within themselves, they would perform most of the functions that other professions do, the only difference being that there would be multiple professional networks, organized regionally or nationally, rather than a single one.

We can imagine two ways in which this policy approach could go awry. The first is that it could develop fairly unsavory insider-outsider dynamics, as the accrediting authorities get captured by existing networks of practice that use their resources and attention to keep out innovative new professional challengers. The second is that the standards for accreditation could become too lax, with networks developing political allies who allow them to opt out of existing state policies without developing the full range of professional infrastructure or without developing sufficiently high standards for student performance. Either of these would defeat the goals of plural professionalism, but we are somewhat encouraged by the fact that there seem to be directly conflicting political incentives in regard to our proposed institutional design that could push against one another. Outsiders will lobby to lower standards, but insiders will probably push back. This could keep the system at equilibrium.

Overall, we think the best way to nudge teaching in the direction of plural professionalism is less weeding (removing bad teachers, closing bad schools) and more watering (nurturing networks that want to vertically integrate, raise their own self-defined standards, and deepen their own connections between knowledge and practice). Rather than attacking the mass of existing institutions and rules, we should create clearer pathways and incentives for networks to escape them entirely. This will allow for a gradual transition from the existing system and minimize political resistance—or at least reduce the political opportunity for stopping plural professionalism from growing.

In the longer run, we might imagine that what is learned through these networks would penetrate back into the traditional system. Ted Kolderie has described a "split-screen" strategy for educational improvement, in which a minority of schools innovates aggressively and the rest do so incrementally, drawing on the lessons of the innovating minority.[15] The greater capacity for deep testing of ideas in professional networks would allow for that split-screen strategy to roll out in an ambitious way. Even if traditional institutions do not become as single-minded as the networks we describe, we can hope that the knowledge they generate can be incorporated into everyday practice in more traditional institutions. When a department wants to run a project, it will draw on the best of the project-based schools, and when it wants to work across disciplines, it will learn from IB, and so forth.

Conclusion: Pluralism but Not Balkanization

The obvious danger in what we are proposing is fragmentation, or balkanization. Much as legal scholar Cass Sunstein hypothesized that the Internet was leading to different groups reading only the news that was already consistent with their assumptions, there is a potential concern that the kind of pluralism we are proposing here could result in parochialism and insularity within each of these various traditions.[16] We think this is a serious concern but that there are ways to potentially mitigate its effects.

The most obvious mechanism of balkanization would be racial or ethnic segregation of schools, especially if networks develop that explicitly or implicitly appeal only to particular groups. On the one hand, there is no way to avoid the fact that networks that have a clear branding will not be proportionally attractive to particular teachers or students. For instance, no-excuses networks will almost certainly have more appeal to relatively disadvantaged families, as do charters in this tradition today. Up to a point, this is a feature rather than a bug; the challenge of teaching such children is, in some respects, different from that of teaching children of wealthier, college-educated parents, and it makes sense to develop a professional culture built around serving their needs. But that does not get professional networks off the hook. While parents or teachers of particular groups may choose at the end of the day not to buy what each network is selling in a proportional way, networks should still face an obligation to try to sell their approach. Accrediting authorities should hold these networks accountable for advertising for students widely across communities and for recruiting teachers from diverse communities.

Another important element of network credentialing would be to require all new entrants to the profession be taught how their respective traditions fit into the landscape of potential approaches, so that they can reflect on the pedagogical choices they are making. We also think that richer traditions will influence one another over time. Our general instinct is that real learning within the teaching profession will come, perhaps paradoxically, when we insist on less uniformity from the start. When members of particular traditions are confident in their ability to develop and implement their own practices, they will be less resistant to learning from others.

What is true of networks of practice is also likely true of individuals. Much as experienced scholars often turn to interdisciplinary work, we think that it is possible that highly skilled teachers might eventually be able to work within multiple pedagogical modes. But it would be best if those teachers had mastered one tradition first, much as scholars generally need to master a particular discipline before they begin to work across fields.

Conventional efforts to achieve teacher professionalization in the United States have been frequently frustrated by the fact that the United States is too diverse, the needs and preferences of students and parents too varied, and the question of "what works" too indeterminate for teaching to become a unitary profession. Working with such a goal has led only to frustration and resistance, and a convergence—if on anything—to the lowest common denominator. But that does not mean that the professional ideal is a pipe dream. By nurturing a range of professional teaching communities to form, to learn, to innovate, and to build their own institutions, we can create a uniquely American teaching profession. We owe the teachers of the future, their students, and the nation nothing less.

—— PART III ——

When Policy Meets Practice

CHAPTER 6

Improving Teacher Quality in Online Schools

More Than a Revolution at the Margins?

DENNIS BECK AND ROBERT MARANTO

MOST OF US can conjure up an image of a schoolteacher standing at the front of a classroom delivering the day's lesson. The role of an online teacher is far less recognizable. No longer holding court in the front of a classroom, cyber teachers can work from home and function as a learning manager—part mentor, part tutor, part cheerleader—helping students work through the material of their class.

Cyber schools (also known as online schools) offer some unique advantages to the traditional schooling model:

- *Distance learning.* Educators and students can work together even while separated by hundreds of miles. This innovation in itself has the potential to end localized teacher shortages and local education monopolies. In the cyber world, any student can take any course from any location. No long bus rides, with their bullying, wasted time, and energy costs. Transportation is no longer a barrier to education. Administrators monitor classes unobtrusively at any time from anywhere.
- *Scheduling flexibility.* Students can take classes any time of the day or night, fitting classes around their real-life needs, like family or work responsibilities. Teachers or coaches are available for help 24/7.

- *Personalization.* Software use enables a teacher to differentiate instruction, providing an individualized education plan (IEP) for every student. Students can review classes until they understand the material. This means that students, including special-needs students, may be promoted based on what they have learned rather than how tall they have grown.
- *Teacher time.* Teachers employ information technology for tutoring, attendance, monitoring student attention, and other routine tasks, freeing them up to teach and build relationships.
- *Twenty-first-century skills.* By integrating technology into course design on a daily basis, by requiring students to use video conferencing, online interface portals, and communicate through e-mail, teachers better prepare students for the modern high-tech workplace.

As anyone who has watched cyber teaching knows, it is something to behold. A teacher might simultaneously lecture, pull individual children into a separate chat room with individual materials, e-mail questions to make sure a particular child is paying attention, and assign individual or group projects—even from home while wearing slippers. New methods of formative evaluation such as instant-result polling, augmented reality applications, and other immersive technologies give immediate feedback to instructors while increasing teacher presence in a novel way. As one might imagine, cyber teaching requires different knowledge, skills, and abilities than those held by traditional public school teachers, which are often not screened for in traditional training programs.

Both common sense and research find that teacher quality is the key school-level determinant of student learning, and for this reason the Obama administration has emphasized improving how public schools recruit, manage, pay, and, at times, separate teachers.[1] But does teacher quality look different across settings? If so, whether or not existing teacher quality–driven policies work well for brick-and-mortar schools, the same policies may not translate directly to an online environment.

Thus, cyber schooling may require distinct personnel pipelines and new personnel systems to attract, train, and retain talent. To what degree have cyber schools reinvented such systems? What can we learn from the way such schools manage human capital that can inform future policy that might be more accommodating of such school models? In order to thrive, cyber schools need to reinvent teacher personnel management. They have demonstrated that they do so by removing teaching from the constraints of time and place and, in part, by systematically substituting technology for labor for administrative tasks that take valuable teacher time.[2] But have cyber charters lived up to their potential? Have they taken advantage of their freedoms from typical personnel management practices like tenure and single salary schedules? Do cyber charter schools hire for mission, systematically mentor new teachers, effectively offer feedback to and evaluate teachers, and base pay, promotion, and termination decisions on teacher work performance rather than traditional trait-based (education, seniority) measures or simple "office politics"? How does the background of leaders affect their personnel management strategies? What effect does school-level leadership have on innovation? How is the morale of cyber teachers? Do regulations inhibit the degree to which cyber charters can reinvent educational personnel systems?

We explore these questions through a mix of quantitative and qualitative inquiries conducted primarily in Pennsylvania. We chose Pennsylvania in part as a convenience, since it is where we have done considerable fieldwork and where we have served on cyber charter boards; but we also chose it because of its well-established cyber charter sector, with the second-largest cyber enrollments in the nation. For the state's cyber charters generally, 8 of the 16 schools account for 95 percent of the sector's 40,000 student enrollment as of spring 2013. While Pennsylvania's 163 brick-and-mortar charter schools serve 77,000 students, with another estimated 44,000 students on waiting lists, the cyber charters have essentially no waitlists because they can expand quickly. The Pennsylvania Department of Education reports that traditional public schools spend a mean of $14,119 per child, compared with $11,625 for the state's cyber charters. Notably, Pennsylvania's cyber charters are funded by the sending districts, which have frequently delayed payment until they are sued. For this reason cyber charters stockpile financial reserves, which has prompted some policy makers to call for funding cuts for cybers.[3]

First, we report data from interviews with the CEOs of eight of Pennsylvania's sixteen cyber charter schools accounting for 24,000 of the sector's 40,000 students. Four of the schools sampled have 1,000 or fewer students, but two have more than 7,000. Five of the eight schools are more than nine years old. Second, we report data from a survey of teachers at two cooperating Pennsylvania cyber charters. Finally, we report data from our national survey of cyber school leaders using questions derived from the survey conducted by researchers Michael Podgursky and Dale Ballou.[4]

To jump ahead, results suggest that, so far, just as most brick-and-mortar charter schools have proven to be incremental rather than "disruptive" innovators, so, too, have cyber charters made modest rather than revolutionary changes. Here are a few defining characteristics:

- *Demographics:* At least within our Pennsylvania sample, cyber teachers resemble their traditional public school counterparts demographically, and the vast majority majored in education as undergraduates, though cyber teachers seem to come from somewhat more selective colleges. Like traditional public school teachers, they also express some skepticism as to whether teachers should be judged in part based on student scores on standardized tests.
- *Contracts:* Very few cyber charters offer tenure; annual contracts are the norm. Collective bargaining is rare.
- *Workplace environment and culture:* Notably, most cyber schools allow significant numbers of teachers to work from home, taking advantage of the digital environment. Yet the supportive culture is not lost. Cyber charter teachers and administrators alike agree that school administrators spend considerable time and effort observing, evaluating, and mentoring teachers. Some schools also give new teachers reduced teaching loads. Cyber teachers seem to respect their school leaders and report that those leaders provide detailed feedback and improve their teaching

- *Evaluation:* Cyber charter leaders report terminating for cause or "counseling out" far more teachers than are typically separated in traditional public schools or other charter schools. These vital decisions reflect purposeful evaluations rather than seniority and official qualifications, as is the case in traditional public schools. It is less clear, however, whether cyber charters systematically incorporate their evaluations into merit pay awards.

Certain factors—including state regulations, the necessity for new schools to build a common culture, and the relatively traditional backgrounds of cyber operators—limit the degree of innovation cyber charters pursue, at least in the short term. Many operators want most teachers, particularly new teachers, in one physical location to facilitate mentoring, evaluation, and teamwork. Most cyber charter leaders come from traditional public school backgrounds, which may bias their thinking about how to deploy teachers. Perhaps more importantly, state regulations keep cyber schools from hiring uncertified teachers for more than 25 percent of positions and from employing teachers from out of state, much less out of country. Perhaps due to state requirements or reflecting market pressures, most cyber schools offer pay and benefits packages comparable to their brick-and-mortar counterparts. In our national sample, CEOs reported a mean starting salary for teachers of $38,200, comparable to the estimated $39,000 for the nation's teachers generally.[5]

In short, as a result of the regulations placed on them and the generally "inside the box" training and backgrounds of teachers and leaders, cyber charter schools have not *reinvented* teacher personnel management. At the same time, particularly regarding evaluation and termination, they have *reformed* it to a greater degree than have brick-and-mortar schools, even other charter schools. Because our particular sample draws from only charter schools, there is some uncertainty as to whether their ability to reinvent stems from the freedoms associated with charter schooling or from their online nature. Cyber teacher management holds the potential for more but currently is something of a revolution at the margins.[6]

Keystone State Cyber Charters

From our interviews of eight Pennsylvania cyber charter CEOs regarding their personnel practices, several themes emerged. First, even when not asked directly, cyber leaders express enthusiasm about leading in a nonunion environment. Second, these school leaders emphasized a strong mission/customer service focus. Third, while hiring practices are not innovative, mentoring is. Fourth, these leaders displayed substantial focus in both monitoring teachers and holding them accountable.

These CEOs, five of whom were founders or co-founders of their schools, had a greater range of experience than the typical school superintendent. One had a career in the information technology industry before working in traditional public schools and then cyber schooling. Others had backgrounds in the health-care industry and religious education. One cyber leader had substantial experience in public education, but only after a career in the military. The other four spent decades in traditional public schools in a range of posts from teacher to superintendent, but three of the four had been mavericks in traditional schools and were quick to latch on to the possibilities of cyber schooling. Everett Rogers refers to them as "early adopters."[7] No CEO was under forty years old, and two were over sixty.

PIPELINE: PREPARATION AND HIRING

Cyber school leaders have somewhat distinct approaches toward hiring. Though it was not part of the interview protocol, most of the CEOs interviewed expressed concerns about the quality of teacher training at schools of education (a theme developed by Billie Gastic in chapter 4), both in small ways, such as technology training and measurement, and in big-picture thinking about goals and accountability. As one CEO with substantial business experience put it, "I haven't found any [schools of education] that do a good job preparing students for an online classroom . . . teachers coming out of education schools are not experiencing online education in a way that is useful to us." A second CEO with substantial experience in both information technology businesses and traditional public schools agreed:

> None of them have good records at teacher preparation. I would not say hire from this university or that university because those teachers rock. These people are not coming out of school understanding anything. Our last interview question was about the Common Core and about the last 15 interviews only one or two could fake it. The others knew nothing about the Common Core. They know nothing about Adequate Yearly Progress, the PSSAs [Pennsylvania System of School Assessment] and the state standards. The colleges are just totally out of touch. One of the professors said, "This too will pass," and I said, "Yes, it shall pass, but in the meantime if you don't make it you close." So the Common Core may pass, but I cannot pretend it is not there, or plan on it going away.

Given the demands of cyber teaching, in which teachers might simultaneously lead a class discussion, e-mail questions to individual students to see they are paying attention, and even move some students into separate chat rooms, the preparation and cognitive demands of cyber teaching mean that teachers normally have a three or four course load (plus additional office e-mail hours, phone hours, and tutoring time), compared to five or six classes in traditional public schools.[8] As one CEO explained, "We had a legislator come in yesterday and watch, and he was stunned that the teacher had four arms. She was doing all these different things. I sometimes forget all the different things they do at one time, and they just love their work. They speak so passionately about it."

Given the skepticism Pennsylvania cyber charter leaders hold toward both traditional public schools and conventional teacher training programs, it is somewhat surprising that, overwhelmingly, the CEOs hire conventionally certified teachers. One clear obstacle for recruiting the teachers they want is Pennsylvania's law limiting charter schools to 25 percent uncertified teachers, even though certification processes have little to say about the skills necessary to teach in a cyber school. But, based on our interviews, only one CEO, who had a background in private education, reported wanting to hire a greater number of uncertified teachers. All of the others reported hiring all or nearly all certified teachers as a matter of course, almost as a sort of seal of approval. Another administrator highlighted a possible second choke point: federal regulations requiring them to only hire certified teachers unless they are making Adequate Yearly Progress (AYP). As a result, the federal regulations superseded the state law. Similarly, only three CEOs said that they gave much weight to a potential teacher's standardized test scores or college record, even though these are among the better (though still weak) predictors of teacher effectiveness.[9]

Given these hiring preferences, it is no surprise that our survey finds that cyber charter teachers resemble traditional public school teachers. They are 83 percent female and more than 90 percent white. Schools tend to hire teachers from nearby communities; and save for one small school, none of the cooperating schools was in Philadelphia or Pittsburgh. Seventy percent of teachers majored in education as undergraduates, and 94 percent were trained through a traditional school of education rather than through alternative certification. Seventy-six percent of teachers were under forty.

There is some evidence that the cyber teachers' college training was more "elite" than that of their counterparts: 27 percent reported studying at a regional state college/university (as typifies teachers generally), compared to 18 percent at one of Pennsylvania's three flagship state universities (the main campuses of Pennsylvania State, Pittsburgh, and Temple universities); 23 percent at a liberal arts college; 18 percent at a private university; and 13 percent out of state. Despite cries from some who might see cyber charters as a conservative movement or even a religious one, Democrats outnumber Republicans 46 to 25 percent, and religiosity seems to reflect that of the state as a whole (28 percent Catholic and 60 percent Protestant, with the latter split between mainline and evangelical churches). Only one of the eight CEOs interviewed came out of a religious schooling tradition.

SUPPORT AND RETENTION

Because traditional paths into the profession offer little preparation to teach in an online environment, each school utilized extensive mentoring, though with radically different approaches. Each school assigned mentors to new teachers. In half of the schools, when possible, teachers either co-taught their first few weeks or had a reduced load their first semester. One small but rapidly growing school had a very intensive and standardized hiring process, followed by an "onboarding process" in which a new teacher would meet with the personnel manager, the principal, the deputy CEO and/or CEO, six separate technology specialists (one who would customize the teacher's laptop), the procurement director, the special education leader, the guidance counselor, the director of pupil service, the assigned mentor, and various others to gain a full understanding of the school, their place in it, and where to go for help. Similarly, the CEO of another school reported having a "two-year induction process where we spend $27,000 on them, including a one-on-one mentor." When possible, "they co-teach everything the first year." New cyber teachers typically teach 60 percent of the class schedules their first year and 80 percent their second year. It is difficult to imagine any brick-and-mortar teachers with similarly gradual inductions.

Given the growth in cyber charters, teacher retention was also fairly stable: only 24 percent had taught at their school for less than 3 years; 37 percent for 3–6 years; 28 percent for 6–10 years; and 12 percent for over 10 years. Sixty-nine percent had taught at other schools, all at traditional public schools. (In part, this reflects Pennsylvania's status as the second-oldest and second-largest cyber market, as well as a job market freezing teachers in place.)

Cyber personnel management was at least somewhat innovative. For example, most CEOs reported allowing experienced employees to do some or all of their work from home. Some saw this as a norm for proven employees. As one CEO put it, "Our virtual classroom teachers can work either at home or on site, but then have to be on-site for at least the first year so they can be mentored by more experienced teachers, but after that we really leave it up to them. Some like the camaraderie of being part of a building, but some want to go home and teach in their pajamas, and then some who are having problems we do ask to teach on-site." Other CEOs seemed to see teaching off-site as a privilege to be earned, as an

incentive to keep good teachers from leaving, or as an accommoda-
tion for teachers who are parents. CEOs, particularly those of new
or rapidly growing schools, were somewhat reluctant to let most
employees work from home, which would make mentoring and
building a school culture more difficult. In our teacher survey, 51
percent reported doing all of their work at a central site, while 20
percent reported doing all of their work from home or at a "third
place," such as a library or coffee shop.

EVALUATING TEACHERS AND HOLDING THEM ACCOUNTABLE

Cyber school leaders report spending a great deal of time monitoring and evaluating teachers, which is seen as part of the mentoring
process. Without school boards, sports teams, transportation, and
extensive facilities to manage as traditional school superintendents
must, cyber charter CEOs feel empowered to dive into the classroom. A CEO with traditional public school experience marveled,
"Without having to focus on everything that a traditional public
school administrator has to do, I am able to concentrate on students.
It is all about the students, and their learning is central to everything I do." Unlike in traditional classrooms, cyber school classes
are nearly always recorded so students can replay lessons until they
learn them, a boon to special-needs students in particular.[10] A side
benefit is that cyber school leaders can easily and unobtrusively
monitor teachers, at a time of their convenience, and even play back
problematic classes to teachers.

Cyber learning breaks down the traditional walls between the
classroom and the principal's office. One CEO reported that he did
not feel comfortable monitoring live classrooms: "I can just see
when the students see me log in, the whole complexion of the class
changes." For the most part, though, CEOs or their teams did both
live and recorded class monitoring. As another CEO described, "We
can observe you. Our teachers are very used to being observed
because all our classes are recorded so anyone can look at it. For
younger teachers we do four recorded observations a semester.
Mostly we just go online and we can see kids' responses and at the
computer you can write it up right then. The principals and I both
do it. I like to get my hand in . . . For midlevel employees we do

two a year." CEOs put enormous trust in classroom observations, as do many high-performing charter schools and traditional public schools.[11] At the same time, each CEO interviewed reported using additional data as well, including data that would be impossible to capture in a brick-and-mortar environment.

> I observe them, but I observe them electronically. I have so much data. I can see how many outstanding assignments they have, and so on. I can look at their grades, how their students are doing. I can look at their students' attendance. I can look to see when they are logging on. I can check their communications with students, what kind of communications—e-mail, phone call, in-person. I have just unbelievable amounts of data. I can look and see if they are not making their weekly calls. I can look and say, "How come you have thirty-five outstanding assignments? You are supposed to get these graded within twenty-four hours. Students cannot move on. If kids are waiting to move on, they need feedback." I do cut the English teachers some slack because of the essays . . . They have classes asynchronously, so if it's Wednesday afternoon at 3:00, I can log in and sit in, if you will, in my office or I can do it from Germany. That's the beauty of the Internet. I can do it from anywhere.

Teachers don't appear to mind the constant monitoring and actually seem to like it. Eighty-nine percent of teachers surveyed reported being evaluated through live and recorded means. Interestingly, 65 percent of teachers (53 percent response rate, n=89) say they are evaluated by administrators quarterly, while only 4 percent report being evaluated weekly, far less often than administrators suggest. It is possible that teachers are referring to formal evaluations while administrators refer to more frequent, informal evaluations. Forty-eight percent of teachers say their administrators provide immediate, detailed feedback, while only 33 percent report annual or semi-annual feedback (perhaps reflecting the relative experience of the sample; novice teachers get more feedback). Sixty-seven percent of teachers working in the same building as their administrator report getting weekly or monthly feedback, while only 20 percent of those working in a different buildings say the same (47 percent of teachers work in a different building). This may be due to a tendency on the part of administrators to rely on more traditional methods of communication such simply "management by walking around" over digital means.

CEOs also report surveying parents and students and using their feedback to evaluate teachers. But most did not make much use of test scores, instead agreeing with some more conventional school leaders that if teachers did good work in the classroom, test scores would follow.[12] Several CEOs mentioned that while they and their staff could train someone how to teach and how to use information technology, they could not train the desire to serve students and parents in a welcoming fashion. As one said, "All of our teachers are highly qualified and certified, but we also look a lot for friendliness. This sounds silly, but this is as much a customer service business as an education system, so making those connections over the phone and the computer—if they can't make those connections, they are of no use to us, because that is what it's all about." All CEOs who mentioned it felt this characteristic was best judged in interviews and by references.

CEOs use all this data—monitoring classes, test scores, attendance, student course completion rates, learning management system usage information, and parent and student surveys—to hold teachers accountable. All report occasionally having to terminate teachers, though, as one put it, "if you do your hiring right you can avoid all that negative activity." Similarly, in our national survey, all the administrators who answered the question reported having fired teachers in one way or another. We asked cyber CEOs the number of full-time teachers they employed and to estimate the number of teachers forcibly separated from their employment in the last school year. By these admittedly imprecise figures, based on the Podgursky and Ballou methodology, we estimate that 3.6 percent of cyber charter teachers left employment after being counseled to do so by their administrator.[13] In addition, 4.3 percent did not have their contracts renewed for performance reasons, and another 2.7 percent were terminated midyear for similar reasons. Thus, we estimate that roughly one-tenth of cyber charter teachers are fired for poor performance in a given year. In short, it would appear that cyber charter leaders resemble private rather than traditional public school leaders in holding teachers accountable. In addition, even though the cyber charter sector as a whole is growing, CEOs report that 0.6 percent of teachers were let go for budgetary reasons, indicating that the sector has the personnel flexibility to adapt to changing economic demands. These numbers suggest that, as one CEO noted, the lack of collective bargaining enables personnel flexibility. In our national survey, 86 percent of CEOs report that their schools do not have collective bargaining agreements. Ninety-five percent of the teachers in our survey report that their schools do not offer tenure.

Most CEOs did not report using merit pay; though they would increase pay to meet counter offers to valued staff. In our survey, only 16 percent of Pennsylvania teachers reported being eligible for merit pay, though 71 percent of those eligible reported earning it. Nationally, CEOs of cyber charters report a much higher use of merit pay; 75 percent of teachers appear to receive it. These apparently conflicting results from the teacher and administrator surveys may be due to a perception that, because most receive it, it isn't really merit pay but just another version of the traditional step system. Interview data appear to confirm this. For example, one CEO who does distribute merit pay does so for the whole school when money is available and school level goals are met, though he maintains that keeping one's job is the best merit pay: "We've done it as a whole group based on our graduation rate, attendance rate, and enrollment for the whole school, but we do not try to fine-tune it for test scores, because people come to us with special needs, and the value-added system is not fine-tuned enough to take account of it. If you can't teach, you are not here."

Interestingly, teachers surveyed downplayed the role of merit in determining salaries. Teachers *disagree* that the personnel rules at their school reward teacher effectiveness. At the same time, teachers agree that they trust their administrators that the leadership consults with teachers regarding matters that affect the school, that their administrators have helped improve their teaching, and that they look forward to coming to work each school day. The 65 percent of respondents (n=58) who have experience at traditional public schools rate their cyber charter schools more favorably (see table 6.1). This is important since considerable research finds that optimism about work predicts teacher self-efficacy, which has been related to teacher quality.[14] Research also has shown that working with like-minded colleagues may contribute to higher teacher self-efficacy and quality.[15]

The imposition of regulations designed to manage traditional brick-and-mortar schools onto online schools cause problems. As one cyber school administer put it, "[Regulators] want to run cyber schools the way they want to run regular schools, and this is a totally different environment. They say charter schools are relieved from the restrictions, and I say, 'Which ones?' I still have to have a school nurse! We are an LEA [local education agency] in the eyes of the law." Cyber schools in Pennsylvania are required to administer the same state tests as their brick-and-mortar counterparts. However, the testing *conditions* are quite different. As one leader explained,

> We have to have our students testing at inconvenient times and in unfamiliar environments all over the state, and our teachers are on the road, staying in hotels, away from their families three, four, five days, testing the kids in big hotel ballrooms, where you have eight-year-olds in strange environments with people they never knew taking tests with dozens of other kids, and then that artificial environment affects their performance. You would think in the twenty-first century the state could come up with a technological fix for this.

If cyber schools and teachers are held accountable in the same way that traditional public schools are by these tests, but their students are forced to take them in environments that risk artificially lowering their scores due to discomfort, then the system is biased against online schools.

Another facet of Pennsylvania law, Act 82, also portends problems for cyber schools. For those teachers with qualifying student test scores:

TABLE 6.1

Teacher ratings of current cyber charter school versus previous brick-and-mortar school (% that agreed to % that disagreed)

Category	Current cyber charter school	Previous brick-and-mortar school	T
The leadership consults with teachers regarding matters that affect the school.	76% to 17%	37% to 31%	3.55***
My administrator has helped improve my teaching.	74% to 13%	57% to 9%	2.36**
I trust my head administrator.	89% to 15%	49% to 20%	1.71*
My colleagues share my beliefs and values about the mission of the school.	81% to 4%	62% to 6%	3.4***
Too many teachers use their classes as a "soap box" for their point of view (disagree to agree).	70% to 9%	40% to 20%	−4.03***
I look forward to each working day at this school.	74% to 9%	60% to 9%	2.17**
Many of the children at this school are just not capable of learning the material (disagree to agree).	72% to 10%	56% to 9%	−1.23
Schools should not be judged on students' test score gains.	59% to 15%	47% to 15%	1.14
There is nothing a teacher can do if a student's family is not supportive.	59% to 20%	49% to 26%	1.00
The personnel rules at this school are clear.	67% to 13%	66% to 3%	.92
The personnel rules at this school reward teacher effectiveness.	33% to 26%	17% to 17%	.73
The administration maintains an atmosphere where the rules and the authority of adults are respected.	67% to 9%	63% to 11%	.76

Notes: $N = 58$. * $p < .10$. ** $p < .05$. *** $p < .01$.

- 50 percent of their evaluation is based on observation based on the Danielson Framework observation instrument
- 15 percent is based on building-level data on the state's School Performance Profile metric
- 20 percent is from teacher-designed Student Learning Objectives, LEA assessments, or nationally normed assessments
- 15 percent is from teacher-specific value-added test scores.

But, as the editors of this volume noted in their introduction, the Danielson Framework is not well positioned as a basis for quality instruction in an online environment. Also, given the decentralized nature of the school, deciding which teachers receive credit in value-added calculations is problematic as well. All of this runs the risk of unfairly and inaccurately evaluating teachers in online schools.

Innovation and Its Barriers

Evidence suggests that cyber charter schools are reinventing certain aspects of teacher personnel management. Not surprisingly, given their medium, the cyber charters are far more likely than brick-and-mortar schools to permit work from home, particularly after a school's initial years and for non-rookie teachers. The cyber charters emphasize customer service in their teacher recruitment, perhaps due to the novel demands of cyber teaching and the need for charter schools generally to satisfy parents. And because cyber CEOs are relieved of some of the more mundane educational support functions (buildings, transportation, most discipline, etc.), cyber charters spend far more thoughtful energy training and mentoring new teachers than do traditional public schools, seeing instructional leadership as a primary role rather than an ancillary responsibility delegated to subordinates. Cyber teachers interact with and get feedback from their administrators.

Possibly for these reasons, teacher morale seems relatively high: teachers with experience in both sectors report higher morale in their cyber charter schools than in the traditional public schools they left, though our small sample demands caution. Teachers are particularly likely to give their cyber administrators higher grades on consulting with teachers and on improving their teaching, which may reflect extensive monitoring and feedback. Having fewer non-academic duties than in traditional public schools, and being aided by technology, which makes it easier to monitor classes both live and later, cyber charter leaders seemingly spend a great deal of time and effort monitoring classes, and offering feedback to teachers. Interestingly, as in the case of the YES Prep (brick and mortar) charter schools, where administrators also offer considerable feedback with high stakes, cyber charter teachers seem to approve of personnel management practices.[16] This may reflect the relative risk acceptance of teachers willing to work jobs without tenure in so novel a place as a cyber school. Perhaps most important, cyber CEOs hold teachers accountable, firing those whose teaching they judge ineffective, an unusual move, generally, in public schools.

But at the same time, several forces prevent a more fruitful reinvention of human capital management practices. These include, but are not limited to, regulations that have been grafted onto cyber schools from brick-and-mortar school management as well as from more traditional cultures and expectations, likely driven by the fact that cyber school administrators nationally (70 percent) and in Pennsylvania (75 percent) have backgrounds in the traditional public systems. (Only 30 percent nationally and 13 percent in Pennsylvania had backgrounds in brick-and-mortar charter schools, with fewer still in private schools.) Extensive reporting rules limit charter administrators' time (though less than for traditional public school counterparts), requirements to hire certified teachers limit their ability to shape their staff, and other regulations (such as having a school nurse) also constrain staffing.

Possibly, universities could increase their entry into the cyber charter business, bringing in new operators with significant educational resources and less tied to the traditional public school personnel management. In addition, limiting reporting requirements, staffing rules, and certification requirements could enable cyber charters to do more to reinvent teacher personnel management. It is not clear, however, what incentives policy makers have to make these changes happen.

Future Implications

In nineteenth-century America's Wild West, the federal government played a supporting role in securing land through treaties and setting up territorial governments while empowering local governments to secure services and public safety. A similar approach to cyber schooling may prove helpful today, with state and federal governments scaffolding and empowering cyber charters to integrate effectively with traditional public school systems to make a high-quality education possible for every student. This may require the following reforms.

- *Higher education to the rescue?* Currently there is little to no infrastructure for training and innovation for cyber charter leaders and teachers. Universities should provide teachers and instructional leadership for K–12 cyber schools. Teacher education remains unprepared for virtual schooling.[17] Additionally, administrator education programs continue, by and large, to ignore training preservice administrators for virtual positions.[18] Administrators can influence teacher quality through personnel practices such as merit pay, tenure, teacher evaluation, and teacher professional development. Demonstrating the dearth of cyber training opportunities for preservice teachers, Jason LaFrance found that of approximately five hundred educational leadership programs accredited by Council for the Accreditation of Educator Preparation (CAEP), only eight offered appropriate field experiences for those aspiring to cyber school leadership. If cyber charters are to succeed long term, they require the support of higher education teacher and administrator preparation programs, with cyber schooling perhaps best conceived as one of a number of "schools" of the education profession (as imagined by Mehta and Teles in chapter 5 in this volume).
- *Statewide employee evaluation* systems must be reimagined to include the knowledge, skills, and abilities required by cyber

school teachers and administrators, whose needs differ from their traditional counterparts. In the area of teacher evaluation, cyber charter leaders have implemented substantial innovations that should be emulated by others. Currently, Pennsylvania has a state-mandated teacher evaluation system for all public schools, the DEBE-333, which is used to rate professional employees for dismissal on the grounds of incompetency or unsatisfactory teaching performance. It has been roundly criticized for being cumbersome and for failing to make meaningful distinctions in teacher quality. Two Pennsylvania cyber charters are currently testing a new system (funded by private grants) focused on student performance *along with* traditional observation of *classroom* practices to inform decisions involving merit pay as well as tenure and retention. Further work in this area has enormous potential. The federal government could facilitate such innovation through expansion of No Child Left Behind (NCLB) waivers regarding school personnel practices. (As of this date, Pennsylvania schools are still waiting to learn whether their application for an NCLB waiver will be approved.) In other states, the waiver has suggested a more targeted approach to student improvement by instituting smaller skill-based subgroups in which to evaluate test scores in reading and math, graduation rates, attendance, and test participation. These smaller skill-based results could help cyber charter schools better distinguish how their schools serve students. For example, cyber charters have long claimed that they serve more at-risk students than traditional schools, and skill-based group data provided through the NCLB waiver may help them demonstrate this claim. This new data may also help cyber charters achieve AYP more frequently. Currently, if one of a cyber charter's many campuses does not meet AYP, none do. New, school-level measures of AYP might more accurately measure teacher quality in cyber environments.

By reforming both the pipeline of teachers and leaders and the regulations that cyber schools are subject to, more space could be created for these innovative schools. That is not to say that every school will take advantage of them; powerful cultural factors within school leadership might continue to wed them to more traditional practices. But we don't know until we try. And until more freedom is created for these schools to truly reinvent human capital management, we do not know what lessons they might have for us.

—————— CHAPTER 7 ——————

The Role of Collective Bargaining Agreements in the Implementation of Education Reforms

Perils and Possibilities

KATHARINE O. STRUNK

ODAY'S K–12 PUBLIC SCHOOL TEACHERS face an evolving profession. Technological innovations, advances in our knowledge about teacher effectiveness, and pursuant shifts in policy have begun to alter our traditional definitions of the teaching role. Policies that encourage or require the implementation of reforms as varied as online instruction, flipped classrooms, multiple measure teacher evaluations, and changed tenure processes have been instituted at all levels of government. Moreover, as technology and knowledge increase at an ever-faster pace, policies and reforms will have to work to keep up. Amid this flurry of policy action, relatively little attention has been paid to important factors and structures that are necessary to implement and enact new reforms, especially those that affect teachers' roles and work. In particular, there has been minimal discussion in policy circles of the impact of collective bargaining agreements (CBAs, or contracts) on states', districts', schools', and teachers' abilities to pursue the many changes and innovations that are being offered as potential solutions to low student achievement and learning gaps.

In the more than thirty states that allow or require collective bargaining, CBAs are negotiated between local teacher unions and district school boards or administrators approximately every three years. Ranging in length from just a few to hundreds of pages, these contracts dictate policy in every facet of the school and district workplace and govern interactions among teachers, students, school personnel, administrators, and parents. For instance, contracts include policies surrounding teachers' school day and year schedules, compensation, evaluations, seniority rules, and assignments. CBAs will greatly impact schools' and districts' abilities to implement policy and program reforms, especially those that affect teachers' roles and working conditions. Many of the regulations included in CBAs constrain district and site operations in some way or another. This is the intent of CBAs: to set parameters for operation so that teachers' rights are protected from arbitrary or unfair decisions made by district and school administrators. These protections are often worthwhile and are historically rooted in responses to very real concerns about administrator patronage and bias. However, because of the myriad and stringent policies they set, these contracts necessarily slow the rate of change in districts, often in ways that hamper the implementation of innovations intended to enhance teacher and school effectiveness and improve student achievement.[1]

In this chapter I explore the role that CBAs may play in implementing new reforms given the current structure and content of the negotiated contracts. I will first offer two examples of reforms that are presently being implemented with the aim of enhancing teacher and school effectiveness in ways that may improve student learning and achievement. I then outline some of the policies found in a sample of 506 California CBAs that governed operations in the 2008–2009 school year that may inhibit how teachers and schools can respond to and implement these reforms. I next highlight some of the flexibilities found in current CBAs that allow for innovation and experimentation with these sorts of policy reforms and then conclude with a discussion of what changes to CBAs and collective bargaining may need to be considered to enable experimentation with and implementation of innovative policy reforms.

Example Reforms

In recent years, a great deal of attention has been given to education reforms that center on two major trends: utilizing rapidly developing technologies in pursuit of higher-quality and more efficient instruction and holding educators accountable for student performance. Although these general types of reform have evolved over time, technology and accountability have had, and will continue to have, a lasting impact on K–12 schooling. In particular, current iterations of these reforms will require relatively extensive changes to teachers' work and practice. Technology-enabled "next-generation" school models that include the use of technology in the classroom and online or hybrid classes and schools will greatly shape the way teachers teach and the structure of their school day. Accountability policies that have shifted their focus from the district and school levels to teachers themselves through the implementation of standards-based multiple-measure teacher evaluation systems will change the way teachers are assessed, supported, promoted, and compensated.

Because of the importance of technology-enabled next-generation school models and teacher-level accountability policies in the current and future education landscape, I focus on the ways in which CBAs may impact the implementation and efficacy of these reforms. Both of these reforms, although quite different from one another, change the nature of teachers' work. As a result, regulations negotiated into CBAs that dictate important aspects of school organization and teachers' work impact districts' and schools' abilities to implement these reforms. To better illustrate this tension, it first helps to unpack the key elements of these two reforms and how they may affect teachers' roles and working environments.

TECHNOLOGY AND NEXT-GENERATION SCHOOL MODELS

As is discussed in other chapters in this volume, schools are adopting technologies that allow for and often require new structures for classrooms, schedules for the school day and year, and instructional roles for teachers. Examples include purely online schools, in which courses are offered online and teachers are remote from their students; hybrid online-brick-and-mortar schools, which meld aspects of traditional schools with online formats; and traditional schools that are using technology such as tablets and computers to change the way teachers teach and students learn.

In all of these cases, teachers' roles necessarily shift from sole content and instruction provider to something akin to a coach or a guide at different times throughout the day. Their roles may shift from standing in front of a classroom to providing more individualized and targeted coaching and instruction to students as they need it, when they need it. Some teachers may never meet their students. School structures also shift in ways that impact teachers' work. Class sizes may and have changed as technology has enabled classroom formats to evolve. The school day and school year schedules have been modified in some cases to allow for 24/7 instruction and learning, for alternative schedules for individual students, and for different uses of students' and teachers' time. Traditional school day schedules that consist of a set number of instructional minutes, lunch periods, preparation periods, and class sessions have been altered or called into question as more technologies are introduced that enable online learning, flipped classrooms, individualized instruction, and small group work. The new and constantly evolving use of technology in schooling is radically shifting what we traditionally think of as "school" and "teacher."

TEACHER-LEVEL ACCOUNTABILITY: EVALUATION AND DEVELOPMENT

As much as technology is triggering a radical shift in our conception of schooling, other elements of traditional schools are evolving in less drastic ways. For instance, teacher evaluation, which has always been an element of traditional schooling, has garnered renewed media and policy attention and is undergoing a shift in format and content. As of 2012, thirty-six states had made significant changes to their state-level teacher evaluation policies, with many resulting in standards-based multiple-measure evaluation systems (MMES).[2] These new systems include multiple measures of teacher effectiveness in teacher evaluations and often require teachers to be evaluated more rigorously and more frequently than in years past. Measures of effectiveness often include value-added measures of teachers' contributions to student achievement gains on standardized tests, site administrators' ratings on detailed and extensive protocols based on observations of teachers' practice multiple times in a given school year, assessments of portfolios of teachers' work and that of their students, and feedback from multiple stakeholder groups, including students and parents. In some cases, evaluation results are intended to drive human capital decisions, such as retention, promotion, tenure, and compensation. In addition, data about teachers' practice and effectiveness are intended to be used to target appropriate professional development to teachers' specific needs.

To make MMES effective, district and site administrators must have the flexibility to collect these data as well as the freedom to observe teachers multiple times throughout the year for varying lengths of time and to offer continuous feedback while promoting collaboration among site administrators, other school personnel, and teachers. Teachers will need protected professional development time and opportunities in order to learn from their evaluation results and incorporate new skills into their teaching practice. Ultimately, administrators will need policy flexibility to base human capital decisions such as promotion, tenure, placement, retention, and possibly layoffs on the outcomes. Although MMES represent a relatively incremental shift in our conception of schooling, the outcomes that result from them have the potential to drastically shift the ways in which teachers receive support throughout their careers and in how school and district administrators make human resource decisions.

UNKNOWN AND INTERACTING CHANGES

Reforms and policies also interact with each other to generate new structures and formats that will inevitably continue to change teachers' roles and school and district structures. For example, the growing incorporation of technology into classrooms will necessarily change teachers' practice and, thus, how teachers are and should be evaluated. Similarly, as new evaluation systems provide teachers and administrators with better data about the areas in which teachers are expert and those in which they need additional support and practice, teachers' roles in providing professional development and coaching to their peers may change the structure of peer assistance and teacher career development. In addition, if MMES are able to uncover true differences in teacher quality, teachers' compensation structures may shift to reward teachers who are particularly effective or who have shown high levels of effectiveness growth. Layered on top of overlapping and evolving district policies are state policies made by legislatures and state boards of education that often contradict or complicate local reforms.

How CBAs Can Stall the Implementation of Reforms

CBAs impact how districts, schools, and teachers respond to reforms because they dictate the rules and policies that regulate teachers' work lives as well as school and district operations. Education reforms and policies are enacted with assumptions about how they will be implemented by districts, schools, and teachers, and their success relies on the autonomy of these implementing agents to act in ways that foster rather than hamper the reforms. However, simply by setting specific rules and regulations, CBAs restrict how innovations, experiments, and reforms can be implemented in schools and districts. In so doing, they interrupt the fidelity with which reforms can be implemented, thus limiting the potential effectiveness of these policies for improving teacher practice, student achievement, and school effectiveness.

In outlining the policies that exist in a sample of California collective bargaining agreements that may hinder the implementation of next-generation school models and educator accountability policies, I use data collected from 506 California CBAs that governed district operations during the 2008–2009 school year. These contracts represent 90 percent of a larger sample of California districts with four or more schools.[3] I coded the contracts using close content analysis and a coding schema developed to isolate individual regulations within a contract.[4] While this contract sample allows for close examination of content across a highly representative population of districts, it is limited by its focus on a single state.[5]

Table 7.1 lists CBA regulations found in five areas of the contract that may impact the implementation of technology-enabled reforms and new school designs, as well as teacher evaluation and development systems, and provides the frequency with which these regulations are found within the sample of CBAs. Provisions labeled with a T likely affect the enactment of technology-oriented reforms, and those with an E may impact the implementation of evaluation programs. Table 7.1 shows that CBAs set multiple policies that are critical to the implementation and enactment of both types of example reforms. Although I use only the two example reforms to illustrate how policies set in collective bargaining agreements can impact reform implementation, it is easy to extrapolate how these same or similar CBA provisions may affect other reform and policy initiatives. In addition, the regulations outlined in table 7.1 are just a sample of the hundreds and sometimes thousands of provisions found in CBAs, all of which intentionally limit administrators' and teachers' discretion in taking actions that are outside the content of the contract. Almost any policy or reform initiative that aims to change the traditional structure of schooling or an element of schooling by altering teachers' working conditions and activities must be reconciled with regulations negotiated into CBAs.

TABLE 7.1
CBA provisions that may impact the implementation of technology or evaluation reforms

CBA provision	%	Tech	Eval
Schedule and hours			
Specifies the length of the school day in instructional minutes	42%	T	
Specifies the amount of time teachers must work each day	63%	T	E
Requires teachers to be on campus at a set time before the beginning of the school day	61%	T	
Requires teachers to be on campus for a set time after the close of the school day	36%	T	

(Continues)

TABLE 7.1
(Continued)

CBA provision	%	Tech	Eval
Specifies the number of work days in a school year	92%	T	E
Class size			
Mentions class size (topic covered)	94%	T	
Specifies a given class size(s)	84%	T	
Requires district to balance class size within a certain amount of time	42%	T	
Requires district to take a specific action if class-size ceiling is exceeded	67%	T	
Specifies maximum caseload of students/day	30%	T	
Evaluation			
Disallows the inclusion of specific factors in teachers' evaluations	47%	T	E
. . . specifically, standardized test scores or student achievement scores	9%		E
Allows permanent/tenured teachers to be evaluated more than once every two years (as stipulated in the CA Education Code)	2%		E
Allows nonpermanent teachers to be evaluated more than once a year (as stipulated in the CA Education Code)	<1%		E
Requires that permanent teachers receive advance notice of formal observations	44%	T	E
Does not contain a clause that allows for additional unannounced observations for permanent teachers	91%	T	E
Requires that nonpermanent teachers receive advance notice of formal observations	44%	T	E
Does not contain a clause that allows for additional unannounced observations for nonpermanent teachers	89%	T	E
Specifies the length of evaluation observations	52%	T	E

TABLE 7.1
(Continued)

CBA provision	%	Tech	Eval
Compensation*			
Includes incentives for teachers with National Board Certification	22%		E
Includes incentives for teachers with master's degrees	93%		E
Includes incentives for teachers with doctorates	53%		E
Includes incentives for teachers with bilingual/English as a Second Language certification	30%		E
Includes incentives for teachers with special education certification	22%		E
Includes incentives for teachers with a math certification	1%		E
Includes incentives for teachers with a science certification	1%		E
Includes incentives for teachers in geographically challenging locations	1%		E
Outlines a "merit pay" program	11%	T	E
... that requires teachers' advancement on salary scale to be contingent on evaluation	10%		E
... that is offered at the school level	10%		E
Requires that teachers receive extra compensation for increased workload	93%	T	
... for covering another class during preparation period	54%	T	
... for exceeding maximum number of course preparations	13%		E
... for being a coach or running an extracurricular activity	73%		E
... for being a consulting teacher for PAR or BTSA programs	67%		E
... for assuming another leadership position	48%		E

(Continues)

TABLE 7.1
(Continued)

CBA provision	%	Tech	Eval
Assignments, transfers, and vacancies			
Addresses seniority in deciding who receives a voluntary transfer			
States that seniority is not a factor	3%	T	E
States that seniority can be considered	20%	T	E
States that seniority shall decide, all else equal	45%	T	E
States that seniority is the deciding factor	7%	T	E
States that certain groups are ineligible for voluntary transfer	6%	T	E
Addresses seniority in deciding who will be involuntarily transferred			
States that seniority is not a factor	1%	T	E
. . . states that seniority can be considered	16%	T	E
. . . states the seniority shall decide, *all else equal*	51%	T	E
. . . states that seniority is the deciding factor	9%	T	E
. . . certain groups are ineligible for involuntary transfer	2%	T	E
CBA outlines causes for which a member may be involuntarily transferred	72%	T	E
. . . for the good of/ best operational needs of the district	49%	T	E
CBA places restrictions on reasons teachers may be involuntarily transferred	46%	T	E
. . . enrollment change	40%	T	E
. . . program change or elimination	27%	T	E
. . . school closure or opening	24%	T	E
. . . downsizing/ reduction in staff	5%	T	E
. . . professional growth reasons	15%	T	E
. . . other reason	16%	T	E

TABLE 7.1
(Continued)

CBA provision	%	Tech	Eval
CBA requires that no teacher can be involuntarily transferred if there is another member as qualified requesting a voluntary transfer to that position	30%	T	E
CBA specifies treatment of involuntarily transferred teachers' preferences for vacancies	38%	T	E
. . . transferee can indicate preferences	31%	T	E
. . . district honors transferees request if transferee meets position requirements	7%	T	E
. . . transfer preferences are dictated by seniority	3%	T	E
. . . transferees displaced by a school closing get vacancy preference	7%	T	E
. . . transferees can bump less senior teachers from their roles/positions	2%	T	E
Order in which the district can consider employees for vacancies			
. . . district is allowed to "fly" vacant positions outside the district before interviewing all within-district teachers	4%	T	E
. . . current employees can apply and/or will be considered for a vacant position before new personnel are considered	28%	T	E
. . . current employees will be assigned to a vacant position before new personnel are considered for the assignment	8%	T	E
CBA outlines causes for which a member may be involuntarily transferred	72%	T	E
. . . for the good of/ best operational needs of the district	49%	T	E
CBA places restrictions on reasons teachers may be involuntarily transferred	46%	T	E
. . . enrollment change	40%	T	E
. . . program change or elimination	27%	T	E

(Continues)

TABLE 7.1
(Continued)

CBA provision	%	Tech	Eval
. . . school closure or opening	24%	T	E
. . . downsizing/ reduction in staff	5%	T	E
. . . professional growth reasons	15%	T	E

Note: *Compensation items regarding incentives, merit pay, and evaluation are based on a sample of 526 CBAs, as the sample includes additional contracts for which only salary schedules are available

SCHOOL DAY AND YEAR SCHEDULE

One basic function of CBAs is to set the schedule for the school day and year. Not only do contracts set the length of the school day and year, but they also specify the amount of time teachers must (or can) be on campus before and after school hours. Table 7.1 shows that 42 percent of California contracts set the number of instructional minutes that can occur within a school day, and nearly two-thirds of contracts set the exact number of hours and minutes a day a teacher can—or must—work. Sixty-one percent of California contracts require teachers to be on campus a set time before the beginning of the school day, and 36 percent specify the amount of time teachers must be present after the close of the school day. Nearly all contracts specify the exact number of days in the school year, and most allocate the number of days devoted to instruction versus preparation or professional growth days (if any). Although perhaps unduly prescriptive in ways that constrain teachers' and principals' autonomy, these provisions conform with the traditional structure of schooling—with a specific start time and end time and clear delineation of instructional time within.

The CBA policies that dictate districts' school day and year schedules will greatly impact how districts and schools can implement reforms that take advantage of technological innovations. For instance, schools across the country are beginning to offer entire curricula or individual courses online. Other schools are operating in a hybrid format that allows students to access course content either in traditional class formats within a brick-and-mortar school building, using technology but inside a school building, or entirely online from home. The intent of these new school formats is not only to improve or change students' instructional experiences but also to allow students who before may have dropped out of school in order to hold down a job or who have other challenges attending school during regular hours to be able to complete their schooling.

The schedule and hours provisions in CBAs will directly impact schools' and districts' abilities to staff these new school models. For instance, in online or hybrid programs, teachers' schedules will likely shift from teaching solely during traditional school hours to teaching some courses before or after students' work days. Regulations that specify exact instructional minutes and hours, and the length of time teachers can be on campus before or after the close of the school day, will need to be amended to account for these new nontraditional schooling schedules. Moreover, the mere definition of "instructional minutes" may need to be considered, as "instruction" may change from in-class delivery of content to online facilitation and more one-on-one interactions and coaching. In addition, as new school models offer courses and modules year-round to accommodate student schedules and desires, CBA provisions that specify days in a school year may need to be changed.

Technology is also being adopted by schools in ways that will have less impact on the actual structure of schooling but have similarly profound impacts on the teachers' roles in instruction. For instance, in California, districts as varied as Riverside Unified and Los Angeles Unified have begun to adopt new technologies such as tablets and laptops in their classrooms and schools. Districts that provide tablets or other computing devices to students will need to consider how students will access content during "nonschool" hours and how teachers may be responsible for assisting them during these times.

The implementation of new multiple-measure teacher evaluation systems will also be impacted by CBA provisions that dictate school day and year schedules. For these systems to be successful, teachers must have the ability to access targeted development opportunities that help them improve. Often these opportunities will come after school hours. By restricting teachers' abilities to come in early or work late, or to work additional days in a year, principals and teachers may find it difficult to provide teachers with additional support and professional development within the current set schedule.

CLASS SIZE

Even though California has had a class-size reduction policy for certain grades in place since 1996, nearly all California contracts still address the topic in some way. Eighty-four percent dictate a specific class-size ceiling and/or average for each grade, and many outline specific actions administrators must take if class sizes are exceeded, often within a set amount of time after school begins. For instance, should districts exceed class-size maximums, administrators may be required to hire or assign new teachers to ease the load (in 13 percent of CBAs), add new classes (18 percent), increase clerical or aide time (19 percent), or provide extra compensation for affected teachers (23 percent).

Such policies can restrict the enactment of new school designs and structures that arise from an increased use of technology in the classroom. For instance, as new technologies are adopted, certain class periods may be conducted entirely using tablets or other computing devices. State policies and CBA regulations that cap class sizes at twenty-two or some other relatively arbitrary number may no longer make sense if students are using computing devices and tablets to learn content and teachers are facilitating group discussions or interacting one-on-one with students. Whereas class sizes were once held to specific levels because it was believed students could not receive sufficient individual attention with larger numbers of students, flipped classrooms may mean that classes should be joined together or made larger with teachers working in teams or in other structures. Similarly, online coursework and content may link students directly to instructors via the Internet, and classrooms may become places for children to access online instruction. Classroom teachers may serve as roaming coaches and facilitators, or segue into online positions where class-size limits make less sense. Regulations within current CBAs (not to mention state laws) will need to be adjusted to accommodate these new learning and teaching styles.

EVALUATION

Teacher evaluation policies are governed both by the California Education Code and by local district CBAs. Although the California Education Code sets policy on the minimum frequency of evaluations for both permanent/tenured (once every other year) and nonpermanent teachers (once a year), it allows districts the right to exceed these minimums. However, as table 7.1 shows, only 2 percent of CBAs allow for more frequent evaluations for permanent teachers and less than 1 percent do so for nonpermanent teachers. In addition, 44 percent of CBAs require that permanent and nonpermanent teachers receive advance notice of formal observations that will be included in evaluations, and approximately 90 percent of CBAs do not allow for additional unannounced evaluative observations. Although not shown in table 7.1, 43 percent of CBAs do not allow for more than one observation as part of an evaluation cycle. In addition, approximately half of all CBAs specify the length of observation, which on average is just under thirty minutes.

CBAs dictate the content of evaluations, as well. Almost all California CBAs include some form of the California Standards for the Teaching Profession as the rubric by which to judge teacher practice. Nearly half of California CBAs include a provision that disallows the inclusion of one or more factors in evaluations, including student achievement, performance on standardized tests (9 percent of CBAs), and other factors, such as performance according to publishers' norms on standardized tests (16 percent) and test results for school improvement plans (2 percent). In addition, the large majority of California CBAs set the number of evaluation categories under which teachers can be rated—almost always two or three different categories.

These regulations found in the evaluation sections of CBAs may hamper many fundamental aspects of MMES. Many MMES include as a measure of teacher effectiveness teachers' contribution to student growth on standardized tests, and most MMES rely on multiple, relatively lengthy, and sometimes unannounced classroom observations in order to accurately observe teachers' practice in ways that allow the teacher to learn from the observation and the administrator to make fair decisions about teachers' performance and growth. Moreover, as districts implement MMES, they will likely wish to work with their teachers to construct a set of standards by which to evaluate teachers, whether these be aligned with the Common Core State Standards or adapted from Charlotte Danielson's Framework for Teaching or entirely district developed. Current CBA requirements that outline specific standards by which teachers must be evaluated constrain teachers and districts from selecting and using another set of standards that they feel may better reflect high-quality teaching in their district.

Current evaluation systems regulated by CBAs may also conflict with reforms that nontraditional school designs or rely heavily on new technologies. Online, flipped, and hybrid settings may shift teachers' roles such that current policies about observation length, frequency, and standards no longer allow administrators to assess teacher practice. What is more, even the new MMES may not be flexible enough to accommodate evaluations of teachers in next-generation schools.

COMPENSATION

Teachers' salaries are traditionally set by step-and-lane salary schedules encoded in the CBAs, with every teacher following the same salary trajectory and receiving raises for each additional year of experience and for achieving some additional amount of educational credits toward or beyond a degree. In addition, teachers can receive differentiated compensation in addition to their schedule-set base salary for various reasons, including obtaining a National Board of Professional Teaching Standards certification (22 percent of CBAs), master's degrees and doctorates (93 and 53 percent, respectively), and certifications to teach English as a second language (30 percent) or special education (22 percent) (see table 7.1).

Similarly, teachers have various noninstructional duties set into their contracts, some of which earn them additional compensation. For instance, over half of California contracts provide extra compensation to teachers for covering another class during their preparation period, and 13 percent provide additional pay for teachers who take on extra course preparations. Nearly three-quarters of CBAs require that teachers are paid extra for being a coach or running an extracurricular activity, and two-thirds stipulate extra pay for acting as a consulting teacher through the Peer Assistance and Review (PAR) or Beginning Teacher Support and Assistance (BTSA) programs.[6] Approximately half of contracts also require that teachers are paid extra for taking on other specified leadership roles, such as participating on a school site council or acting as a teacher-in-charge. Only 11 percent of district contracts allow for some form of merit pay structure, and nearly all of them (87 percent) simply require that teachers' advancement along the salary schedule be contingent on the receipt of a satisfactory evaluation. Only four CBAs (less than 1 percent of the sample) allow for test score data to be incorporated into a merit pay program, always at the school level.

This structure of step-and-lane compensation, along with various pay differentials, has implications for new evaluation systems, the results of which may be used in compensation decisions. In particular, there is little room for compensation for individual merit or growth as indicated by performance on evaluations. In addition, some proposed MMES will give teachers "credit" for contributing to the district or school community; teachers who offer to take on extra duties, such as coaching or serving in a leadership capacity, may be given higher evaluation marks on the school/district community measure for serving in this capacity. Districts will need to consider if they should still offer separate pay differentials for teachers who take on these roles, effectively compensating these teachers twice under the new evaluation systems—once through their evaluation score and once through their stipend/pay differential.

Current compensation structures also have implications for the implementation of reforms that foster new school designs and/or the increased use of technology. Under current structures, there is little room to provide extra compensation to teachers who are not in traditional school settings. For instance, teachers who offer most of their instruction online or who work in schools with longer school days may be less able to act as coaches or extracurricular coordinators or to assume site-based responsibilities. Similarly, the sorts of extra duties in which they participate, such as developing online or computer-based assessments and curriculum, may not be rewarded under the current system of differentials. Moreover, teachers in nontraditional settings, such as online or hybrid schools, may best serve schools and students by offering online courses to students from multiple districts. Current CBAs that dictate raises based on full-time teaching experience in a single district are not equipped to compensate such teachers fairly.

ASSIGNMENTS, TRANSFERS, AND VACANCIES

The last set of regulations embedded in CBAs has to do with how teachers are assigned to positions, including how they are transferred between assignments and how open vacancies can be filled. These staffing policies are critical to district human resource management and are almost entirely dictated at the local district level by the CBAs. There are two main kinds of transfers in school districts: voluntary, in which teachers ask to be transferred into a new role, and involuntary, in which administrators transfer teachers into a new position. Much has been made in recent years about the role of teacher seniority in transfer decisions, particularly because seniority and other requirements for transfer placement may inhibit administrators' abilities to most efficiently and effectively match teachers with schools and students.[7] Approximately three-quarters of CBAs address the role of seniority in voluntary and involuntary transfer decisions. Seniority decides who is transferred as long as all other factors are equal between two transfer candidates in about one-half of CBAs. The "all else equal" language is often vague, and when it is specified it often encompasses having the correct credentials and experience for a role. Seniority is the absolute deciding factor in voluntary transfer decisions in 7 percent of CBAs and in involuntary transfer decisions in 9 percent of CBAs.

CBAs also contain policies that regulate who may be transferred. Nearly half of all contracts place clear restrictions on the reasons for which administrators may involuntarily transfer teachers between positions. Among the most common reasons districts may do so are changes in enrollment in the district (40 percent), changes in or elimination of programs (27 percent), school closures or openings (24 percent), and downsizing and/or reductions in staff (5 percent). Only 15 percent of CBAs allow administrators to involuntarily transfer teachers for reasons related to professional growth. In addition, nearly a third of CBAs require that a teacher cannot be involuntarily transferred if there is another member as qualified who wishes to transfer to that position.

Once teachers are involuntarily transferred, over a third of CBAs specify how administrators must incorporate transferees' desires into placement decisions. Notably, in 7 percent of districts, administrators must allow the transferee to move to his location of choice if he meets position requirements, such as certification level. In 3 percent of CBAs, the most senior involuntarily transferred teachers get their pick of open vacancies each year; in 2 percent of districts, transferees can actually displace less senior teachers from their roles or positions. In addition, in 40 percent of districts, administrators must abide by strict vacancy posting and interview guidelines, and in 8 percent of them administrators must assign current employees to vacant positions before new personnel can be considered for the assignment, regardless of position fit or employee quality.

These staffing regulations have direct and far-reaching implications for any policy or reform intended to help improve teacher and school effectiveness. MMES are intended to integrate with human capital decision making so that teachers can be matched with students, classrooms, and schools where they are most needed and/or most effective. Policies that dictate staffing rules and procedures constrain administrators' abilities to use teacher effectiveness data provided by MMES to staff their schools with teachers who best fit their needs. In addition, MMES are designed to allow for a coaching and support relationship among administrators and teachers and teachers and other teachers. Provisions that allow for more senior teachers to "bump" less senior teachers from their positions or that restrict how teachers can be transferred between schools and classrooms may unintentionally interrupt progress that teachers and administrators are making together. In short, assignment provisions like those described in table 7.1 will make it difficult, if not impossible, to act on the MMES-provided data and place teachers where they can best be supported.

The success of next-generation school models also relies on administrators' abilities to match staff with the appropriate schools and positions and may be similarly hampered by current CBA provisions that dictate staffing procedures. For instance, as some schools become partly or entirely Internet based and/or begin to rely more on technology to facilitate student learning, certain teachers will be more willing and more able to take on the new teaching roles that emerge from these changes. Current contract restrictions on who can transfer or be hired into open positions because of seniority, current district employment, or other reasons will again make the efficient staffing of positions in new school structures difficult.

How Current CBAs Provide Opportunities for the Implementation of Reforms

Although this paints a somewhat grim picture of the ways in which typical CBAs may impact the implementation of school reforms, CBAs also provide some allowance for new programs and policies to take hold. It is important to remember that CBAs are negotiated between teacher unions and district administrators or school boards. Contracts arise not simply because one side or the other makes demands but through compromise and negotiation. Because of this, it is possible that both parties may work to include in their contract policies to enable the implementation of worthwhile school reforms.

In fact, flexibility can be built into contracts to allow for the inclusion of new policies during the contract term. Although CBAs must be negotiated every three years, three-quarters of CBAs include provisions that allow for the contracts to be reopened during the contract term, usually annually. This reopening option allows unions and administrators to come together to negotiate on topics that may not have been relevant or fully developed during initial negotiations. In addition, 16 percent of CBAs include provisions that give unions ongoing consultation rights that go beyond the limited set required by California law so that unions and district administrations may work together to establish policies on areas such as school day and year schedule, district and school budgets, class size, and site-specific issues. Similarly, many CBAs include provisions that allow for administrator discretion in important areas like setting class size (one-fifth of CBAs) and evaluation frequency (half of CBAs)

It is also important to consider some policies in a more forgiving light. For instance, CBAs that require seniority to be considered but not determinative (either wholly or "all else equal) allow administrators to work with teachers to find their best fit based on results from new evaluation systems or in new school structures. Similarly, CBAs that allow involuntarily transferred teachers to indicate their preference of vacancies or that ensure that teachers displaced by school closings can select their preference of vacant positions provide fair protections for teachers who are displaced for reasons out of their control. Moreover, where regulations don't exist in CBAs, administrators and teachers are not bound by them. This is important in cases such as teacher hiring: although 40 percent of CBAs regulate whether administrators can offer vacant positions to external applicants before considering or hiring existing teachers, 60 percent of districts administrators have more discretion to hire the best teacher—external or internal—for the post. Administrators and teachers have the opportunity to work within the open spaces of CBAs to aid the implementation of reforms and programs that may not conform to traditional school structures and operations.

Moving Forward: Collective Bargaining Agreements 2.0

Reforms such as the use of new technologies in instruction and schooling and the adoption of MMES will change education and teachers' roles. Today's CBAs in many ways hamper the implementation of these reforms and, as a result, may diminish their efficacy in improving teacher practice and student achievement. However, the myriad policies set within CBAs were negotiated in large part to protect teachers' professional working environments. Given the historical role of contracts in protecting teachers from unfair or arbitrary decisions that impact their rights and working conditions, how can CBAs evolve so that they continue to protect teachers but also allow educators to implement new reforms?

This dilemma is not a new one. Just as education reform itself is not new news, neither is the concept that the contracts negotiated between administrators and unions are restrictive and impede these reforms and must evolve to allow for improvements in public education. To that end, in the 1980s and 1990s, after the release of *A Nation at Risk* and the ensuing concern about K–12 education in the United States, various union leaders instituted "new unionism," or "reform unionism." The intent of this new brand of unions was to work collaboratively with administrators to broaden the scope of collective bargaining outside of traditional teachers' working conditions and regulations to encompass education policy. In so doing, teachers and administrators in the schools might be able to help implement reforms that would truly improve teacher effectiveness and student outcomes. Reform unions worked to negotiate new collective bargaining agreements that were interest based rather than adversarial, holding at their core a mission to improve student achievement in public schools.

Unfortunately, although some progress was made during this time to step away from traditional industrial-style contracts, reform unionism has largely given way to the same old same old, with a few examples of true collaboration interspersed across the country.[8] Even the contracts and partnerships that did emerge successfully from reform unions and collaborative administrations still were prescriptive in nature. Although they included some new reforms ideas, they continued to set restrictive regulations and policies that held administrators and teachers to predetermined structures. There was little room for innovation beyond those that had already occurred.

If the original 1960s-style industrial contracts were CBAs 1.0, and interest-based contracts moved the needle to CBAs 1.5, it is now time for CBAs 2.0. CBAs will need to evolve to allow for teachers and administrators to work together to implement new programs such as multiple measure evaluation systems and reforms based on the increased use of technology in schooling. Yet, it is not solely, or even mostly, the content of CBAs that should change. The structure of CBAs will need to evolve if current education reforms and innovations are to be implemented and tested. Specifically, next-generation CBAs will need to have two key features, both of which will require drastic changes from the way contracts are today, and even from the way contracts were envisioned under reform unionism. CBAs must be both *simpler* and *more flexible* in order to provide sufficient protections for teachers' working conditions while allowing for the implementation of new innovations and reforms.

KEY FEATURES OF NEXT-GENERATION CBAS: SIMPLICITY AND FLEXIBILITY

Current contracts consist of a laundry list of policies that have been included over time in response to perceived or actual injustices or the threat of such actions. Rather than working together to address important policy concerns, union leaders and administrators have negotiated into their CBAs elaborate webs of procedures and operations that are intended to address any possible infraction or outcome. The result is the sort of detailed and prescriptive policies shown in table 7.1 that frequently leave little or no room for innovation.

For example, in many district CBAs, class-size policies are complex and highly prescriptive. Not only do CBAs outline the average and maximum class size for each grade and subject taught in the district, but many also dictate the exact processes and procedures that must be taken should class sizes be exceeded within set periods of time. Such regulations were likely made because at some point in time teachers were required, or were worried that they would be required, to take on too many students and class-size overages were not adequately addressed. In response, negotiators came to the table to specify exact class sizes in each grade and/or subject and to delineate exactly what actions administrators would take, and by what times, to resolve or accommodate for class-size overages. The resulting web of regulations, while protecting teachers and clarifying policy for administrators, stifles districts' abilities to implement new reforms.

However, these policies do not need to be so complex. Districts and unions could together decide on a set of guiding principles to underscore the district's approach to class size. Such a clause might require that districts attempt to minimize class sizes subject to the changing and evolving needs of the district—for instance, based on districts' adoption of technologies that change how classes are structured or due to budget constraints or other realities. Such clauses are not so far-fetched. In fact, 21 percent of California CBAs contain class-size regulations that allow class sizes to be decided according to the needs of the district. These kinds of clauses leave space for teachers and administrators to work together to determine what programs and policies might be best given the specific district context—a context that might not have been foreseeable years before.

Flexible and simple policies exemplify how next-generation CBAs can refrain from dictating the specific details of policies. Instead, contracts should outline a set of guiding principles that are intended to allow for innovation and experimentation while at the same time protecting teachers' working conditions in ways that enable them to continue to provide high-quality instruction to their students. It is not enough to change CBAs to incorporate additional flexibilities to allow for the reforms that are currently being implemented; CBAs must evolve in ways that enable teachers and administrators to work together to nimbly adapt to changing policies and contexts as reforms interact and lessons are learned and incorporated into current and new programs and structures.

It is easy to extrapolate from the class-size clause to a similar provision that might shape a district's approach to teacher evaluation. A first-generation CBA outlines the specific protocols on which teachers are evaluated (usually mirroring the California Standards for the Teaching Profession), dictates the exact ratings a teacher can receive (usually two to three levels), and sets policies about the length, frequency, and timing of observations. A reform CBA might include some discussion of a Peer Assistance and Review program. However, while most states and districts have now moved beyond PAR to new MMES, few would argue that we know the correct way to evaluate teachers.

As new teacher evaluation policies are implemented by states and local districts, a simplified and flexible next-generation CBA might include regulations that require district administrators and teachers to work together to institute teacher evaluation systems based on a set of guiding principles. For example, rather than include the specific standards and processes by which teachers can be evaluated, guiding principles in CBAs might require districts to include in teacher evaluations multiple measures that allow them to discriminate between teachers by their effectiveness and to link data from evaluations with professional development and support systems to help teachers improve. By setting guiding principles for evaluation systems in CBAs, administrators then have the flexibility to try new systems and adjust them based on their successes and failures.

CHALLENGES TO IMPLEMENTING NEXT-GENERATION CBAS

Crafting next-generation CBAs that rely on guiding principles rather than on strict regulations will not be easy. First, CBAs 2.0 will require a great deal of trust between teachers and administrators that both parties will come to the table focused on the core mission of schooling: to improve student learning. Decades of industrial-style bargaining have left many district-union relationships acrimonious at worst and cautious at best. More recently, years of budgetary difficulties required districts to make difficult decisions, many at the expense of teachers' jobs and compensation. Trust in schools and districts is not an easy commodity, and it will need to be earned on both sides.

In order to build trust, next-generation CBAs will likely need to incorporate some version of an oversight committee that includes both teachers and administrators, and possibly parents and other stakeholders. Such a committee would be responsible for ensuring that policy and reform decisions are made based on the set of guiding principles rather than for arbitrary or capricious reasons. However, there needs to be a fine balance so that such a committee does not itself hamper reforms due to excess caution or political maneuvering.

In addition, restrictive and prescriptive state policies complicate the ability of teachers and administrators to collaborate in the ways required by new education reform ideas. Although there is a place for state guidance, uniformity, and accountability, many state education codes have grown into behemoths, dictating minutiae of district and school operations.[9] State policy, like local CBAs, can heavily constrain local administrators and teachers from enacting reforms in ways that are best suited for their own schools, districts, and students. When these state-level policies interact with local contracts they generate a web of regulations and rules that leave administrators and teachers with little ability to determine and act on what works.

State and local policy makers are facing an exciting and challenging time. Enhanced technologies, increased and increasing knowledge about what does and does not work, and rising national interest in education policy are coming together to bring about new and inventive reforms in education. Many of these programs will, in some way or another, change the ways teachers work and schools operate. Rather than sticking to old structures that limit schools and schooling, teachers, and teaching to what we knew before, policy makers at all levels need to give administrators and teachers the flexibility to enact and experiment with new reforms. To do this, they must loosen the leash of CBAs and work to implement flexible structures that enable rather than inhibit reform.

CHAPTER 8

The Future of Value-Added

From Whether *to* How

MATTHEW DI CARLO

I N EDUCATION, *value-added* is a class of statistical models designed to measure teachers' impact on their students' test score growth.[1] In many respects, however, that description is an understatement. These models, and the research that employs them, play a central role in the debates and policy making surrounding teacher quality in the United States.

In fact, many of the arguments supporting the drive for teacher quality reforms come directly from the value-added literature. The core finding from this body of research—that teachers' impact on testing outcomes varies widely—provides the empirical backbone for an urgent push to achieve even small improvements in the distribution of teacher effectiveness, as the potential for such shifts to affect millions of students' lives seems so enormous.[2]

"Improving teacher quality," however, is an outcome, not a policy. In other words, the relevant policy issue is not the shape of the distribution but, rather, how to affect it. Having played a huge role in establishing such improvement as a priority, value-added is now being used in high-stakes accountability systems to measure the performance of individual teachers.

This transition from research method to component in high-stakes personnel policy is the next phase for these models. There is much potential for these models to help increase our ability to improve the teacher workforce. But there is also a great deal of risk.

In contrast, the debate about using value-added in teacher accountability systems is characterized by striking certainty. Supporters argue that teacher performance assessments are meaningless unless they include value-added as the predominant component. Opponents, however, view these models as overly dependent on standardized tests and too unreliable to be at all useful.

It is tempting to respond with the mundane argument that the truth is somewhere in between these two viewpoints, but it is more accurate to assert that the mind-set underlying them is inappropriate for the current situation. Lost in this endless back and forth about *whether* to use value-added is the more important question of *how* to do so. There are productive and counterproductive roles for these measures, and how they are incorporated into evaluations and other policies will go a long way toward determining their eventual impact. There is, however, a rather massive snag: the research as to how these measures should be deployed as part of a system of evaluation remains quite thin.

In this chapter I focus on aspects of such usage going forward that share a common theme beyond their substantive importance in the design and implementation process: their illustration of how policy makers and other stakeholders—surrounded by intense controversy, time constraints, and well-funded advocacy groups with strong preferences—aren't making right or wrong decisions about the use of value-added as much as trade-offs between the technical and human considerations that so often define the uncertain arena of accountability policy.

The High-Stakes Institutionalization of Value-Added

When it comes to accountability systems, good policy makers must be part technocrat, part psychologist. That is, they must balance the need to differentiate by performance using necessarily imperfect measures with the equally important goals of incentivizing desirable behavior and maintaining the credibility of the system as a whole.

These two aspects are, of course, interdependent: The properties and use of performance measures affect how educators view and respond to them, and vice versa. This is particularly salient in the case of value-added, given the controversy surrounding these measures and unfortunate incidents such as the publication of teachers' names and scores by newspapers in New York City and Los Angeles. Policy makers cannot directly control responses to and attitudes toward value-added, but they can use it in a manner that acknowledges that these outcomes matter as much as any technical considerations.

Fortunately, although value-added is still unfamiliar to many educators and other members of the education community, the research on these models is quite well developed, arguably more so than that focused on other components being used in evaluations, including classroom observations. In addition to their important role in increasing our understanding of the magnitude and persistence of teachers' impact on their students, value-added models have also been a direct player in teacher policy for some time.

Economist Douglas Harris draws a distinction between two different uses: value-added models for policy evaluation (VAM-P) and value-added models for accountability (VAM-A).[3] VAM-P refers to the use of the estimates as an outcome in evaluating different types of policies and interventions. For example, in the context of teacher accountability, researchers have examined the association between teacher value-added and characteristics that influence compensation, such as master's degrees.[4] They have also assessed interventions such as mentoring programs in terms of whether they improve teachers' test-based productivity.[5]

Over the past five to ten years, however, there has also been a focus on finding ways to use value-added to measure *individual* teacher (as well as school and district) performance for the purposes of accountability (VAM-A). VAM-A might include low-stakes applications like targeting professional development, but the big push has been for more high-stakes uses, most notably incorporating the scores into teacher evaluation systems and using them for important personnel decisions, including hiring, transfer, tenure, compensation, and dismissal.

This is an important development. It is one thing to evaluate a mentoring program based on its effect on value-added (VAM-P).

It's quite another to use individual teachers' scores to make personnel decisions. The information is the same, but it is being used in a substantively different manner.

For instance, there has been some experimentation with test-based incentives for teachers, like granting bonuses based on scores. Studies of a few of these programs have found little or no impact on short-term teacher performance.[6] This suggests that teachers are not withholding effort, which is an important finding. At the same time, personnel policies such as performance-based compensation systems may be conceptualized as a means of influencing other types of behavior—that is, attracting better candidates and keeping them around, as well as providing a disincentive for ineffective teachers to remain.

These goals, as well as the potential for spurring improvement via strong, actionable feedback, drive the current proliferation of comprehensive, multiple-measure teacher evaluations in the United States, often with value-added in a starring role.

A full review of the evidence and arguments surrounding whether states and districts should use value-added in teacher accountability systems is beyond the scope of this chapter. Such a discussion is important, and there are legitimate arguments on both sides, but the reality is that the decision to use them in evaluations and other personnel policies has already been made. At present, more than thirty states are moving ahead with new evaluations, and the vast majority is requiring value-added or some type of growth model as a significant component in these systems.[7] Moreover, many will soon be tying the results of these evaluations to high-stakes decisions.

Put differently, like it or not, high-stakes VAM-A is now the status quo. And that requires a change in how policy makers and other stakeholders view these measures, the information they transmit, and the impact they will have.

This shift can be illustrated in the debate over the impact of dismissing low-performing teachers, specifically the influential simulation showing that removing the 5–10 percent of teachers with the lowest value-added scores in math and replacing them with "average" teachers would, over the course of a decade or so, boost average scores rather dramatically, perhaps even to the point where they were comparable to those of high-performing nations such as Canada and Finland.[8]

What this calculation illustrates, rather vividly, is the wide variation in measured teacher effects on math test growth. In other words, it demonstrates that teachers matter; there is a big gap between the lowest scores and highest (or, in this case, the lowest and the average). This is clearly an important point, and it does carry real-world policy implications. But it does not account for behavior and other effects that we might expect from an actual deselection policy.

In addition to the obvious fact that value-added scores are only available for a minority of teachers, there is the issue of labor supply—that is, whether schools, particularly hard-to-staff schools, would be able to fill their vacancies. On a related note, districts cannot simply begin removing teachers without having some effect on the behavior of current and prospective teachers, especially if those teachers don't trust or understand the measures used for dismissals. Teachers, like all employees, consider risks and rewards in their decisions to enter and remain in their jobs. For example, one more recent deselection analysis focused on modeling teacher responses, such as how current and prospective teachers assess the risk of being fired versus their prospects elsewhere in the labor market. This simulation found that there may be a meaningful, cost-effective impact, but it is comparatively modest and depends to no small extent on the actual and perceived quality of measurement, especially whether teachers are paid more to compensate for the greater risk.[9]

My purpose here is not to imply that one simulation is better than the other, or that either is more accurate in the impacts it projects. My point, rather, is that the effect of any teacher accountability system depends not just on the ability to differentiate teachers by performance but also on the behavioral responses of current and prospective teachers. If large proportions of educators do not trust or understand value-added (and/or other measures used to evaluate their performance), they will react accordingly. They may opt for other professions, where the uncertainty is lower and/or more commensurate with the rewards. Or they may try to get assigned to students who do not take state assessments or avoid students who are traditionally harder to serve, such as those with disabilities. And finally, of course, teachers may alter their practice in undesirable ways, such as "teaching to the test" or focusing on students who they perceive to be most likely to make gains.[10]

Virtually all educators would agree that they have underperforming colleagues, that talented teachers routinely leave the profession for preventable reasons, and that many subpar teachers would improve dramatically if only they received the right feedback. Good measurement is important for all these outcomes, but its impact will be compromised, perhaps severely, without buy-in from those being evaluated.

And the reality is that many teachers are not particularly sanguine about the use of measures based on state standardized tests in high-stakes personnel decisions.[11] Without question, such distrust is far from universal, and some of what does exist is less about value-added per se than negative views, often justified, about the quality of standardized tests, as well as fatigue from years of relentless high-stakes testing. So the skepticism about value-added is probably inevitable, but addressing it is nonetheless important going forward. In the context of accountability systems, perception is reality.

The Future of Value-Added

Looking ahead, there are four key issues surrounding the use of value-added in high-stakes accountability systems that not only are substantively important in terms of design and implementation but also illustrate the trade-offs being made in seeking the right balance of good measurement and productive incentives.

To be sure, this is far from a comprehensive list of the numerous decisions and factors pertaining to value-added's role, and it is largely focused on one particular accountability policy application: teacher evaluations. Nevertheless, as whole, these factors provide an efficient overview of where we are heading with these measures.

THE CALIBRATION OF VALUE-ADDED'S ROLE IN EVALUATIONS

When it comes to teacher accountability systems, value-added models are more than just another measure. Given their strong research foundation and their compatibility with the test-based goals of existing accountability systems, including No Child Left Behind (NCLB), there is a natural incentive not only to assign a relatively high weight to these estimates when incorporating them directly into evaluations but also to rely heavily on them in the selection and incorporation of other measures—that is, to use value-added as the benchmark against which the validity of other measures is judged.

In both contexts, it is important to *exploit the strengths of value-added models while also acknowledging their weaknesses*, and this difficult calibration may benefit from some creativity in how policy makers conceptualize these measures and their role in policies such as evaluations. For example, among the most prominent existing studies pertaining to teacher quality is the Measures of Effective Teaching Project (MET), a massive endeavor funded by the Bill & Melinda Gates Foundation. MET's primary purpose was to demonstrate that it is possible to identify effective and ineffective teachers and to propose a template of sorts for a multiple-measure system best suited for doing so.[12] This is an important and worthwhile goal. And, with generous funding, full cooperation from several districts, and some of the best education researchers in the nation, this project indeed produced a desperately needed barrage of policy-relevant findings and also gathered an unprecedented wealth of data that will keep scholars busy for years to come.

One feature of MET was its assumptions, shared by many, that not only should teacher evaluations include measures of "student achievement gains" but also that any other measures incorporated into these systems "should be demonstrably related" to such gains. Put simply, this means an association with value-added is a necessary (but not sufficient) criterion for establishing the validity of all other measures, such as observations and student perception surveys.[13] In addition, while the project was very thorough in its examination of how to combine the different measures into a final composite score, most of the public attention paid to findings focused on the configuration that best predicted a teacher's future value-added.[14]

On the one hand, the premises underlying this approach have merit. We cannot directly measure or observe "true teacher performance" and must therefore rely on comparing measures with outcomes that are available and gauge meaningful student outcomes. Value-added is focused explicitly on standardized tests, which, while controversial, are among the only common measures of student performance available (for its part, MET was exceedingly thorough and compared the associations using different tests, observation protocols, etc.). In addition, recent research suggests that the impact of teachers, as measured by their value-added scores, is associated with small but meaningful changes in students' future outcomes, including earnings, college attendance, and even teenage pregnancy.[15]

It is therefore appropriate to consider value-added as one benchmark (recall that VAM-P is based on a similar premise), especially when it is done in as deliberate and rigorous a manner as it was the case in the MET project. It may even be fair to argue that value-added is the best benchmark available, at least for now. Alternatives are difficult to come by.

In practice, however, reliance on this premise may go too far. Either we believe in "multiple measures," or we do not. If we do, then it's not entirely clear whether we should require a significant association between value-added and other measures or combine multiple measures in a manner that best predicts future value-added. Teachers who are adept at increasing students' scores on state assessments are not always the best at imparting other skills, and the outcomes and traits that are desirable may vary by context. If we set up teacher accountability policies to select primarily on the ability to boost test scores, we will get teachers who boost test scores. That may be a rather narrow definition of not only educators' effectiveness but student performance as well.[16]

The behind-the-scenes role of value-added—driving the selection and incorporation of other measures—reflects a somewhat rigid, formulaic approach to new teacher evaluations, one that is also evident in how the estimates are actually being incorporated into these systems. For example, in the vast majority of districts, due in no small part to state laws that specify general guidelines for how evaluations are to be designed, teachers' ratings are calculated using one of two general methods: (1) combining subcomponent measures with different weights into an index score and sorting those scores into final rating categories, such as "highly effective" and "ineffective," or (2) first sorting each subcomponent measure into categories and then assigning final ratings based on different combinations of subcomponent ratings.

There are alternative approaches that might be better-suited for exploiting the signal of value-added while accounting for its shortcomings, and without taking it so far that it drives the selection and role of other measures. For instance, Doug Harris, Steven Glazerman, and other researchers have proposed using value-added measures as a kind of "screening device."[17] Harris suggests that instead of combining multiple performance measures into one index or matrix, evaluation should be viewed and designed as a process. In the first stage, value-added models, along with one or two other measures, are used to identify potentially low-performing teachers. In the second stage, these teachers are subject to intensive classroom observations and other interventions to ensure that the "diagnosis" is accurate and, importantly, to provide them with feedback that will hopefully spur improvement (failing that, the teacher might be dismissed). Finally, to complete the process, value-added is also used as a check on the implementation of other measures, such as classroom observations. If the correlations between value-added estimates and observation scores are too low, the observer may be failing to identify high- and low-performing teachers. But if there is an unusually high relationship between the two measures, this may serve as a signal that the observers (namely, principals) are allowing teachers' value-added scores to unduly influence their judgments of classroom performance.[18]

Notice how instead of choosing and combining measures in a manner that presumes value-added is the best player on the team, the screening approach exploits the signal and low cost of value-added to target more intensive, formative intervention, such as additional observations. Similarly, in the "feedback loop" component of the process, value-added serves to verify the results of observations or other components in a manner that acknowledges these estimates' signal but accounts for the possibility of undesirable stakeholder behavior (such as unusually high or low correlations that suggest possible observer bias).

This is not to say that the screening approach is superior or the way to go in every district but, rather, that there may be creative ways to calibrate the direct and behind-the-scenes roles of value-added so that it goes far enough, but not too far, in driving the design and implementation of policies such as evaluations. Although value-added scores are often used interchangeably with "teacher quality" and "teacher effectiveness," they are not the same thing, and states and districts need to be careful not to use them in a manner that implies otherwise.

THE IMPORTANCE OF THE UNDER-THE-HOOD DETAILS OF VALUE-ADDED IN EVALUATIONS

One of the most salient features of teacher evaluation reform in the United States, which bears directly on the nuts and bolts of using value-added, is the remarkably rapid pace of policy making and implementation. Just a few years ago there were virtually no districts using test-based productivity measures in formal personnel policies. Now, due largely to the Obama administration's Race to the Top competitive grant program, most states are either already using them or will be relatively soon.

Much of the design and implementation burden is falling to individual districts, many of which are already understaffed and dealing with recent budget cuts. In these situations, attention to detail can sometimes suffer. Making things worse, to reiterate, there is still only a relatively thin evidence base that might guide this process. As a result, officials are making choices that, while not sexy and generally ignored by the public, can play a huge role in determining the outcomes of these new evaluations.

This importance of such details is illustrated very well in a recent working paper by researchers Elizabeth Davidson, Randall Reback, Jonah Rockoff, and Heather Schwartz, who present a simple but effective analysis that examines why the proportion of schools making Adequate Yearly Progress (AYP) varied widely between states during the first few years of NCLB.[19] What they found was somewhat surprising: it wasn't differences in actual student performance driving the AYP rates as much as arcane little implementation decisions, such as the choice of "confidence intervals" (lower targets set for smaller samples), how students were included in schools' testing samples, and which student subgroups were separated out. In other words, details that seemed unimportant and received little public attention actually ended up driving measured outcomes.

The same basic lesson applies in the case of teacher evaluations, including, of course, value-added. Actually, the heterogeneity in teacher evaluations will almost certainly surpass that of states' NCLB plans, given that the former is being at least partially determined at the district rather than state level. A full discussion of the many choices states and districts have to make, or will have to make, when incorporating value-added into evaluations would be burdensome to say the least, but three choices in particular stand out as effective examples of the trade-offs that must be considered in the design process.

MODEL CHOICE AND SPECIFICATION. There are a few different types of models being chosen for use in evaluations. The two most common are loosely classified as value-added models and student growth percentile (SGP) models. (Although the terms are often conflated, value-added is just one type of growth model.) These two approaches share the same basic features, including setting growth expectations using prior student achievement in regression models, but they do so differently.

Recent research suggests that estimates from SGPs and value-added models, despite their different approaches, tend to be highly correlated. Yet, this overall agreement masks a stronger association between student characteristics (for example, free/reduced-price lunch, special education) and SGP scores than the association between these traits and value-added estimates.[20]

A highly related issue, one that is independent of the type of model used, is the choice of variables to include. For example, although the differences are often overstated, models that do not control for student characteristics such as race and free or reduced-price lunch eligibility will tend to give higher scores to teachers in schools (or classes) serving more advantaged students.[21] Thus, including these factors in the models may level the playing field, and/or, just as importantly, be perceived as doing so, and help avoid perverse incentives (such as switching to schools in more affluent areas). Yet controlling for race or poverty in a value-added model may be viewed as maintaining different expectations for different groups of students.

The big point here is that no model is perfectly accurate or perfectly fair. There are not necessarily right or wrong choices here. At this early stage, it is difficult to say whether and how teachers will respond to different models, but this choice may very well matter in terms of both results and teachers' reactions to them.[22]

THE TREATMENT OF ERROR.   Value-added and other growth models produce imprecise estimates, particularly at the classroom level. Classes tend to be small, and smaller samples result in more imprecise scores in any given year, which in turn produces the well-documented tendency of value-added estimates to fluctuate between years.[23]

Such imprecision has been a massive sticking point among value-added opponents. These reactions are sometimes overblown. Value-added is error prone, but so are virtually all other performance measures worth their salt, including classroom observations.[24] Nevertheless, the point is well taken: if value-added is to be used in high-stakes decisions, error matters. Unlike observations and many other measures, however, value-added models can *in practice* provide a direct estimation of that error, and this information can be used when incorporating the estimates into final evaluation scores/ratings. For example, states and districts might account directly for margins of error (for example, via significance tests) and/or use multiple years of data (when available). Finally, there is a statistical technique, called "shrinkage" that adjusts teachers' scores based on sample size.

In one sense, these are statistical estimates, and there is a strong case for careful interpretation, particularly when the scores are attached to stakes. Accounting directly for error is also fairer to teachers and might mitigate their concerns regarding the imprecision of value-added and the manner in which that uncertainty influences their labor market choices. Once again, however, there are few easy choices here, as some of these techniques also entail costs. For example, requiring minimum sample sizes for teacher value-added would boost precision, but it would mean that those teachers without a sufficient number of students would not receive estimates. Similarly, incorporating scores based in part on statistical significance sacrifices potentially valuable data and reduces differentiation in the results. Finally, one must consider that different classification errors—such as false negatives versus false positives—may have different implications for students.

THE WEIGHTING GAME. The debate over the role that value-added should play in evaluation has tended to concentrate mostly on just one detail: the importance, or weight, assigned to these estimates in evaluations. In most states that specify them, these weights range from 20 percent to 50 percent. To no small extent, initial opinions about the overall quality of these new systems depends on how large a role test-based measures play in determining teachers' final scores. The weights reflect value judgments about the importance (and perhaps reliability) of each measure. These are difficult decisions for policy makers, and they must consider a range of issues, measurement-related and political, when making them. For example, there may be a temptation for policy makers, under tremendous pressure to boost average test scores, to mandate a relatively high weight to value-added scores, which are direct (albeit imperfect) measures of teachers' effectiveness in boosting test scores. But doing so also tends to evoke pushback from educators and advocates concerned about the proliferation of high-stakes testing. It may also, in a sense, exacerbate differences between teachers of tested and nontested students.

Moreover, regardless of the weights that are chosen, the specific manner in which value-added estimates are incorporated into evaluations, in combination with the properties and incorporation of the other measures, can have a substantial influence on the true importance, or "effective weight," of these estimates within a larger evaluation system. In other words, the weight you choose is not always the weight you get.

In general, if teachers' scores on classroom observations or any other component vary less than their value-added scores, then value-added may play a larger role in determining the variation in overall scores than it was intended to play. This issue is especially relevant given that value-added models essentially impose a distribution on the results; by design, they ensure that teachers' scores will vary, whereas observation systems do not.[25] In several states, for example, districts are required to assign a predetermined weight to state-generated value-added scores (at least for tested teachers) but are given more leeway in choosing (and, in some cases, weighting) the other components of the systems, such as observations, alternative learning measures, student surveys, etc. This means that the effective weight of value-added might vary rather substantially by district depending on the other components they choose. From this perspective, mandating minimum weights for value-added in exchange for more flexibility in choosing the other components may have unintended consequences. Regardless of the technique, preserving the intended importance of value-added measures is a critical detail that will affect not only results but perceptions and credibility as well. There are no unimportant decisions about weighting.

These three issues are not even close to a comprehensive list of the "under the hood" details surrounding how to use value-added. They do illustrate, however, that many of the most important decisions do not have definitive right or wrong answers and that they entail both technical and human considerations that are often not in harmony. To the degree possible, districts should be allowed to experiment with different configurations, and states should monitor how and whether these differences in design are associated with variation in results and reactions among educators. Greater flexibility for districts not only encourages innovation and facilitates policy research, but it can also increase local buy-in and allow districts to tailor their use of value-added to their specific needs. There is, however, a risk that too much flexibility might compromise the comparability and quality of the new systems and perhaps place undue burden on smaller districts with fewer resources to devote to the task.

This is always a difficult path to negotiate, but the "under-the-hood" details of how value-added is incorporated into teacher evaluations will play a major role in determining how these new systems work and how teachers respond to them. Policy makers, advocates, and other stakeholders must therefore ensure that these details are receiving enough attention so that the trade-offs are examined and informed choices are made.

THE PROLIFERATION OF VALUE-ADDED AND ITS COMPETITORS

Any discussion of the future of value-added must address one basic fact, which is somewhat ironic given all the controversy over these estimates and what effect using them will have: at present, most teachers do not receive these scores. In general, the proportion of teachers "eligible" for value-added is constrained by the availability of standardized testing data. In many states, such data are only available in math and reading for grades 3–8 (though teachers in the earliest tested grade cannot receive estimates, since the models require at least two consecutive years of scores). Percentages vary by state, but roughly three out of four teachers do not yet receive scores.[26]

This presents challenges for new evaluation design and implementation. Policy makers are understandably eager to ensure that all teachers are evaluated in part using measures that, to the degree possible, reflect meaningful student learning outcomes. In addition, if teachers are being judged differently, or even if they simply perceive that they are being judged differently, that may undermine the credibility of systems and create perverse incentives, such as efforts among teachers to be assigned to classes or even transfer schools based on preferences for how they want to be evaluated.

Going forward, states might choose to expand the sample of teachers who receive value-added estimates by developing (or adopting) standardized tests for additional grades and subjects. In the meantime, in some systems, *school-wide* value-added is more heavily weighted for teachers who do not receive their own scores.

This confers benefits such as cost effectiveness and the possibility of promoting teamwork among educators in the same school, but there are also downsides, including the fact that it holds teachers accountable for students they may not teach.

It is more than plausible that non-tested grades and subjects will eventually become a rarity. However, any attempts to expand the use of these of tests will be costly, take time, and likely encounter resistance from parents and advocates. Also, some subjects, such as art and physical education, are not particularly well-suited for the kind of standardized tests that value-added models require, and there is still scant research as to the properties of value-added estimates in grades and subjects beyond those currently available.[27] It is important to avoid proliferation for the sake of proliferation.[28]

But this "value-added for (almost) everyone" future may face challenges beyond the cost and difficulty, logistical and political, of installing new tests. There is an alternative group of teacher performance indicators being adopted throughout the nation, and it's not entirely clear how this market will play out. Among the more common examples are student learning objectives (SLOs), which are now being required as a component of evaluations in states such as Maine, New York, Massachusetts, and Connecticut. SLOs vary widely in their parameters, but their overarching feature is that they permit district- and, in some cases, school- and classroom-level autonomy in how targets are set and, perhaps, the selection of assessments. For example, teachers, with approval from their principals and a centralized review board, might choose an objective for each of their students, such as a specified amount of improvement on a locally designed assessment. They are then evaluated based on the proportion of students who meet the target. Some districts, including Denver and Austin, have used SLO-type measures for years and maintain intricate systems to track and approve the measures and monitor their results.[29]

As with any performance indicator, SLOs have strengths and weaknesses, and assessing them vis-à-vis value-added entails trade-offs. For instance, whereas all districts within a given state tend to use the same value-added model, the design of SLOs necessarily varies far more widely. They also have virtually no research base, are arguably more expensive and difficult to administer, and are perhaps more susceptible to gaming strategies. Nevertheless, in addition to their primary advantage—that they theoretically can be calculated for all teachers—SLOs also have other positive features. Teachers may prefer these kinds of locally designed models over state tests and formal value-added, and there is a good case to make that they provide more formative information about performance than sanitized growth model estimates from a state-generated report.

It is at least possible that states' and districts' decisions to use SLOs may end up complicating the proliferation of value-added proper to additional grades and subjects. Suppose, for example, teachers of grades 1–3 are evaluated using SLOs over the next several years, and the measures are generally well-executed, widely supported, and require a lot of time and resources to set up. If the state suddenly requires all districts to discontinue or, more likely, "downweight" these measures in order to incorporate value-added estimates that use new state assessments in these grades, there may be considerable pushback. In other words, once established, SLOs and similar measures may be difficult to supplant.[30]

But alternative measures such as SLOs need not compete with value-added. The two measures might play a complementary role in evaluations and other policies. Similar to the screening idea discussed earlier, value-added estimates might serve to partially validate SLO scores (and vice versa). If, for example, SLO scores were unusually highly or weakly correlated with value-added in a given school, this might be a red flag for how the measures are being implemented in that location.

One of the districts that has demonstrated what can be done about nontested grades and subjects is Hillsborough County, Florida. Over the course of five years, beginning in 2005–2006, administrators, union leaders, and teachers worked together to build a comprehensive teacher evaluation system. One of the key components of this system was its development of growth-based measures for the vast majority of teachers, which employed a combination of state tests, third-party assessments, and more than five hundred end-of-course exams and other assessments. Just as multiple observers improve the quality of classroom observations, the district's value-added measure includes data from multiple tests whenever possible.

The price of building this kind of system, of course, is that it is extraordinarily difficult, time-consuming, and costly. Designing and implementing the new measures in Hillsborough required the erection of a rather impressive infrastructure, constant maintenance, as well as communication with and feedback from teachers on the ground and their union leaders (not to mention generous funding, including a $100 million grant from the Gates Foundation). Over time, however, the time and effort served to lay the groundwork for a carefully designed system that, apparently, is generally viewed as credible by educators who will be evaluated by it.[31]

This kind of project, of course, may not be possible for or desired by many districts, and it remains to be seen if the measures and local assessments on which they're partially based will retain their credibility under high-stakes implementation, as well as whether they will hold up under empirical scrutiny (validation).[32] Nevertheless, Hillsborough may serve as a model for what a long-term, comprehensive strategy with sufficient investment can accomplish. If so, then the primary lesson may be that the proliferation of value-added and/or alternative learning measures should proceed slowly, cautiously, and with sufficient resources to be done correctly.

VALUE-ADDED IN ALTERNATIVE SCHOOLING CONTEXTS

Just as policy makers and researchers take the first steps toward getting a handle on the use of value-added in high-stakes teacher accountability systems, education itself is changing, and thus the teaching profession with it. There is a rapidly expanding sector of schools and models that do not fit the traditional mold. Perhaps the most notable among these are online schools. Virtually all states provide at least some form of online educational opportunities for students, and more than half operate full-time online schools. Although the proportion of all public school students using these services remains relatively small, all signs point to significant growth in the short and long terms.[33]

There are several variants of online education models. For instance, some students attend virtual schools full-time and receive all their instruction online. In other cases, students attend a traditional brick-and-mortar school part time and take some of their classes online. There is blended learning, which, although it too takes many forms, entails a mix of face-to-face and online instruction. Students might get all their instruction virtually but in a lab supervised by paraprofessionals. Or teachers might provide traditional instruction for part of the curriculum and some of it online. In short, the forms and contexts of online education, as well as the technology, keep evolving. The lines between brick-and-mortar and online schools continue to blur.[34]

Given the rapid proliferation of technology in K–12 education, there is an increasingly pressing need for a greater understanding of teacher performance in online and similar alternative schooling settings. In other words, this not necessarily a compartmentalized issue; it is something that traditional schools will also have to address, at least eventually, as they continue to incorporate education technologies as instructional tools in the classroom.

Unfortunately, there is still relatively little in the way of best practices or standards for teachers of online or blended courses. What is certain is that the job of teachers in these and similar alternative settings is substantively different from that of teachers in traditional classrooms. Moreover, what makes for effective online or blended teaching almost certainly differs from effective instruction in standard face-to-face contexts. The ability to communicate effectively in writing, for instance, is arguably more important among online teachers, as are, of course, technological skills. The lack of standards and best practices serves as an obstacle to any attempt to develop valid and reliable measures of these teachers' performance, as does the striking variation in the forms and contexts of alternative learning. The choice facing policy makers who are already immersed in the earlier stages of figuring out value-added's role in traditional contexts is whether to delve into the even-more-uncharted waters of these nontraditional forms, particularly in states where these sectors are large and/or growing rapidly.

One of the most basic issues is the fact that value-added models are designed to attribute student progress to a single teacher or clearly defined group of teachers (for example, co-teachers).

Granted, such attribution is often far from clear-cut even in brick-and-mortar schools (for example, coteaching, special education classes), but it is severely complicated in the case of online and blended learning environments. For instance, it may be the case that some students enrolled in virtual schools are receiving some degree of home schooling from parents and/or tutors. They are also, of course, likely to receive part of their instruction from software programs and/or from rotating teams of teachers working more one-on-one or in small groups than is the case in traditional classrooms. Even when testing data are available, therefore, linking teachers and students in a straightforward manner is a particularly thorny proposition.

Another problem here is that there is as yet no published research on value-added for educators teaching online or similar courses, to say nothing of evidence as to how the measures should be deployed in these alternative contexts.[35] Where value-added scores are available for these teachers, they should be compared with those of teachers in traditional classrooms in terms of reliability, association with student characteristics, and, especially, whether and how the scores vary among teachers who switch between traditional and nontraditional classrooms. It may also be helpful to look to higher education for guidance, as the use of alternative learning forms, online classes in particular, is at a more advanced stage.

Among the particularly interesting potential areas for this research is the comparison of value-added with alternative learning and performance measures. For instance, standard classroom observations cannot be conducted for teachers of online courses. This may carve out a more important role for student and parent surveys than is the case in traditional evaluations. It might also lead to adaptations of widely used observation rubrics for use in online courses (such as administrators observing the communication between teacher and students on discussion boards). The correlation of these measures with value-added estimates will be an important initial examination, and it's not entirely clear how the results should be interpreted (particularly if the associations differ from those found in traditional settings). The behaviors and practices associated with stronger student testing growth may differ between contexts.

In the final analysis, the primary outcome of interest in evaluating teachers in nontraditional contexts—student learning—is the same. However, whether it is the use of technology in traditional classrooms or virtual schools, the teaching profession is changing in ways that may influence the information that value-added estimates transmit and the manner in which they should and should not be used. Policy makers (and researchers) will have to address this if value-added is to play a role in the evaluation of teachers working in this growing sector.

Conclusion

Education is a personnel-intensive enterprise. Schooling systems are complex, and there are rapid changes under way in terms of delivery. But, for the foreseeable future, there is a degree to which everything comes down to a group of students receiving instruction from a teacher or group of teachers. In this sense, the impressive body of research on value-added has contributed a great deal to the important social scientific goal of confirming and elaborating on what we already suspect is true: The ability and performance of a teacher is the key input under a school's jurisdiction, and thus among the most potentially powerful sources for improvement.

Accordingly, advocates and policy makers repeatedly invoke the large differences in test-based effects between the highest- and lowest-scoring teachers as a justification for the relentless push to improve teacher quality in the United States. Although such arguments tend toward overly casual conflation of teacher quality with teachers' estimated impacts on math and reading scores, the underlying logic is sound. Even small shifts in the distribution of teacher performance may translate into large, meaningful improvements in student outcomes.

The frantic rush in many states to put new evaluations in place as quickly as possible, sometimes without so much as a pilot year, seems to reflect an attitude among some policy makers and advocates that identifying and exiting the lowest-performing teachers, and retaining the best, will generate discernible, immediate improvement in outcomes, even if the measures are implemented carelessly and are not credible among educators. This is a fantasy, and a dangerous one at that. Used properly, value-added measures, like evaluations in general, can play a productive role in both measuring performance and compelling behavioral changes that lead to improvement. Used poorly, they may lead to attrition, gaming, and resentment and may actually threaten not only the nonaccountability uses of these measures, such as policy evaluation, but also the entire evaluation enterprise.

This will be difficult to assess in the short and medium terms, and it will be similarly tough to separate the specific contribution of value-added to such outcomes from that of all the other components and features of teacher accountability systems. In the meantime, however, it bears remembering that policy is inherently a trial-and-error endeavor. The education realm is currently in a transition phase, during which it is moving rapidly from a state of having virtually no information about using value-added in teacher performance evaluations to having more information than can be handled easily. The first versions of these new systems will range from somewhat to substantially flawed, and the ability to make smart adjustments will play a significant role in determining outcomes.

While I have focused here primarily on the decisions and dilemmas facing policy makers, in most important respects, the future of value-added is in the hands of teachers. Over the next five to ten years, vocal supporters and critics alike may continue to dig in their heels, but the true test will be how educators, at least those in tested grades and subjects, respond to them. The outcome of this trial will play a major role in the future of the push to improve teacher quality in the United States.

CHAPTER 9

Unfinished Lessons?

What We Can—and Can't—Learn from Innovations
in Teacher Quality in Other Countries

JONATHAN PLUCKER

I N ANY EXPLORATION of psychological constructs, and creativity and innovation are no exception, defining terms is very important. In other words, what is the standard to which we should hold educational interventions?

Fortunately, we have such a definition for creativity, with the most popular conception being "the interaction among aptitude, process, and environment by which an individual or group produces a perceptible product that is both novel and useful as defined in a social context."[1] For the purposes of my analysis, the most important part of that definition is that a particular intervention be "novel and useful as defined in a social context."[2] An innovation has to be unique, and it has to have some promise of success (if not outright evidence of success).

The social context criterion is a critically important part of the definition. Essentially, it means that an intervention can be creative in one country's particular educational and cultural context but not in another. Putting all the pieces of the definition together, a particular policy—paying teachers much higher salaries in exchange for more rigorous licensing requirements and larger class sizes— might be novel in many countries, but in some countries, such an innovation wouldn't be useful (too expensive, class sizes already too large) or the political or cultural context won't support the implementation of the idea. Teacher preparation systems not able to train prospective teachers to teach large classes, or perhaps the majority of citizens, do not perceive teachers to be highly trained enough to justify six-figure salaries. The big takeaway from this definition is that context matters, not just for feasibility and implementation but for determining originality and usefulness.

Most humans are curious about other countries and cultures. We are constantly comparing ourselves to others. Americans tend to do this as much if not more than people in other countries; maybe it's the natural function of being a nation of immigrants. But there is also a creative benefit from looking at other countries. Innovation research makes a strong case that it is very difficult to predict which ideas will be successful and which will not.[3] Rather than invest heavily in one or two ideas and hope for the best, creative individuals and groups tend to spread their investment (and risk) across several potential solutions, therefore increasing the odds that one of them is useful for solving the problem at hand.[4]

One of the time-tested ways to try out more ideas while lowering one's investment and risk is to study those that others are using to solve similar problems. Technically, in some contexts (business, art) this is often called "stealing," but some of our most revered creators—Edison, Picasso, Steve Jobs—used this strategy freely. And we use it every day as we watch coworkers, neighbors, family, and friends try out solutions to problems we also face, learning from their successes and failures while they watch us try out our solutions. In policy contexts, the "let a thousand flowers bloom" approach is probably the best way to promote innovation without bankrupting a country, allowing for a healthy balance of creative effectiveness and efficiency. With all this in mind, my analysis of educational policy at the *national* level begins with countries where I work closely with colleagues on research and policy projects, such as China, South Korea, and several Western European countries.

China, at first glance, appears to be a good case study. Contrary to popular conceptions, Chinese education policy, while centrally planned, is often regionally or locally directed. This is largely the case for teacher education, which was modeled after the Soviet system of teacher training in the 1950s. This approach focused initially on addressing very large teacher shortages that forced untrained people into classrooms. The Soviet model was, interestingly, fairly dependent on local implementation, which has largely become the Chinese tradition, with collaborative planning, demonstration lessons, and teacher-teacher mentoring representing a somewhat social cognitive, mentorship-based approach to teacher development. At the same time, educational priorities are set by the central government, with the national five-year education plans setting broad priorities (the current twelfth training plan runs from 2008 to 2013). Until the advent of market-based reforms in 1978, in a period roughly coinciding with the Cultural Revolution, the purposes of Chinese education were largely political.[5] Since the late 1970s, the main goal of education has been to advance economic growth, with an increasing emphasis on creativity, problem solving, and innovation with each five-year national education plan.[6] In the No Child Left Behind (NCLB) era, with the U.S. federal government implicitly (and often explicitly) directing state and local education policy, the Chinese-American comparisons can be viewed, with a grain of salt, as somewhat similar.

China also contends with extreme wealth gaps, and leveling this playing field is a major focus of Chinese education policy. A Chinese colleague (both an academic and a Ministry of Education official) once described teacher quality improvement initiatives in China. He talked about a range of issues and interventions, including efforts to increase teacher efficacy regarding problem-based learning, teaching interactively with large class sizes, and improving teacher education programs. But then he paused, pulled out his laptop, and showed some pictures of someone in a coal mine. He pointed to the screen and said, "This is what a friend of mine, who's a high school teacher, does when he's not teaching." The point was effectively made: teachers in China, especially in rural areas, have a tough time of it. Pay is low, working conditions are challenging, and things like "improving teacher quality" take a back seat to improving basic living and working conditions for teachers.

The twelfth training plan is representative of the government's broader emphasis on lifelong learning, with a focus on professional development throughout a teacher's career, especially in the area of learning about student-centered instructional techniques. In 2007, the National Congress identified online education as an avenue through which to achieve its goals of lifelong learning for all Chinese citizens.

The push to make better use of technology-based solutions for teacher development makes sense on several fronts. First, the quality and availability of technology in China is quite high, although cutting-edge technology is not ubiquitous. China is a large country, roughly the size of the United States, with the population concentrated on the eastern edge and becoming less dense as one moves west. Resources also vary along the same pattern, making online education an appealing avenue through which to level the playing field, especially for educators who do not have readily available access to in-person resources. And, of course, any interventions that provide higher-quality services to some teachers rather than others will only further worsen gaps between the haves and have-nots in China, which is a hot policy topic. As many other commentators have observed, the growth of private education, inequities regarding access to higher education, and rural/urban differences serve to heighten inequality in China rather than reduce it.

Many of these online teacher development tools are innovative in the Chinese context and would be considered well-constructed and well-conceptualized in most countries. But as I have talked to colleagues over the last few years and read about many of these online efforts, few aspects of these Chinese projects are not being implemented elsewhere, especially in the United States. For example, one distance education system in China, which essentially archives and annotates videos and instructional materials in any classroom with a Web-enabled camera, is impressive in scope and ambition and will clearly promote teacher professional development. But as impressive as this system is, I recall National Science Foundation–funded efforts at Indiana University and elsewhere that essentially built the same system—back in the late 1990s. The Chinese system clearly has several unique, effective aspects, but these are innovations at the margins, leaving little to inspire highly meaningful teacher quality innovations in the United States.

When I dug into other countries' widely discussed education reform success stories, I came away with similar conclusions. For example, when one talks to educators in other high-performing countries, you hear generalities ("We changed the emphasis in our K–12 system"), interventions that are very country and/or culture specific, or interventions that are already being implemented here at home.

Take Finland, for example, with its impressive performance on the Program for International Student Assessment (PISA) and, to a lesser extent, Trends in International Mathematics and Science Studies (TIMSS). Teacher quality reforms are often given much of the credit for this improvement, including raising entrance requirements for the profession and greatly increasing compensation.[7] These reforms feel innovative to Americans primarily because we have short memories (or don't know our own history). The crux of teacher quality reforms in the Northeast United States in the late 1980s involved raising certification and licensing requirements (often dramatically), and, at the same time, many of the country's top public schools of education raised entrance requirements for their teacher preparation programs.[8] Finland and the United States aren't all that similar. Many, many other countries have more similar policy, education, and political contexts, making any direct lessons drawn from Finnish educational innovation tricky. And when I asked the "What can we learn from you?" question of a Finnish high school principal recently, she looked at me quizzically for a moment and then said with a slightly pedantic air, "America is a very different country from Finland." Indeed.

So my investigations into the reforms and innovations of the "usual suspects" were not fruitful—but what about the unusual suspects? After all, who has the most to gain by attempting bold, innovative reforms? Certainly not the established high performers, which have the most to lose; in any field they are the least likely to risk what they already have by rolling the dice on new initiatives. Which company has been more innovative over the past fifteen years, Apple or Microsoft? In the mid-1990s, Microsoft was on top of the world, while Apple appeared to be disintegrating. Which company rolled the dice by bringing back a somewhat disgraced ex-CEO, who promptly went big with several very risky new product lines that only look like inevitable no-brainers in hindsight?

One could argue that the most established companies should be innovating and taking strategic risks more frequently, but the fact is that they do not.

Similarly, and more to the point, American business schools, often among the most high-powered, prestigious schools on major university campuses in the modern age, went through a period in the 1950s where they were widely derided and had little of their current prestige.[9] Predictably, the business schools that took the biggest risks were not the first-tier, über-prestigious schools but, rather, second-tier schools with less to lose and more to gain. The innovations at these less-prestigious, less-obvious business schools were eventually adapted by the first-tier schools (when reputation risk was pretty much off the table and the innovations were largely proven). Following this logic, perhaps the most impressive examples of organizational innovation will be occurring in countries that are doing good things but are not heralded for being at the top of the PISA, TIMSS, and Progress in International Reading Literacy Study (PIRLS) league tables.

In my research for this chapter, I asked some of my friends, widely respected experts in international education, international testing, and related areas, to nominate countries that they think are doing cool things with teacher quality. Interestingly, they named only a handful of countries. In studying the teacher quality reforms in each of them, I was surprised to find that the same pattern emerged: interesting changes in most of the countries, many of which appear to be quite innovative (novel and useful) in a particular country, but in almost every case, the innovation was something that is already being tried in the United States, and in some cases has been for a long period of time.

For example, Norway was nominated as a country that has turned around its reading instruction in response to a run of poor reading scores on national and international tests. Norway seems to be a good comparison case: Norwegian has two distinct dialects, and students receive instruction in their preferred dialect. While not a perfect match to the English language learner (ELL) issues faced by many American schools, it's not terribly different either. The population is also unevenly distributed across the country, with a wide range in school sizes as a result. Recent interventions include the 2006 Knowledge Promotion curriculum, which delineated competency goals in core subject areas by grade, additional admissions requirements in language and math for entrance into teacher preparation programs, and a transition from a general teacher certification to a differentiated system with separate grades 1–7 and 5–10 teaching credentials.[10] Professional development generally takes place during a week added to the school year for in-service teachers. These strategies have a lot of face validity (in other words, they make sense), student test performance appears to be improving, and there's no question that they represent a departure from previous practices. That makes them creative *for Norway*, but are they innovative within the American context? That appears to be a harder case to make, given that most of these reforms have been present in many states predating NCLB.

The Netherlands was also nominated, and it is easy to see why. In response to solid but stagnant (or declining) international test performance, a series of major, national reforms have been undertaken by the Ministry of Education, Culture, and Science, including the Quality Agenda in 2007 and the Basis for Performance Plan in 2011.[11] Teacher quality efforts at the elementary school level within these broad reforms include language and math competency testing for prospective teacher education students, along with a focus on evidence-based teaching strategies and dissemination of effective teaching practices, all while preserving the Dutch tradition of teacher and school autonomy.[12] Over the past few years, the growth in curriculum-embedded assessments and student-based data monitoring systems is also notable. The VTB-Pro initiative, part of the Platform Beta Techniek reform plan, is particularly interesting, with its focus on increasing preservice and in-service teacher ability to provide engaging instruction in STEM areas, with a primary outcome being student self-efficacy in these fields.

The Dutch reforms are compelling and logical, with their increased focus and complexity over time, and many aspects are personally appealing to me—citizenship as a primary student outcome, focus on excellence versus minimum competency, emphasis on teacher autonomy, increased rigor of entrance requirements to some teacher preparation programs—but the teacher quality reforms are not dissimilar to those being attempted in many U.S. states.

The patterns are the same with the other counties my colleagues nominated. Several are making serious efforts to improve schools and student learning, often via teacher quality reforms, but most intervention would either be considered marginally creative (small innovations on the fringe of broader reforms that are already widely applied) or not creative at all in the American context.

In response to these observations, one reviewer of this chapter provided a list of teacher quality reforms in other countries, many at the local level, that she considered to be truly innovative and far ahead of any American efforts. Putting aside the fact that several of her examples were simply wrong (no one should be able to say with a straight face that *no* American teacher preparation programs have ever tried to be more exclusive in their admissions criteria), the criticism actually supports my broader observation: if you have to point to local interventions in order to find unique programs, you're having trouble finding relevant national innovations.

I am in no way saying that the reforms in these countries are not important, effective, well-suited to their context, or successful. In fact, a case can be made that many of these reforms are quite innovative in their social context. In China, the attempts to move away from test-based factual recall to creativity via problem-based learning are well-intentioned. And if my Chinese colleagues can find ways to systematically address teacher training issues to facilitate this, the resulting increase in creativity from Chinese students could be a model for all other countries to study. The Netherlands' emphasis on education reform within a context of teacher autonomy is intriguing, as is the Dutch value of excellence in educational performance. But there is little evidence that the reforms should be considered unique within the context of American educational systems. A particular reform may be more or less emphasized, which is interesting and potentially very important, but that is different from "they are innovating and we are not." What's more, interventions that could be potentially innovative would also have to overcome tremendous cultural hurdles to even be seriously considered in most

American schools. For example, many urban Chinese students do quite well on tests of factual knowledge. The "secret to success" is widely known: study like crazy all day long, seven days a week, nearly fifty-two weeks per year, with few extracurricular activities, no part-time jobs, etc. As much as some reformers call for American students to be "more Chinese," this is unlikely to happen for a range of cultural reasons.[13]

So where does this leave us? My two big takeaways concern the nature of making international comparisons and renewed optimism (tempered with considerable caution) regarding American innovativeness in teacher quality reform.

Regarding international comparisons, I once proposed "The Three Undeniable Tenets of International Education Comparisons." They were meant to be tongue in cheek, but over the past few years the tenets have largely held true, and after this comparison exercise I'm more convinced in their validity than ever before. The first tenet is that Americans will always think other countries are doing much, much better. From Mexico in the 1950s and 1960s, Russia throughout the Cold War, Japan and the Asian Tigers in the 1980s and 1990s, and Ireland (innovation, high-tech manufacturing) and Britain (finance) during the most recent financial bubble, Americans usually find themselves worrying about the latest international success story, with the American way of life in imminent peril unless *we change everything right here and now, darn it*. This attitude is not necessarily a bad thing, as fear of others is ingrained in the American public consciousness as a competitive motivator. One reason why Eisenhower downplayed the importance of *Sputnik* was because he knew we had better technology and had little to fear from the satellite, but his reputation was battered by overwhelming public concern that the Russians had somehow moved far ahead of us.[14]

Conversely, both in my personal experiences and my research for this chapter, I found evidence that many other countries base their reforms on American innovations. The emphasis on problem-based learning in China is a good example, as is the oft-stated Chinese goal of reducing the role of testing and emphasizing the role of creativity (which makes our movement in the opposite direction quite ironic). Many of the teacher quality reforms I discovered in other countries—having preservice teachers major in a content area, detailed teacher quality standards and competencies, distance education-based professional development—appear to be based on similar changes that were largely pioneered in the United States some decades ago. With the benefit of hindsight, this phenomenon should not be surprising given the country's reputation for fostering global innovation.[15]

The second tenet is that test scores usually show that we are not that different from other countries. The PISA results are most often quoted, and they just happen to be the most negative results from the U.S. perspective. But other international results, such as TIMSS and PIRLS, provide a more nuanced assessment of American students' performance. Sure, Finland outperforms the United States on PISA, but the differences on TIMSS are much smaller. And if the results of specific states like Massachusetts are factored into the results, at least some of our students look world-class. Granted, as our students get older, they don't compare as well, and in general the collection of international assessments suggests that we have a lot of work to do, but the differences are usually overstated. Are we the best in the world? No. But we shouldn't panic either.

The final tenet is that when there are significant differences between the United States and other countries, we almost always emerge with the wrong takeaways. I'm a bigger fan of TIMSS than PISA, as sampling by grade (TIMSS) just feels more appropriate than sampling by age (PISA), but even the PISA results suggest that the situation isn't as simple as "the U.S. ranks 15th in reading." As my colleague David Rutkowski and I have observed, American results look different if student performance is broken out by student racial groups: Asian Americans score in the top five, Caucasians score in the top ten, and Hispanic-Americans and African Americans score well down the rankings.[16]

These disparities should not be surprising given our size and economic disparities (the United States is the largest country participating in these assessments; China and India do not report nationwide results). The question shouldn't be, "What is Country X doing that we can copy?" Rather, we should be asking, "Why do we have such huge disparities within our country?" or, "What allows Asian American and white students to be successful, and how can we help black and Hispanic students perform similarly well?" Other than child poverty reduction programs, I find little success around the globe in solving the issues we are tackling in the United States, with not much in the way of teacher quality reforms to guide our efforts.[17] Our tendency to ignore our successes, overgeneralize our failures, and become fascinated with other countries' efforts is understandable given the first tenet, but ignoring the huge differences in context between countries is shortsighted.

Regarding American innovativeness in teacher quality reform, this exercise has forced me to reconsider my impatience with American educational innovation. Perhaps, in the end, I am frustrated with the pace of innovation and inability to implementing existing innovations at scale. Maybe we are already producing a great deal of innovation but not disseminating it widely enough or, in a related vein, not learning enough from our pilot implementations of innovations. And we may be holding unrealistic expectations that creative reforms that work in Boston should be equally successful in very different places like Seattle, Los Angeles, and South Harrison County Schools in Indiana. This would argue in favor of limited regional or even local pilot evaluations of potential reforms rather than large, national studies (for example, examining whether an intervention improves teacher effectiveness in a specific type of charter school rather than *all* charter schools).

And perhaps this is where we can learn from our colleagues in other countries. How have they encouraged (and avoided barriers to) widespread implementation of reforms? Or are they all facing implementation issues, regardless of the potential innovations they are attempting to implement? Many of the reforms in the countries I studied are treated positively in the media and academic literature, but one can be forgiven for skepticism if similar reform programs are announced every two to three years or if successive five-year plans deal with new approaches to the same problems with each new iteration. In the end, the most promising ideas, implemented most effectively with the most convincing evidence of success, can be easily derailed by political and cultural issues that have little to do with the intervention.

As a case in point, consider the major research university schools of education that drastically raised their entrance requirements for teacher preparation programs, seriously downsized their programs, and assertively transitioned to the Professional Development Schools model.[18] The collected evidence of these reforms' effectiveness is convincing if not overwhelming, yet I have heard from academics within those programs that the pressure from state policy makers to increase class sizes is considerable. This is not surprising given that the United States, with the third-largest population in the world, has lots of students and needs lots of teachers. "Be more exclusive" and "Train more teachers" are mutually exclusive concepts, yet those conflicting messages are often heard by those responsible for preparing teachers. The history of American education reform is replete with examples of promising initiatives that were derailed because of cost, local politics, or changes in federal policy that forced changes in state policy, among other factors. Policy makers, school boards, public opinion, among other actors, can be parochial and anti-innovation even when faced with overwhelming evidence that certain new reforms would provide maximum benefit at low cost. We can truly be our own worst enemy regarding education innovation.

Where do we go from here? If nothing else, we need to rethink our units of analysis in global comparisons. Comparing U.S. policy to that in much smaller countries is not fruitful; our size is both bigger than we often realize (of the world's population, one in twenty is American), and that size is unique. The two countries with larger populations are massively larger, and their policy structures couldn't be more different from ours; our population is also roughly 80 million people more than the next-biggest country (Indonesia) and more than *120 million* more than the fourth largest, Brazil. And again, our policy structures couldn't be more different. Comparing U.S. policy to that in Finland (just under 5.5 million people), Hong Kong (7 million), or even Chile (about 17 million) just doesn't make a lot of sense.

But comparing national innovations in those countries with individual American *states* does make a lot more sense. First, it acknowledges that the majority of American education policy is created and implemented at the state level. And comparing the countries mentioned above with Massachusetts (just under 6.7 million people), Minnesota (5.4 million), and Florida (19 million) makes more sense. If nothing else, such comparisons lead to better policy questions. Rather than asking what the United States can learn from Chilean choice experiments, we can ask how the outcomes of various choice interventions in Florida and Chile compare to each another. More to the point, rather than ask what the United States can learn from Finland about teacher quality, we can ask what the Finns can learn from Massachusetts (6.6 million), whose students were among the top in the world during the last TIMSS round.[19]

Similarly, a more fruitful global analysis of teacher quality innovation would probably involve *systems* for innovation, even if the interventions and reforms in question already exist within the United States. For instance, how was Finland able to raise teacher quality to current levels? More importantly, how do those efforts compare to those in states like New Jersey and Connecticut that made similar efforts in the late 1980s and early 1990s? What can we learn about the contrasting implementations that helps us understand the differential outcomes and provide lessons from others? I'm not completely convinced that even these comparisons will yield a great deal of helpful guidance, primarily because of cultural differences in attitudes toward government and education; but changing our units of analysis and comparing innovation systems strikes me as infinitely more helpful than comparing the United States with other countries and looking for specific innovations from which to learn and borrow.

More to the point, traditional teacher preparation programs are another area that appears to be light on innovation. Condemnations surrounding a lack of rigor in these programs have always felt overblown to me, but criticisms about being stuck in the status quo carry some weight, and I suspect many critics would be surprised at the number of university schools of education faculty who share similar concerns behind closed doors. But policy maker solutions, which are usually very prescriptive, are just as likely to produce status quo behaviors as the current system.

For example, Indiana revised its teacher licensure rules four years ago. The initial draft, which the governor publicly declared was intended to address perceived quality issues at the state's teacher preparation programs, was very directive, with limits on what could and couldn't be taught, down to details about how many credits of certain reading instruction needed to be included in each program. This approach was unlikely to produce much innovation, as it replaced one prescriptive model with another and allowed for little flexibility in program design. Essentially, Indiana was playing teacher preparation roulette by playing one number on the board. That's a good strategy if your number comes up, but odds are it will not, leading to a new status quo situation that is unlikely to produce meaningful change.

The state superintendent at the time, Tony Bennett, elected to move the new rules in a different direction, using market-based forces to promote innovation. In the first step, the draft rules were made less prescriptive, with the promise that later reforms would publicize each program's decisions about program inputs (required numbers of credits, cost per credit, average time to degree completion) along with outputs (licensure rates, percent of graduates who are hired to teach full time on graduation). Such an approach would create a market in which future teachers (consumers) could "vote with their feet" based on how they balance the various combinations of inputs and outputs across programs.

Someone suggested to me, directly and forcefully, that the latest report from the National Council on Teacher Quality (NCTQ) has data that provides the necessary information to help people choose the most effective teacher preparation programs.[20] The report, which grades more than 2,400 American preparation programs using a range of indicators, has received a great deal of publicity. In describing the report, NCTQ states that "as a consumer tool, [the report] allows aspiring teachers, parents and school districts to compare programs and determine which are doing the best—and worst—job of training new teachers."[21] But on closer examination, nearly all of the data points are inputs, with only a cursory examination of outcomes (usually surveys of graduates or employers). I don't necessarily disagree with many of the report's conclusions and recommendations, but to point to the report as a helpful guide within a more energetic, innovative teacher preparation marketplace is a big stretch. Hopefully, future editions of the report will do a better job of providing outcome data, because, as the report itself notes, "measures of effectiveness are ultimately what is most important."[22]

Regarding the use of market forces to encourage innovation, a colleague of mine, Ted Hall at Indiana University, took this basic idea a step further and once proposed the idea of promoting innovation *within* schools of education using similar principles. Why not allow faculty to propose new teacher education programs that fit their interests and understanding of the research on teacher quality, without regard to whether the faculty were in the teacher education or curriculum and instruction programs? For example, a science educator, educational psychologist, and educational philosopher, along with a professor from a public policy program, could design and propose a creative approach to teacher education. Performance criteria would be established on the front end, so each new program would be accountable for reaching certain levels of success. If those criteria were met, then the program could continue; if not, the program would be dissolved. Throughout the process, the new programs would be rigorously studied, informing both formative program improvement and summative lessons for similar and future efforts. Such a program would be very challenging to implement, but the potential payoff could be extremely promising. Risk aversion will not lead to improvements in teacher quality.

Similarly, the federal role in education could be transformed to promote much greater innovation than we currently observe. One approach, although not directly focused on education, is the U.S. Agency for International Development's (USAID) Development Innovation Ventures (DIV) project, which provides funding for ideas that have significant potential for innovation within the global development context.[23] The most promising ideas are funded, implemented on a small scale, and rigorously evaluated. If the ideas appear successful on a small scale, bigger implementation trials are possible. USAID promotes DIV as a "venture capital approach," but it is essentially a basic strategy for fostering creativity. USAID staff cannot predict which development ideas will be the most creative, nor can they generate every possible idea themselves. DIV solicits a large number of ideas, manages risk by selecting a portfolio of ideas to implement, and studies the effects of those programs carefully to determine which are most successful. Unsurprisingly, the program is receiving rave reviews. If it works for others, why not try it more extensively within education?

Many U.S. Department of Education programs developed over the past two administrations, such as Race to the Top, Investing in Innovation Fund, or the creation of the Institute of Education Sciences, partially hold to this model. At the same time, the programs often come with odd preconditions. The first Race to the Top competition is a good example of how the federal government decided which "innovations" needed to be included in state applications, assuming it knew best about how to improve teacher quality and student learning. The inevitable stories about implementation challenges in funded states may not have been surprising, but they also did not need to be so predictable. The role of educational entrepreneurs and private enterprise should also continue to be encouraged. I admit to being squeamish about the philosophical dilemmas involved (e.g., privatization in a public system; schools are perceived to be too expensive yet we are opening the system to for-profit ventures), but there is no question that the creative potential of such involvement is worth the risks.[24]

The American tendency to look beyond our borders, with the dual motivations of competition and the desire to copy foreign practices, has been an issue in education for decades. But while we should compare our student outcomes to those in other countries and carefully study other nations' innovations, many of those interventions already exist in the United States, and others are not culturally compatible. We are better served promoting educational creativity here at home, where more innovation exists than is commonly acknowledged. Still, there is a great deal left to be done.

CHAPTER 10

Into the Looking Glass

Teacher Quality Research over the Next Decade

DAN GOLDHABER

THIS CHAPTER BEGINS with the assumption, implicit throughout this volume, that a revolution in teaching quality would mean that the teaching profession looks quite different in the future. Such a revolution would likely mean that teachers have more specialized career options and, at the same time, that their roles are broadened beyond simply instructing single groups of students over a specific time period in brick-and-mortar classrooms. Given this, a 2.0 teacher research agenda should also be different than research on the existing teacher workforce, though some old research questions will still be relevant, even under a new teacher policy regime.

Other chapters have outlined the ways in which schooling might be affected over the next decade by the increasing availability and use of digital tools, computer-assisted instruction, and hybrid schooling models. Yet, the success of new learning tools and schooling models is, much as today, likely to depend on the quality of people in the "classrooms" (a term used loosely to represent the group of students over which teachers have responsibility) of the future and how they are utilized. We will need to know, for instance:

- Are the skills a teacher needs for online instruction similar to or distinct from what's needed in a traditional brick-and-mortar classroom?
- How should we think about evaluating the quality of new teacher tools?

- How might we start to figure out whether quality teachers are good at a whole bundle of tasks, or if the skills are discrete?
- How desirable are different types of new teacher career options?
- What are the best means of training teachers of the future?

It is well-trod ground to note that education research over the last decade showed three key findings: teacher quality appears to be the biggest schooling influence on student achievement; teachers differ substantially from each other in their effectiveness; and what makes teachers effective or ineffective is only weakly, at best, linked to the characteristics used for such high-stakes purposes as determining employment eligibility and compensation. These findings, along with the lack of variation in existing performance evaluations, form the empirical basis for the 1.0 reform agenda that provides more diverse pathways into the teaching profession, emphasizes differentiating teacher evaluations (often with the use of student growth/value-added measures as a component), and changes the basis of teacher compensation so it relies less on degree and experience levels. Given the potential for research to influence policy, outlining a 2.0 teacher research agenda is not merely an academic exercise. Framing the questions we need to answer about a 2.0 agenda has the potential to influence the agenda itself.

It is no great leap to suggest that teacher quality research over the last decade helped shape existing 1.0 teacher quality reforms. And while the 1.0 reforms seem sensible given what we know about teachers, we cannot help but wonder if the agenda might have been different given different research. As an example, teacher effectiveness research has been hampered to some extent by the fact that year-after-year testing is typically in grades 3–8 and because existing administrative data sets, especially early in the last decade, tended to only link teachers and students (and track them over time) at the elementary level. Consequently, the vast majority of value-added research is based on elementary students and teachers. A plausible argument can be made that value-added at the elementary level works well, at least as compared to other means of teacher evaluation. But there is also work showing that value-added might not work quite so well at the high school level, where students move from class to class and the academic tracking of students is more prevalent. Might the 1.0 reforms have had less emphasis on the value-added of individual teachers, or rewarding individual teacher performance, had research focused on high schools rather than elementary schools? And might a different research agenda leave room for some different types of innovation? The answer to both of these questions is most likely yes.

The point I am making here is not that 1.0 reforms are misplaced; it is that there is a value in conceptualizing what a 2.0 research agenda might look like so that we do not find ourselves in a situation where the availability of data on particular teacher innovations leads to specific kinds of research that then ends up driving a 2.0 policy agenda. The hope is that outlining the big questions that we need to answer about 2.0 innovations helps ensure that we collect the data that allows researchers to answer these questions so as to avoid a situation where the research tail wags the policy dog.

Before going too far down the road to imagining the teacher quality 2.0 research agenda, it is worth noting that the next decade of teacher quality research would be incomplete in the absence of research focused on 1.0 policy reforms—reforms encouraged by initiatives such as Race to the Top (RTTT) and the Teacher Incentive Fund, which create new models for evaluating teachers and that attach stakes (employment eligibility and compensation) to new evaluations.

Many of the potentially important consequences of 1.0 reforms cannot be assessed over a short period of time because they depend on how institutions and individuals respond to new information about teacher performance. Hence, there are many open questions about how the 1.0 reforms will ultimately affect the quality of the teacher workforce.

What's Left on the 1.0 Research Agenda

We know a good deal about the *properties* of existing ways of measuring teacher performance, value-added in particular, but we

know very little about the impacts of *using* performance evaluations. Research on value-added, for instance, assesses the degree to
which value-added treats teachers fairly, reveals how predictive it is
of future student test achievement and other longer-run outcomes,
and shows how stable it is from year to year or across different tests.[1]
There is some research on teacher observation-based evaluations,
and we are beginning to learn about the relationship between new
means of evaluating teachers, like student perceptions surveys or
student growth objectives, and student test performance.[2]

Yet, knowing the properties of teacher performance evaluations
only gets us so far. Most theories of action linking evaluations to
workforce quality improvements suggest that they are connected
to personnel decisions, such as what type of professional development teachers receive, their compensation, or which teachers are
retained. Analysts can use the properties, combined with assumptions about how measures are used, to simulate how the use of
evaluations affect the quality of the workforce, but this is a pretty
speculative exercise for two reasons.

First, many of the 1.0 teacher policy reforms are only now being
implemented at scale, and we have little idea of how differentiated
teacher evaluations and performance categorization will be under
new evaluation regimes. Delaware and Tennessee, for instance, the
first two states to win RTTT grants in 2010, have only recently (in
the 2013–2014 school year) fully implemented their new teacher
evaluation systems. New systems like these are formulaic in the
sense that states and districts mandate precisely how teachers are
to be judged; there is little in the way of supervisor judgments about
how teachers are evaluated. But there is still a human element to
this, for instance, in terms of the student achievement goal setting
that is required of teachers under many of the 1.0 reforms. Will
supervisors and teachers settle on aggressive student achievement
goals? Will more structured classroom observations change teacher
practice ratings? The answer to these sorts of questions will help
determine the degree to which teachers are differentiated from one
another and then how their performance is categorized. There is no
absolute standard for what constitutes an acceptable level of teacher

effectiveness, so it would not be surprising if standards vary from state to state or locality to locality. But the early evidence suggests that new evaluation systems result in performance evaluations that do not look all that different from the old ones, at least in terms of the *categorization* (for example, the proportion of teachers rated as "highly effective," "effective," or "ineffective") of teacher performance. But assume that this changes over time. If so, old questions about the validity and reliability of new evaluations will continue to be relevant.

Second, even if we do see more variation in teacher performance ratings, the full effect of the reforms depends on how teachers (and prospective teachers) respond to this. Also, learning about behavioral responses may take some time; the reaction to evaluation (and the stakes attached to evaluations) may not be immediate. With this in mind, I outline two important classes of questions about the 1.0 reforms.

1.0 TEACHER PRACTICES AND PREPARATION

The first class of questions has to do with teacher practices and training. Are some rubrics used to judge performance better than others at identifying effective teaching practices? Do teachers teach to the rubric? If so, is teaching to the rubric good or bad? Are there important differences in training programs in terms of the teaching practices they instill in their graduates? Are there teacher practices that are more effective with some types of students than others?

These questions are not new, but one of the reasons that we know relatively little about what constitutes effective teacher practices is, arguably, that there is little standardization in the rubrics used to do classroom observations. Obviously, the lack of variation in existing performance evaluations (most of which are based on classroom observations) is also problematic; we know empirically that teachers differ from one another, so performance evaluations that do not vary are, by definition, not going to be very valid. Of course, the whole notion behind the teacher policy 1.0 reforms is to change teacher evaluation systems, making evaluation a more rigorous process that does recognize the true differences among

teachers. If this does come to pass, we will be able to better con-
nect teaching practices to student outcomes and teaching practices
to teacher training.

BEHAVIORAL RESPONSE TO 1.0 REFORMS

The second class of questions has to do with the behavioral response
of teachers (and prospective teachers) to 1.0 policy reforms.[3] Does
feedback on evaluations or the incentives connected with evaluations improve teacher effectiveness? Are teacher career paths
shaped by evaluations and the stakes attached to them? The answers
to these kinds of questions are fundamentally connected to how
teachers respond to the performance information they receive as
well as its implications for employment status and compensation.

It is worth recognizing that teacher responses to performance
information could be contingent on the nature of an evaluation
system, such as what evaluations are based on. The reliability and
validity of performance evaluations are certainly important, but
issues of trust, understanding, and emotional salience will likely
also influence the way teachers react to the feedback they receive
about performance. For instance, teachers may easily discount
value-added measures as statistical mumbo jumbo or doubt that a
brief classroom observation or two really capture what is going on
during the course of a school year. Or the perceptions of a teacher's
students could have a powerful emotional effect, regardless of their
statistical properties.

Behavioral responses may also depend on a performance rating's implications for personnel actions. Here we know a bit about
some 1.0 reforms, pay for performance in particular. Specifically,
there are now a number of well-designed experimental studies
showing that teachers who are provided with monetary incentives
to increase student test achievement do not appear to be more effective in the short run.[4] But detecting the effects of pay for performance, or evaluation reform more generally, could take time. The
behavioral response to incentives or performance feedback may
work through changes in the types of professional development
required or sought by teachers. The existing experimental studies
of performance incentives focus on whether teachers are working

harder or smarter (in ways that show up in student test perfor-mance), but this may not be enough to lead to change. It is also possible that more systemic changes to human capital systems will follow teacher policy 1.0 reforms, so that teachers get better infor-mation about how to improve their practice (through professional development). But this, too, would take some time.[5]

Moreover, the short-run focus on the effects of performance incentives may miss the fact that incentives influence the com-position of the teacher workforce by encouraging the retention or attrition of teachers.[6] This raises the issue of whether teacher career path decisions are shaped by teacher policy 1.0 pay reforms. Do poor-performing teachers who are not dismissed for perfor-mance but regularly receive smaller-than-average pay increases opt to leave the teaching profession? Do performance rewards for highly effective teachers keep them in the profession longer? Are teachers removed from the workforce for poor performance? How do 1.0 policy reforms affect the talent that goes into teaching? The answers to these sorts of questions are not as straightforward as they might appear. For instance, 1.0 reforms likely make teaching a less secure occupation, but at the same time they are designed to reward teacher effectiveness. The net impact of these changes on prospective teachers will depend a great deal on how they are per-ceived by teachers (or prospective teachers), and that will depend, to some degree, on how the reforms are communicated to them. The answers to all of these questions will depend in part on how teacher performance under the 1.0 policy reforms is categorized, and this is an open question.

A 2.0 Research Agenda

Technology offers the potential to change schooling and a teacher's job in a number of ways, though it is important to acknowledge that there are significant political and cultural reasons why this might not come to pass.[7] For the sake of argument (and the meat of this chapter), however, assume that instruction is changed by technology in two fundamental ways: teachers and students are less bound to brick-and-mortar classrooms, and new digital tools provide teachers with better information about individual student needs and new ways to address those needs. While I do not delve deeply into the specifics of these computer-based or digital tools, it is not hard to envision this future; it is already here on a small scale.

Will the availability of these tools affect the quality of the teacher workforce? The answer depends on a host of connected issues. For instance, we will need to know the answers to questions like: Are teachers successful in different contexts? How can evaluations be used to match a more varied/differentiated teacher career? What influence do institutions and incentives have on the kinds of people who end up in teaching? In order to make discussion of the research connected to these complex questions more tractable, I break it down into three interrelated components:

- *The use of digital targeting and digital engagement tools.* Sophisticated computer algorithms that pinpoint students' academic needs, along with computer-based and online learning tools, offer the potential to change teaching and make teachers far more effective. But we will need to learn a good deal about the effective use of these tools. For instance, tools may be used to tailor the kinds of academic experiences that specific students have with teachers or technology. They may also indirectly affect students by changing the composition of their classmates during the course of a day.
- *Novel school designs and teacher teams.* Digital tools may change school structures and use teacher talent differently, requiring teachers to have more specialized knowledge (for example, an elementary teacher might be expected to specialize in teaching students about fractions) and to carry out very different kinds of tasks (such as the development of online learning modules). To inform school designs, research will need to determine whether teacher talents appear to be transferable across different roles or whether they are more suited to discrete tasks, and how evaluation systems should be best designed to recognize the potential importance of the team aspects of teaching under new models.
- *Institutions, governance structures, and the labor market.* There is little doubt that the talents of teachers will continue to be

fundamental to school quality; the effective use of digital tools will depend on sound judgments made by teachers. This means research on the institutions and governance structures that shape the teacher workforce, and how these interact with a changing labor market, will be as important to a 2.0 research agenda as it has been to shaping our current understanding of the quality of the teacher workforce.

THE USE OF DIGITAL TARGETING AND DIGITAL ENGAGEMENT TOOLS

New digital tools, both those that might help understand individual student needs and those used to address those needs, should in theory equip teachers to be more effective. A first-order question is, Are new digital teaching tools being used? This simplistic question seems almost silly until one recognizes that virtually all public schools have Internet access, yet there are schools across the country where computer labs sit unused. The tools used to store, manage, and analyze individual student needs exist in some school systems today, but the nascent literature on teacher use of these tools suggests low utilization.

For the sake of simplifying the discussion that follows, I break digital tools into two broad categories: digital *teacher targeting tools*, designed to help teachers better assess and address individual student needs; and digital *student engagement tools* for student use, designed to provide more tailored instruction (such as computer-based learning games).

As sophisticated as digital targeting tools may become, they ultimately will depend on the information about students that is put into the system and the capacity of teachers to use any of that information. In some cases, new student information will represent a significant enhancement to what teachers know about their students. Tools that track student achievement and assess student needs would be particularly valuable for students new to a school or school district, since getting detailed information about these students would be quite costly if it has to be acquired from teachers outside of a school. But no amount of information and computer-based recommendations about how to tailor instruction (level of a lesson, type of assignment, type of learning environment) to students will supersede the judgments of highly skilled teachers interacting with students. Instead, digital targeting tools are likely, in most cases, to represent somewhat marginal enhancements to the types of information that teachers currently have about students or could easily acquire from their colleagues down the hall.

A fundamental question about these tools is: Do teachers adapt their pedagogical approach to students because the tool provides better information about student needs? Differences in the ability of teachers to diagnose and then address individual student needs through their instructional choices is certainly one contributing factor to why there is such a great variation in teacher effectiveness in the workforce. It is conceivable that future digital targeting tools will be helpful to the kind of teachers who are not terribly good at these tasks performed with the information about students typically available now. If so, a narrowing of the distribution of teacher effectiveness in districts where digital targeting tools are available to teachers may take place. But it is also plausible that the kind of teachers who tend to be effective today are the ones who might best exploit the information digital targeting tools provide, widening the distribution of teacher effectiveness.

The impact of digital targeting tools on teacher practices and productivity is also likely to depend a great deal on the incentives they face. For instance, we know that accountability pressures (for example, incentives under NCLB to push students beyond a cut point on a state test) lead teachers to target their instructional efforts toward students who are near proficiency cutoffs.[8] Thus, it would also make sense to see whether there are important interactions between the availability of digital targeting tools and the type of student achievement incentives that teachers face.

Different from the tools teachers use to diagnose and tailor instruction for students are the tools designed to interact with and engage students in their learning. Teachers might address student needs by assigning them to work with these digital *engagement* tools. There are already good examples of what such tools look like—online lessons, computer-based math games—and their use actually goes back to the 1970s.[9] The existing empirical evidence on the efficacy of schools using some of the more prosaic existing tools is pretty mixed, which should serve as a caution to unbridled optimism about the impacts of digital tools on student achievement.[10] There is no doubt that digital engagement tools will become much more sophisticated in the future, but that does not necessarily mean all students will benefit from using them.[11] Given this, one could question whether teachers tend to make good decisions about which students are assigned to use digital engagement tools.

These tools could have both direct and indirect effects on teacher productivity. As the name suggests, engagement tools have the potential to directly impact those students who use them. Learning modules that are tailored to an individual student's needs and that allow them to progress at their own pace may be more engaging to students than being at the back of the classroom lost during a teacher's lecture, or sitting in class bored because the teacher is covering material that the student has already mastered. Depending on which students are targeted to receive digital instruction, and the impact of this instruction, we might expect the availability of digital engagement tools to differentially affect student achievement at different points in the achievement distribution. Research should be attentive to this and the potential that these tools have to affect achievement gaps.

When students are receiving digital instruction, a teacher's effective class size is smaller.[12] The benefits of the smaller classroom alone are likely marginal, but to the degree that teachers pick out the academic outliers in the class to receive digital instruction, the remaining students should be more academically homogeneous, allowing for a teacher to better target instruction to the remaining students.[13] Given this theory of action, research should focus not just on the direct impact of digital engagement tools but on the potential for indirect effects on students not using them.

Teachers already have access to an abundance of lesson plans and other digital resources, but will they make good choices among them? The effective use of digital targeting or engagement tools, making these tools truly transformative, requires that teachers make good judgments and adapt their own practices. This raises the issue of whether there are certain types of teachers who are more successful in using these tools. For instance, teachers newer to the profession are more likely to use and be successful with digital tools, since they are likely more familiar with using various digital aids in their personal lives. As is the case with existing research on teachers, we will want to assess whether there is an association between various teacher characteristics and/or experiences (such as preservice training or professional development) and their effectiveness when schools are using digital tools. Moreover, there is a good argument for contextualizing this line of research to explore, for instance, whether there might be networking effects associated with the coherent use of tools across schools or districts, where the impact of one teacher's use of a digital tool depends on the extent to which the tool is also being used by other teachers. For instance, there may be benefits associated with teachers working off of a common platform, or students becoming familiar with particular computer-based learning interfaces.

NOVEL SCHOOL DESIGNS AND TEACHER TEAMS

The kinds of questions I've outlined so far are not all that different from those long addressed by researchers when a new instructional model is introduced into schools. There are ways, however, that digital tools could lead to more fundamental changes to school structures and teachers' roles in them. The discussion has treated teachers' use of digital tools as if they are simple one-offs rather than as central to a school design, but recent innovations seen in schools fundamentally change school structures and teachers' roles in them. In Rocketship Education, for instance, students rotate between online and face-to-face modules. In the "flipped classroom" students are first taught key concepts online at home, and teachers play more of a facilitator role in helping students do (homework) problems and apply the concepts they've been introduced to. Technologies will also dissolve many of the barriers that place a teacher in just one building and with just one classroom of students. Imagine the physics teacher who is present in one bricks-and-mortar school but is also charged with providing instruction to students in other remote rural schools. Emphasizing different modalities for learning will require some teachers to become expert in the utilization of a more diverse set of learning models and at the same time create the potential for new, more specialized teaching roles. These changes are likely to make teaching a more collective enterprise challenging our current models for assessing teacher quality.

These types of arrangements represent much more radical departures from our current understanding of teaching and the role of teachers. Under such models, teachers might play the role of traditional, up-in-front-of-the-classroom lecturer and facilitator and, in some cases, also be called on to develop online content. The potential change in roles means there is a need to reconceptualize the very definition of what it means to be a teacher. Under these circumstances, *teacher* is more of a catch-all defining those adults who bear some direct responsibility for the instruction of students, whether because they are in front of them delivering a lecture or because they have designed the online curriculum students will receive. Changing teacher roles imply that teachers might need to develop more specialized skills, in terms of the delivery of particular lessons such as complex fractions, and/or be able to handle more varied duties, such as being responsible for instruction of both traditional brick-and-mortar and online classrooms.

On the whole, teacher roles in a 2.0 world might be characterized as having the potential to be both more specialized and more diverse, and research can help determine the degree to which teachers' skills vary across these roles. Of course, these skills may be readily observable; they might be associated with characteristics, like teacher experience, or they might vary from teacher to teacher. Either way, this research should help inform the organization and staffing of schools. For instance, if individual teachers turn out to be good at a whole bundle of tasks, it could indicate that school staffing might be pretty flexible; but if it turned out that teacher skills tend to be more discrete, it could suggest teachers hired into schools implementing a new type of structure might be better off hiring teachers into specific roles.

New schooling models also raise fundamental questions around the collectiveness of teaching. Many of the 1.0 policy reforms in place implicitly assume that the responsibility for student learning can be tied to individual teachers (even when that may not be the reality), but the 2.0 reforms that envision more teacher specialization may make this far less likely. This means that there needs to be some thinking around what the plausible units of responsibility for student learning are. In the majority of today's elementary schools, for instance, it is pretty clear which teachers in self-contained classrooms are contributing to students' test score growth in mathematics, but this would not be the case if students in the future are learning distinct math modules from specialist teachers.[14]

The issue of the unit of responsibility is closely linked to issues about teacher evaluation. In cases where the unit of responsibility is a team, evaluation should focus, at least in part, on effectiveness at the team level (there is no reason to have evaluation be solely individual or solely team based).[15] But there is no clear right way to target the unit of responsibility for student achievement. Under new schooling models where multiple teachers interact with students during the course of the day, it is more difficult to isolate the contributions of one member of a team, and there is an increased likelihood of "spillovers" (for example, team collaboration that leads to student achievement benefits), suggesting a team-based approach. But team approaches increase the likelihood of "free rider" problems, possibly leading to a reduction in teacher effort.[16] Indeed there is already suggestive evidence from 1.0 policy reforms that individual versus team responsibility for student learning in an evaluation system can impact teacher effectiveness.[17]

Beyond the issue of the unit of responsibility for student learning, 2.0 evaluation may look less standardized than it does under 1.0 policy reforms. Reforms of evaluation systems under Race to the Top, for instance, are formulaic; they tend to rely on specific components (value-added, student growth objectives, classroom observations, student perceptions) that are weighted to create summative measures. The formulas do not vary from school to school; the specific components that factor into the formulas do vary given that not all components—that is, value-added—are available for all teachers. Evaluation in a 2.0 world, by contrast, should be different because teacher roles might vary from school to school. It will call for assessments about the extent to which allowing for flexibility in evaluation designs might result in different distributions of teacher performance and/or whether designs appear to have a causal impact on performance itself.

The bottom line is that it is an open question as to how evaluation systems should be best designed to recognize the potential importance of the team aspects of teaching under new models. Research can help address this issue (for example, by assessing the extent to which the variation in student achievement is explained by different units of responsibility). But in order to frame this type of research, policy makers themselves must provide some structure for which teachers are plausibly responsible for student learning.

INSTITUTIONS, GOVERNANCE STRUCTURES, AND THE LABOR MARKET

A 2.0 research agenda would be incomplete without a focus on how institutions and governance structures influence the propensity of individuals to pursue a teaching career and their career paths in teaching. In particular, it will need to look at how these interact with broader changes in society, for the labor market associated with greater geographic, job, and occupational mobility may well have ramifications for the teaching profession.

While the profession has changed a good deal over the last decade in terms of providing additional alternative pathways into the profession, it is still largely structured as a career that people enter in their early twenties and remain in for an entire career.[18] Alternatives to this basic career path are often frowned on given a belief that it is those individuals fully committed to teaching who are likely to be most effective, and one proposed path forward envisions more structure around early recruitment and training of teachers.[19] But a more mobile workforce may not want a job that requires twenty years' experience to attain leadership positions, or one in which cross-state mobility is inhibited (by state licensure systems). Should the labor market continue to evolve in the direction of more occupational and job mobility, the teaching profession, if it does not adapt, could find itself increasingly out of step with these trends, perhaps making it more difficult to recruit talent into the profession. Given this, it is important to generate research on the aspects of a teaching career that are appealing or unappealing.

Institutions and governance structures play a role in determining the desirability of teaching jobs, and, as other chapters in this volume make clear, teacher preparation and collective bargaining may also look different in the future.[20] Is there a connection between preservice training and teacher effectiveness? Do specific provisions in collective bargaining agreements influence the distribution of teacher talent in school systems? Do training requirements imposed by licensure systems, or collective bargaining provisions, affect the desirability of pursuing a career in teaching?

Questions like these about a 2.0 world are not different from the policy issues that exist today. Still, it is an important reminder that a 2.0 research agenda should not treat either the composition of the teacher workforce or the organization of teachers in schools as "givens." Training institutions and licensure requirements explicitly delineate specific pathways into the labor market, and collective bargaining agreements influence the ways that teacher talents may be used. For instance, that physics teacher working in a rural area—will collective bargaining agreements and licensure systems allow her to instruct students across district or state boundaries? Answers to questions like this will go a long way toward determining the extent to which digital tools permit innovation in teacher roles.

Governance structures may also implicitly affect the distribution of teacher talent through the incentives they create. Given that teacher talent will continue to be important, we will need to know whether the institutional or governance arrangements that exist in a 2.0 world affect the desirability of the teaching profession. Moreover, 2.0 research should draw connections between these governance structures and the use of digital tools and novel school designs. Do licensure requirements inhibit cross-state employment relationships between teachers and schools? Do some provisions in collective bargaining agreements make it difficult to use teachers in schools in novel ways?

2.0 governance questions may not be all that different than those asked today, but what is likely to change is the diversity of methods by which teachers receive training and the nature of the teacher labor market. Technological innovation that is spurring changes in the K–12 environment is also changing the nature of teacher training. Right now that typically means that teachers are getting certified through online college programs, but we are also beginning to see alternative models, like residency programs that more closely link certification to K–12 experiences by having teacher trainees work with in-service teachers in a classroom for long periods of time before they become full-fledged teachers.[21] It is not hard to imagine that these ideas could be combined so that teachers could get very specialized training on the job without needing trainers in the same room with them. The general point is that we are likely to see the emergence of new types of preservice training and will want research to assess whether these appear to provide teachers with valuable skills.

Finally, in a 2.0 future, some teacher specialists may not even have teaching as their primary occupation. A Boeing engineer might contract with a school system to teach advanced math models.[22] We will need continued work that directly tackles the question of whether teachers who come into the profession through alternative routes or have nontraditional careers are more or less effective than those who have more traditional careers.[23]

Policy Implications and Conclusions

New digital tools have emerged that make it possible to dramatically enhance the impact and reach of individual teachers. Schools might be able to leverage these tools to determine new ways to engage individual students or to find the best match between a teacher's talents and his or her job. All this affords us the opportunity to make teaching radically more productive. But we have also seen this promise before. For instance, in a recent *Education Week* column about advertisements for educational technology, Larry Cuban wrote:

> For more than a century, educational technology ads have glistened with hope. Newly invented devices from the typewriter to film projectors, from the overhead projector to instructional

> television, from the Apple IIe to the iPad, have painted pictures
> of engaged students who will learn more, faster, and better. They
> have pictured teachers using new technologies to teach effec-
> tively. Of course, it is the nature of advertising to promise a rosier
> future, appealing to what policymakers, administrators, and, yes,
> parents yearn for . . . a better, easier, and even enjoyable way for
> teachers and students to teach and learn. And that is what these
> ads do. They assure readers that both teachers and students will
> be better off using these machines.

As this indicates, a rosy future connected to technology has been
promised many times before. I am somewhat skeptical about
whether this bright future will truly transform K–12 schooling.
Such radical improvement will require complementary changes to
the ways that teachers are trained, drawn into the workforce, and
used in schools. And absent changes to K–12 governance structures,
a good deal of innovation is likely to be stifled.

In fact, much of the 2.0 research agenda implicitly assumes a
significant level of policy experimentation with the way teachers
are used. But there is a bit of a catch-22 here: it is typical for people
to hold changes to common practice up to a higher standard of
evidence than the status quo. Debates over new teacher evaluation
systems are illustrative of this phenomenon. The statistical properties of value-added, for instance, are being thoroughly vetted by
policy makers and in the public sphere, yet there is little focus on
the properties of classroom observations, the most commonly used
means of measuring teacher performance. Perhaps this particular
measure would not look so good when held under the same micro-
scope. But, at the same time, bold experimentation requires a leap
of faith that cannot be supported by research, because research on
significant changes in policy or practice is incomplete without some
variation, or point of comparison, on which it can be based.[24]

Making significant progress at scale will depend a great deal on
policy makers being very purposeful about figuring what is working and, importantly, what isn't. This, of course, requires research.
But for research on 2.0 reforms to be well-grounded, policy makers
must think carefully about the theory of action that underlies the

use of digital tools and be sure to collect the data that allows for research that can adequately assess the theory. I cannot emphasize strongly enough the importance of collecting the right kinds of data. It will likely have to be different than the kind of information that is commonly available in the administrative state data sets that have formed the backbone of 1.0 teacher policy research. It is no coincidence that there are literally thousands of teacher studies that include controls for a teacher's degree and experience levels; these are the characteristics that are maintained in state databases, usually for pay purposes. Lest we fall into the trap of letting existing data frame 2.0 research and reform, we will need much more fine-grained information about which teachers are using which kinds of digital tools with which students, and for how long. Without this type of information, it will be very difficult, if not impossible, to understand the influence of the teams of teachers that interact with students in a 2.0 environment. This is what is necessary in order for researchers to help policy makers get a handle on the implications of the value of digital tools for improving teaching.

Conclusion

Making Room for Both Trains and Planes

MICHAEL Q. McSHANE AND TARYN HOCHLEITNER

To invent an airplane is nothing. To build one is something. But to fly is everything.

Otto Lilienthal, German pioneer of aviation

A T 5:21 A.M. ON JULY 4, 1912, a Delaware, Lackawanna & Western Railroad mail train heading to Buffalo, New York, from Hoboken, New Jersey, plowed into the back of a passenger train that was stopped on the tracks in East Corning, New York. The next day's *Ogdensburg Advance and St. Lawrence Weekly Democrat* reported, "The dead, which filled to overflowing the morgues of the little town are in many instances so mangled that identification is almost impossible."[1] Thirty-nine people were killed and eighty-eight were injured.

The subsequent investigation by the U.S. Interstate Commerce Commission (ICC) found several factors that may have caused the wreck. The mail train's engineer had imbibed a few "medicinal" gins that morning and had failed to notice the stop signal, barely visible through the thick fog, because he was preoccupied with some malfunctioning steam injectors. He also did not hear the exploding noise made by two warning "torpedoes," which had been placed on the tracks to alert trains of dangerous conditions. The investigation also found that the steel passenger cars held up much better than those made of wood; only two people in the steel cars died.

In the wake of the tragedy, the ICC made several recommendations. It clarified when and how to use the torpedoes most effectively. It called for more automatic blocking signals that would repeatedly warn trains to stop. And it declared that "the substitution of all steel equipment for wooden equipment in high speed passenger service shall be required at the earliest practical date."[2]

These proposals seem perfectly rational. After all, if the warning system in place fails to warn trains, it does no good. Improvements to the torpedo procedures gave engineers a better chance of avoiding a crash, especially during poor weather. Automatic signal upgrades addressed the risk posed by having only one signal, which could be too easily missed. Making rail cars out of steel makes them a lot safer than making them out of wood.

As sensible as these train safety provisions were, what would have happened if the ICC had decided to apply them to all forms of interstate travel? Close to a decade before the East Corning wreck, on December 17, 1903, Orville and Wilbur Wright first took flight in Kitty Hawk, North Carolina, in an aircraft made of wood. In 1911, just one year before the Corning collision, Calbraith Perry Rodgers became the first person to fly across the continental United States, from Sheepshead Bay, New York, to Pasadena, California.[3] He did so in a wooden Wright biplane. Indeed, the first decades of air flight were dominated by airliners, like the de Haviland Dragon (which operated well into the 1940s), made primarily of wood.

Imagine how different the history of American transportation might have been if a well-intentioned but overzealous ICC had, in 1912, decided that its efforts to promote passenger rail should also apply to any and all interstate travel. A regulation requiring the substitution of steel for wood that may have made good sense for rail travel would have grounded those pioneering American air travel.

This tale should hold a particular resonance for those enmeshed today, a century later, in efforts to improve teacher quality in the nation's schools. The reform effort of the past decade, with its emphasis on teacher evaluation and tenure reform, has been focused on addressing areas of obvious concern in the existing system. Think of this as the "improve rail travel" strategy. Perhaps multiple-measure evaluations are the automatic signal upgrades of teacher quality policy. If previous teacher evaluations provided an inaccurate and unhelpful picture of teacher performance, moving to systems that give more weight to value-added measures makes sense. But, just as it would have been a mistake to heedlessly apply the ICC's recommendations to all modes of transportation, so is it equally vital that we don't permit the sensible measures of the past decade to stifle emerging school models that have the potential to transform schooling in the same way that airplanes revolutionized travel.

The Role of 1.0 Reform

What we call 1.0 reforms are akin to measures to improve railroad travel, efforts focused on making an early-twentieth-century model of teaching work better. Vital here is keeping in mind the fact that railroads were getting safer, faster, and cheaper even as air travel was first emerging. The shift from steam to diesel to electric greatly increased the fuel efficiency of trains. The passenger experience was enhanced with air conditioning and refrigerator-equipped dining cars. Faster trains have shortened travel time. It is possible to improve both trains *and* planes at the same time—but they will require different strategies. What we advocate for in this book, therefore, is a policy and research agenda that can simultaneously further those 1.0 efforts *as well as* those that support and encourage new school models. This pursuit is what we refer to as teacher quality 2.0.

Similar to necessary and important improvements made to railroad travel, 1.0 reform has fulfilled a dire need to take steps toward improving the quality of teaching in traditional schools. At the start of the twenty-first century, there were few meaningful measures of student progress in relation to the teacher, teacher evaluation systems were largely symbolic and ineffectual, and—not surprisingly, given those conditions—seniority almost uniformly trumped performance when it came to layoffs and teacher assignment. Over the course of the past decade, much has changed to grease the wheels of traditional systems and structures. Researchers have pioneered increasingly sophisticated value-added models, offering schools a way to measure the academic progress of students assigned to a given teacher. States have adopted evaluation systems that combine those test-based measures with increasingly structured and consequential observational protocols. Tenure, teacher assignment, and teacher pay systems have been modified in a number of states and districts. Meanwhile, sensible efforts are under way to improve teacher preparation and provide more clinical experience to pre-service teachers.

Yet, there is still plenty of work to do if the 1.0 reform agenda is to deliver on its promise. Consider newly minted teacher evaluation systems. When results of new state evaluations were released in the spring of 2013, 97 percent of teachers in Florida were still ranked "effective" or "highly effective," 98 percent of teachers in Tennessee were found to meet expectations, and 98 percent of teachers in Michigan were rated "effective" or better.[4] New York City's revamped multiple-measures evaluation system found only 6 percent of its grades 4–8 teachers to be "ineffective"—not much of a change from the previous 3 percent rated as such.[5] A tremendous amount of work still lies ahead if these reforms are to change a culture of symbolic evaluation. The challenges may be even steeper when it comes to improving the quality of teacher preparation or identifying value-added metrics for the 70–80 percent of teachers not currently covered by value-added metrics in reading and math.

Given that this 1.0 effort has only just begun, many proponents of these reforms might wonder whether it's even necessary or useful to start talking about teacher quality 2.0. Are we getting ahead of ourselves? Is this just another distraction?

The reason to risk this "distraction," we believe, is because 1.0 reform is unlikely to fulfill the grand ambitions of many of its advocates on its own. We're skeptical that it's possible to fill all of today's teaching positions with highly effective educators, given the current structure of schools, school systems, and the teaching job. For instance, in chapter 2 contributors Bryan Hassel, Emily Ayscue Hassel, and Sharon Kebschull Barrett document the problem of scale in teacher quality reform. Today there are approximately 3.4 million teachers in the United States, only 25 percent of whom generate the year-plus gains in learning desired to keep students on pace to graduate ready for college or careers.[6] Even with the most rigorous 1.0 reforms—aggressively recruiting high-potential teachers and dismissing ineffective teachers—Hassel, Hassel, and Barrett estimate that the percentage of classrooms with a "high-quality" teacher would only increase to 40 percent.[7]

Teacher quality 1.0 has adopted a narrow vision of what great schooling entails. The labor force and the tools at our disposal have changed profoundly over time. It's now increasingly difficult to recruit a few hundred thousand new teachers a year who are eager and willing to do the same job for decades. Solving this problem today doesn't just require managing yesterday's model better but, instead, imagining new school models that tap available talent and tools.

Could Today's Teacher Quality Reforms Get in the Way of Tomorrow's Innovative School Models?

Pioneering education leaders and entrepreneurs who seek to design and build new schools still have to operate within structures created for traditional schools. Today's teacher quality policy proposals codify traditional definitions of schools, teachers, and classrooms into new laws and routines and, in the process, threaten to make it more difficult for 2.0 school and staffing models to thrive. New policies and strategies aim to revise familiar infrastructures (certification, tenure, step-and-lane pay scales, and job descriptions) that 2.0 school models, by nature, may not be aligned with or follow.

Even more troubling is new state legislation requiring schools to comply with laws around teacher evaluation, which, intentionally or not, pressures them to conform to particular staffing arrangements. Teacher evaluation policies threaten to make it difficult for schools to obey the law. Multiple-measure teacher evaluations, or those that consider more than one standard by which to assess teacher performance, are the backbone of 1.0 teacher quality policy. As articulated in state No Child Left Behind waiver applications, most states' models follow much the same pattern. For teachers in tested subjects and grades, 25–50 percent of the score is determined by student value-added test scores and 25–50 percent by observations, almost always following an established protocol like Charlotte Danielson's Framework for Teaching; whatever percentage is left over is dedicated to locally determined measures of performance, be they alternative assessments, school-level learning goals, or other national- or state-normed assessments.

The problem is that all three of those elements present difficulties for next-generation school models. It is worth examining each in greater depth.

VALUE-ADDED MODELS AND "OWNING" STUDENTS

Value-added models represent a clear step forward for student assessment. Rather than relying on single-shot proficiency exams to measure how many students clear the hurdle set by the state for a particular grade and subject, value-added tests attempt to measure growth over time, correcting for demographic characteristics. This leads to a more accurate and fine-tuned measure of student performance. As Matthew Di Carlo points out in chapter 8, however, value-added models pose challenges for innovative classrooms. As he explains, value-added models are "designed to attribute student progress to a single teacher or clearly defined group of teachers (for example, co-teachers)," not a loosely defined or shifting team or an in-person/technology shared instructional program.

Di Carlo also raises the important point that while there is a robust literature on the relationship between value-added measures and traditional brick-and-mortar teaching practices, there is "no published research on value-added for educators teaching online or similar courses, to say nothing as to how the measures should be deployed in these alternative contexts." Using the same tools to evaluate employees with different jobs raises serious questions about both the reliability and validity of these measures across contexts.

OBSERVATION IN NONTRADITIONAL ENVIRONMENTS

In Pennsylvania, the site of Dennis Beck and Robert Maranto's case study of cyber schools presented in chapter 6, 50 percent of a teacher's evaluation, by law, is derived from observations based on Danielson's Framework for Teaching. As Beck and Maranto point out, much of what teachers do in online environments is unique to their particular school model, and traditional evaluation instruments based on uniform instructional frameworks are simply ill-equipped to evaluate how well they are doing their jobs.

For example, Danielson's framework offers standards for maintaining order in a classroom, but teachers in an online school may do this in a much different way than their brick-and-mortar counterparts. Rather than making sure students are in their seats and keeping their attention on the front of the classroom, cyber instructors are monitoring language in chat rooms or patrolling class message boards. The fundamental task—ensuring that students do not misbehave—is the same, but the execution is different. Even when it doesn't make a lot of sense in an online context, Pennsylvania's Act 82 forces schools to use this tool. This runs the risk of both inaccurately measuring a teacher's performance and wasting the time of the administrator performing the observation.

Hybrid schools and schools with innovative staffing arrangements run into the same problems. As documented in chapter 2 by Hassel, Hassel, and Barrett, teachers who work as part of an instructional team simply don't perform many of the activities measured by traditional observation frameworks. Teachers who focus on instructional design need instruments to measure their ability to design effective instruction. Teachers who focus on assessment need instruments that focus on designing quality assessments. Teachers who act as mentors, when evaluated with the same blunt instrument designed to evaluate their traditional peers, can be scored on domains that are not part of their day-to-day responsibilities. Similarly, schools that divide instruction between computers and teachers need observation instruments that measure what teachers are actually doing. It is worth repeating that these are not flaws in the Danielson Framework per se, which is designed to accomplish a particular task in a particular environment; rather, this is a criticism of the application of this model in teacher evaluations wholesale, without care for schools that may operate differently.

STUDENT TESTING FOR TEACHER EVALUATION

Nontraditional models raise an important question about how to measure student learning in a manner that is accurate, consistent, and reliable. After all, testing circumstances can greatly affect student performance on assessments. In Pennsylvania, students in online schools are required to travel to a central location in order to take tests overseen by state officials. One administrator described it to Beck and Maranto as "teachers on the road, staying in hotels, away from their families three, four, five days, testing the kids in big hotel ballrooms, where you have eight-year-olds in strange environments with people they never knew." It's an open question whether such conditions may affect student performance and, consequently, evaluations of teacher effectiveness. This is particularly relevant if those students' assessment results are compared to those of peers who are tested in more comfortable, familiar surroundings. Testing-condition bias may color teacher evaluation, creating an inaccurate picture of how educators in nontraditional schools are doing and setting an artificial bar for such school models.

Where Do We Start?

Continuing sensible 1.0 teacher quality improvements without closing the door on 2.0 staffing and school models will be a tremendous challenge. Yet, contributors to this volume offer steps that policy makers, education leaders, higher education institutions, and private actors can take to improve current, traditionally structured schools while leaving room for future innovation. They fall under four themes: creating meaningful accountability systems for alternative school models, building a pipeline of 2.0 teachers and leaders, balancing short-term goals with long-term priorities, and developing a 2.0 research base.

CREATING MEANINGFUL ACCOUNTABILITY SYSTEMS FOR ALTERNATIVE SCHOOL MODELS

Current accountability systems hold states to standards and requirements based on certain assumptions about how schools are organized and staffed. Contributors offer two possible avenues for creating systems better suited for a more diverse landscape.

STATES COULD ESTABLISH MODEL-SPECIFIC ACCREDITING BODIES. Schools with unique missions and models could be evaluated by bodies that understand and are respectful of their particular pedagogical approach. Current accountability policies are implemented at a state level and are, purposefully, school-model agnostic. This runs into problems when tools designed to measure traditional teaching practice are applied wholesale to teachers who do a completely different set of tasks. To prevent this, as Jal Mehta and Steven Teles suggest in chapter 5, the state could empower model-specific accrediting bodies to oversee the management of individual sets of schools. There could be a cyber accreditor, a hybrid technology accreditor, a team teaching accreditor, or accreditors for new models that emerge. Those bodies would work with the state to develop and monitor appropriate, model-specific metrics for teacher performance.

DISTRICTS CAN WORK WITH UNION LEADERS TO DEVELOP FLEXIBLE CONTRACT CLAUSES. Contracts and collective bargaining agreements that too rigidly codify how teachers are to educate students can leave little room for innovation. In chapter 7, Katharine Strunk offers a way to avoid this. School and unions can establish guiding principles for certain items, like class size or evaluation, rather than strict codification of instructional minutes or student teacher ratios. For example, guiding principles in CBAs might require districts to link data from evaluations with professional development and support systems to help teachers improve. Then, as Strunk writes, administrators "have the flexibility to try new systems and adjust them based on their successes and failures."

SCHOOL LEADERS COULD INSTITUTE TEACHER-CHOSEN, TEAM-BASED EVALUATIONS. One of the hallmarks of 1.0 teacher quality policy is multiple-measure evaluations for *individual* teachers. This might be less useful in schools were teachers work in a team, dividing up instruction among several different specialized actors. Rather than individually evaluating teachers, it could be possible to allow teacher teams to decide to be held accountable *together*. Hassel, Hassel, and Barrett argue in chapter 2 that one of the best ways to mitigate pushback from teachers is to give them power in choosing their instructional teams. Then, rather than trying to parse out individual member contributions, students' value-added results could apply equally to all members of the team. This gets around the "who owns which students" problem and empowers teachers in the evaluation process at the same time.

BUILDING A PIPELINE OF 2.0 TEACHERS

The successful emergence of 2.0 approaches to teaching and schooling faces something of a "chicken or egg" problem. Regulators, accreditors, institutions of teacher preparation, and professional organizations don't feel much need to accommodate new school models because there simply aren't that many of them. Why would a large, public college of education that graduates hundreds of students per year prepare students to teach in an online school that may have one or two spots open in the entire state? At the same time, it's hard for these nascent school models to grow or succeed when they are constantly scrambling to find trained staff, cobbling together materials and training, and butting heads with credentialing bodies. Escaping this dilemma will require simultaneous movement by parties on both sides and by new providers collaborating with training programs, accreditors, and designers of instructional resources

STATES, DISTRICTS, AND PRIVATE PHILANTHROPY COULD ENCOURAGE INSTITUTIONS OF TEACHER PREPARATION TO PARTNER WITH LOCAL SCHOOLS. In chapter 3, Gross and DeArmond suggest that states and districts have a role to play when it comes to bringing top talent to their jurisdictions. They can establish partnerships with alternative sources of talent (like TFA), build residency programs, and be supportive of new programs. What's more, schools that staff differently or leverage technology in new ways need teachers trained in the skills necessary to work in these nontraditional environments. The birth of Relay Graduate School of Education described by Billie Gastic in chapter 4 offers a framework for how a school of education can effectively partner with new school models. First, teacher preparation programs can work closely with school models to identify what skills and knowledge are needed by teachers in those environments and create a curriculum to prepare teachers for those roles. Second, schools will need to develop quality clinical experiences for preservice teachers seeking to work in these new school models.

Performing the observations and student teaching necessary to earn a degree or certification in teaching in traditional schools will likely be of little help to a teacher preparing for a role in a 2.0 school. Next-generation teacher preparation programs can place practicum and student teachers in hybrid schools, online schools, and schools with innovative staffing arrangements.

STATES AND DISTRICTS CAN CREATE AND FUND INNOVATION ZONES. As Sara Mead, Andy Rotherham, and Rachael Brown argue in chapter 1, many of these new school models are untested and need more research to determine their efficacy—they're building the plane while flying it, with respect to pedagogical practice and teacher quality management. As a result, they are evolving and changing faster than even the most nimble of waivers could feasibly keep up with. To get around sticky issues of compliance and oversight, individual districts could invite new model schools into designated innovation zones as demonstration projects. Built into the model could be a rigorous evaluation, particularly in the short term, of the kinds of blanket statewide or district accountability systems such new models need to participate in.

UNIVERSITY PRESIDENTS AND DEANS COULD PROMOTE INNOVATION WITHIN EXISTING SCHOOLS OF EDUCATION. Creating enough new teacher preparation programs to fill the need for possibly hundreds of thousands of new teachers is a desperately tall order. Most likely, innovative school models are going to need to work with existing colleges of education to develop a supply of adequately prepared teachers. In chapter 9, Jonathan Plucker proposes that schools of education may be able to foster innovation within their programs by allowing faculty to propose new teacher education programs. For example, Plucker suggests that "a science educator, educational psychologist, and educational philosopher, along with a professor from a public policy program, could design and propose a creative approach to teacher education." They could work with a particular school model to identify needs or propose a more general path for new models of education. The college would establish certain performance goals at the outset and hold program creators accountable.

DEVELOPING A 2.0 RESEARCH BASE

It's hard to overstate the role of research in driving the teacher quality 1.0 research agenda. With this in mind, Dan Goldhaber identifies in chapter 10 research queries that could fuel a generation of 2.0 research. Researchers and potential funders would do well to consider carefully the agenda that Goldhaber outlines, while considering three recommendations critical to its successful execution.

GET IN ON THE GROUND FLOOR BY PARTNERING WITH NEW SCHOOL MODELS. In order to develop 2.0 research questions, researchers could partner with new schools and access data in exchange for analysis and advice based on the results—because that's where the 2.0 data are. The availability of large, statewide data sets has allowed many researchers to dig into 1.0 research questions. But 2.0 questions like, "How do we isolate a teacher's contribution to student learning in a classroom where students receive part of their instruction online?" require working with such organizations as Rocketship Education or such districts as Mooresville Graded School District.

LOOK AROUND THE BEND FOR THE QUESTIONS THAT WILL SHAPE TOMORROW'S PRACTICE. Researchers like Goldhaber pioneered the use of value-added to measure teacher effects at a time when such techniques were considered marginal, at best. Indeed, it was William Sanders, a professor of agricultural genetics in Tennessee, who initiated the use of reading and math scores to gauge learning during the 1990s because faculty in schools of education had no interest in doing so. By refusing to limit themselves to familiar correlational inquiries and case studies of professional development and curriculum implementation, researchers of that era helped illuminate a whole new world of possibilities for policy and practice.

THERE'S PLENTY OF 1.0 WORK TO BE DONE. As Goldhaber notes, there is still an array of 1.0 questions to be pursued. Perhaps more tellingly, these include understanding how teachers and the labor markets respond to today's new evaluation systems—and the changes to tenure and pay that go along with them. Learning how these systems work in reality will provide critical insights that can help inform the next generation of policy making, preparation, and practice.

Preparing for Takeoff

The unknown looms large. Most 2.0 schools are still in their infancy and are few and far between. Technology critics fear that virtual or blended approaches that require students to spend a great deal of time working in front of a screen will have deleterious effects, and supporters have little evidence to negate these trepidations. Indeed, it's possible that some 2.0 schools may not be as successful as some high-performing traditional schools. Yet, this hard work is important work if we hope to breed thoughtful redesign within the nation's system of public education.

Calbraith Perry Rodgers's successful transcontinental flight in 1911—the first ever made across the United States—followed many failed attempts made by his peers and took him forty-nine days and countless stops, delays, and accidents.[8] Less than forty years later, Chuck Yeager broke the sound barrier. Ten years after Yeager, in 1954, Boeing launched the first 707 jet airliner. Today, the airline industry has made long-distance travel fast, affordable, safe, and accessible to an extent unimaginable a century ago. We take for granted that we can fly direct from New York City to Los Angeles in less than six hours, a far cry from the forty-nine days Rodgers spent on his journey. Yet it would have been impossible in 1911 to imagine just how far air travel would advance in the ensuing years.

It's equally hard today to guess which emerging school models might make a big difference, or how they will evolve. It would be a tragedy if, twenty-five years from now, we look back ruefully at our inability to harness new tools to improve schooling because our sensible commitment to improving yesterday's schools led us to accidentally stifle the possibilities of tomorrow's.

Notes

Introduction

1. Trevor Thompson, Jennifer Benz, and Jennifer Agiesta, *Parents Attitudes on the Quality of Education in the United States* (report, Associated Press–NORC Center for Public Affairs Research, Chicago, August 2013), http://www.apnorc.org/projects/Pages/parents-attitudes-on-the-quality-of-education-in-the-united-states.aspx.
2. Raj Chetty, John Friedman, and Jonah Rockoff, "The Long-Term Impacts of Teachers: Teacher Value-Added and Student Outcomes in Adulthood" (Working Paper No. w17699, National Bureau of Economic Research, December 2011).
3. Robert Gordon, Thomas J. Kane, and Douglas O. Staiger, *Identifying Effective Teachers Using Performance on the Job* (Washington, DC: Brookings Institution, 2006); Steven Rivkin, Eric Hanushek, and John Kain, "Teachers, Schools, and Academic Achievement," *Econometrica* 73, no. 2 (2005): 417–458.
4. Horace Mann, *First Annual Report of the Board of Education Together with the First Annual Report of the Secretary of the Board* (Boston: Dutton & Wentworth, 1837), 58.
5. The National Commission on Teaching and America's Future, *What Matters Most: Teaching for America's Future* (New York: National Commission on Teaching and America's Future, 1996).
6. Daniel Weisberg, Susan Sexton, Jennifer Mulhern, and David Keeling, "The Widget Effect: Our National Failure to Acknowledge and Act on Differences in Teacher Effectiveness," TNTP, 2009, http://widgeteffect.org/downloads/TheWidgetEffect.pdf.
7. U.S. Department of Education, "ESEA Flexibility," 2013, http://www2.ed.gov/policy/elsec/guid/esea-flexibility/index.html.
8. "Moving America Forward: 2012 Democratic National Platform," http://www.presidency.ucsb.edu/ws/?pid=101962; "We Believe in America," http://www.gop.com/2012-republican-platform_Renewing/.
9. Lexis Nexis headline search, August 12, 2013.
10. John Watson, Amy Murin, Lauren Vashaw, Butch Gemin, and Chris Rapp. *Keeping Pace with K–12 Online and Blended Learning: An Annual Review of Policy and Practice* (Mountain View, CA: Evergreen Education Group, 2013), available at http://kpk12.com/cms/wp-content/uploads/EEG_KP2013-lr.pdf.

11. Nick Pandolfo, "Education Nation: In Arizona Desert, a Charter School Competes," *The Hechinger Report*, September 24, 2012, http://hechingerreport.org/content/education-nation-in-arizona-desert-a-charter-school-competes_9687/.

12. Douglas Ready, Ellen Meier, Dawn Horton, Caron Mineo, and Jessica Yusatis Pike, "Student Mathematics Performance in Year One Implementation of Teach to One: Math" (report, Center for Technology and School Change, Teachers College, Columbia University, New York, November 2013), http://www.newclassrooms.org/resources/teach-to-one-report-ctsc-fall2013.pdf.

13. Watson et al., *Keeping Pace*.

14. Ibid.

15. Florida, "ESEA Flexibility Request," submitted to U.S. Department of Education, January 31, 2012, http://www2.ed.gov/policy/eseaflex/approved-requests/fl.pdf.

16. Charlotte Danielson, *The Framework for Teaching Evaluation Instrument*. (Princeton, NJ: Danielson Group, 2013).

17. Council for the Accreditation of Educator Preparation, "Annual Report to the Public, the States, Policymakers, and the Education Profession," 2013, http://caepnet.files.wordpress.com/2013/05/annualreport_final.pdf.

18. Council of Chief State School Officers and Interstate Teacher Assessment and Support Consortium, *Model Core Teaching Standards and Learning Progressions for Teachers 1.0: A Resource for Ongoing Teacher Development* (Washington, DC: Council of Chief State School Officers and Interstate Teacher Assessment and Support Consortium, 2013).

19. Frederick M. Hess and Jess Castle, "Teacher Pay and 21st-Century School Reform," in *21st Century Education: A Reference Handbook*, ed. Thomas Good (Thousand Oaks, CA: Sage, 2008), II.68–II.76.

20. "Agreement between the Board of Education of The City of Chicago and Chicago Teachers Union Local 1, American Federation of Teachers, AFL-CIO," October 2012, http://www.ctunet.com/for-members/text/CTU_Contract_As_Printed_2012_2015.pdf.

Chapter 1

1. Andrew Rotherham and Sara Mead, "Back to the Future: The History and Politics of State Teacher Licensure and Certification," in *A Qualified Teacher in Every Classroom?* ed. Frederick M. Hess, Andrew Rotherham, and Kate Walsh (Cambridge, MA: Harvard Education Press, 2004), 11–48.

2. Sandra L. Stotsky, "Revising Teacher Licensing Regulations to Advance Education Reform in Massachusetts," in *Education Success Stories* (Amherst, MA: National Evaluation Systems, 2001), www.pearsonassessments.com/hai/images/NES_Publications/2001_14Stotsky_466_1.pdf.

3. Emma Smith and Stephen Gorard, "Improving Teacher Quality: Lessons from America's No Child Left Behind," *Cambridge Journal of Education* 37, no. 2 (2007): 191–206, available online atwww.tandfonline.com/doi/abs/10.1080/03057640701372426; Robert Rothman and Patte Barth, "Does

Highly Qualified Mean Highly Effective?" Center for Public Education, 2009, www.centerforpubliceducation.org/Main-Menu/Staffingstudents/How-good-are-your-teachers-Trying-to-define-teacher-quality/Does-highly-qualified-mean-highly-effective.html.

4. Dan D. Goldhaber, "The Mystery of Good Teaching," *Education Next* 2, no. 1 (2002): 50–55.

5. Charles Clotfelter, Helen Ladd, and Jacob Vigdor, "Teacher Credentials and Student Achievement: Longitudinal Analysis with Student Fixed Effects," *Economics of Education Review* 26, no. 6 (2007): 673–682; Goldhaber, "The Mystery of Good Teaching."

6. Jennifer Rice King, "The Impact of Teacher Experience: Examining the Evidence and Policy Implications," *CALDER Policy Brief* 11 (August 2010), www.urban.org/uploadedpdf/1001455-impact-teacher-experience.pdf.

7. Dan D. Goldhaber and Dominic J. Brewer, "Why Don't Schools and Teachers Seem to Matter? Assessing the Impact of Unobservables on Educational Productivity," *Journal of Human Resources* 32, no. 3 (1997): 505–523.

8. June C. Rivers and William L. Sanders, *Cumulative and Residual Effects of Teachers on Future Student Academic Achievement* (Knoxville: University of Tennessee Value-Added Research and Assessment Center, 1996), 9, available online at http://heartland.org/sites/all/modules/custom/heartland_migration/files/pdfs/3048.pdf; Kati Haycock, "Good Teaching Matters: How Well-Qualified Teachers Can Close the Achievement Gap," Education Trust, 1998, www.take2theweb.com/pub/sso/eastlinton/images/Good_teaching_matters.pdf.

9. William L. Sanders and Sandra P. Horn, "The Tennessee Value-Added Assessment System (TVAAS): Mixed Model Methodology in Educational Assessment," *Journal of Personnel Evaluation in Education* 8 (1994): 299–311, available online at www.redmond.k12.or.us/145410515152938173/lib/145410515152938173/The_Tennessee_Value-Added_Assessment_System-_Mixed-Model_Methodology_in_Ed_Assessment.pdf.

10. Kevin Carey, "The Real Value of Teachers: Using New Information about Teacher Effectiveness to Close the Achievement Gap," *Thinking K–16* 8, no. 1 (2004): 3–42, available online at www.edtrust.org/dc/publication/the-real-value-of-teachers-using-new-information-about-teacher-effectiveness-to-close.

11. Robert Gordon, Thomas Kaine, and Douglas Staiger, "Identifying Effective Teachers Using Performance on the Job," Brookings Institution, 2006, www.brookings.edu/papers/2006/04education_gordon.aspx.

12. Daniel Weisberg, Susan Sexton, Jennifer Mulhern, and David Keeling, "The Widget Effect: Our National Failure to Acknowledge and Act on Differences in Teacher Effectiveness," TNTP, 2009, p. 6, http://widgeteffect.org/downloads/TheWidgetEffect.pdf.

13. Ibid.

14. U.S. Department of Education, "Race to the Top Program Executive Summary," November 2009, www2.ed.gov/programs/racetothetop/executive-summary.pdf.

15. Bellwether Education Partners staff, including two coauthors of this paper, were involved in writing or advising state RTTT applications.

16. Learning Point Associates, "State Legislation: Emerging Trends Reflected in State Phase 1 Race to the Top Applications," June 2011, www.learningpt.org/pdfs/RttT_State_Legislation.pdf.

17. While TNTP referred to this style of evaluation as 2.0, we would consider it 1.5—an improvement on the current system but not necessarily a system designed for next-generation school models. TNTP, "Teacher Evaluation 2.0," 2010, tntp.org/files/Teacher-Evaluation-Oct10F.pdf.

18. Ron Tupa, Jocelyn Huber, and Barbara Martinez, "Built to Succeed? Ranking New Statewide Teacher Evaluation Practices," Democrats for Education Reform, October 17, 2011, http://www.dfer.org/Report%20-%20Evaluation%20Ratings%20DRAFT9.pdf; National Council on Teacher Quality, "State of the States: Trends and Early Lessons on Teacher Evaluation and Effectiveness Policies," 2011, www.nctq.org/p/publications/docs/nctq_stateOfTheStates.pdf; Sara Mead, "Recent State Action on Teacher Effectiveness: What's in State Laws and Regulations?" Bellwether Education Partners, August 2012, http://bellwethereducation.org/ideas/publications.

19. U.S. Department of Education, "ESEA Flexibility," September 23, 2011, www.ed.gov/esea/flexibility.

20. Ibid., 7.

21. Michael Winerip, "In Tennessee, Following the Rules for Evaluation Off a Cliff," *New York Times*, November 6, 2011.

22. U.S. Department of Education, "Race to the Top Annual Performance Report," 2012, www.ed.gov/programs/racetothetop/annual-report.pdf.

23. Gordon, Kane, and Staiger, "Identifying Effective Teachers Using Performance on the Job."

Chapter 2

1. Bryan C. Hassel and Emily A. Hassel, *Opportunity at the Top: How America's Best Teachers Could Close the Gaps, Raise the Bar, and Keep Our Nation Great* (Chapel Hill, NC: Public Impact, 2010), http://www.opportunityculture.org/images/stories/opportunity_execsum_web.pdf.

2. National Center for Education Statistics, "Table 83: Estimated Average Annual Salary of Teachers in Public Elementary and Secondary Schools: Selected Years, 1959–60 through 2010–11," http://nces.ed.gov/programs/digest/d11/tables/dt11_083.asp.

3. Frederick M. Hess, "How to Get the Teachers We Want," *Education Next* 9, no. 3 (2009): 35–39; *Re-Imagining Teaching: Five Structures to Transform the Profession* (Washington, DC: National Network of State Teachers of the Year, 2013); Teach Plus, "T3 Initiative," http://www.teachplus.org/page/t3-initiative-8.html; National Education Association, "NEA Policy Statement on Digital Learning," 2013, http://www.nea.org/home/55434.htm; Barnett Berry, *The Teachers of 2030: Creating a Student Centered Profession for the 21st Century* (Hillsborough, NC: Center for Teaching Quality, 2009); Jane Coggshall, Molly Lasagna, and Sabrina Laine, *Toward the Structural Transformation of Schools: Innovations in Staffing* (Naperville, IL: Learning Point Associates, 2009).

4. Emily A. Hassel and Bryan C. Hassel, *3X for All: Extending the Reach of Education's Best* (Chapel Hill, NC: Public Impact, 2009), available at http://www.publicimpact.com/images/stories/3x_for_all-public_impact.pdf; Hassel and Hassel, *Opportunity at the Top*; Opportunity Culture, www.opportunityculture.org.

5. For a detailed description of the vision for a selective, opportunity-rich, well-paid teaching profession, see Emily A. Hassel & Bryan C. Hassel, *An Opportunity Culture for All: Making Teaching a Highly Paid, High-Impact Profession* (Chapel Hill, NC: Public Impact, 2013), http://opportunityculture.org/wpcontent/uploads/2013/09/An_Opportunity_Culture_for_All-PublicImpact.pdf.

6. For more detail, see "Redesigning Schools to Extend Excellent Teachers' Reach," Opportunity Culture, http://opportunityculture.org/reach/.

7. For a typology of blended learning models, see Heather Staker and Michael B. Horn, *Classifying K–12 Blended Learning* (San Mateo, CA: Innosight Institute, 2012), available online at http://www.christenseninstitute.org/wp-content/uploads/2013/04/Classifying-K-12-blended-learning.pdf. For more on how staffing models can enhance the use of digital instruction, see Joe Able-idinger, Jiye G. Han, Bryan C. Hassel, and Emily A. Hassel, *A Better Blend: A Vision for Boosting Student Outcomes with Digital Learning* (Chapel Hill, NC: Public Impact, 2013), available online at http://opportunityculture.org/wp-content/uploads/2013/04/A_Better_Blend_A_Vision_for_Boosting_Student_Outcomes_with_Digital_Learning-Public_Impact.pdf.

8. For detailed models of these potential financial savings and reallocation to teacher pay, see http://opportunityculture.org/reach/pay-teachers-more.

9. For more on career paths related to these models, see http://opportunityculture.org/reach/career-paths.

10. Organisation of Economic Co-operation and Development, *Strong Performers and Successful Reformers in Education: Lessons from PISA for the United States*, 2011, http://www.oecd.org/pisa/46623978.pdf.

Chapter 3

1. For example, see Jessica Levin and Meredith Quinn, "Missed Opportunities: How We Keep High-Quality Teachers Out of Urban Classrooms," TNTP, 2003, http://tntp.org/assets/documents/MissedOpportunities.pdf; Jessica Levin, Jennifer Mulher, and Joan Schunck, "Unintended Consequences: The Case for Reforming the Staffing Rules in Urban Teachers Contracts," TNTP, 2005, http://files.eric.ed.gov/fulltext/ED515654.pdf; Edward Liu and Susan Moore Johnson, "New Teachers' Experiences of Hiring: Late, Rushed, and Information-Poor," *Educational Administration Quarterly* 42, no. 3 (2006): 324–360; Daniel Weisberg, Susan Sexton, Jennifer Mulhern, and David Keeling, "The Widget Effect: Our National Failure to Acknowledge and Act on Differences in Teacher Effectiveness," TNTP, 2009, http://widgeteffect.org/downloads/TheWidgetEffect.pdf; Jessica Levin and Meredith Quinn, "Missed Opportunities: How We Keep High Quality Teachers Out of Urban Classrooms," TNTP, 2003, http://tntp.org/assets/documents/MissedOpportunities.pdf.

2. For example, see Patrick M. Wright and Gary C. McMahan, "Theoretical Perspectives on Strategic Human Resource Management," *Journal of Management* 18, no. 2 (1992): 295–320; Casey Ichniowski, Kathryn L. Shaw, and Giovanna Prennushi, "The Effects of Human Resource Management Practices on Productivity: A Study of Steel Finishing Lines," *American Economic Review* 87, no. 3 (1997): 291–313; Casey Ichniowski and Kathryn Shaw, "The Effectives of Human Resource Management Systems on Economic Performance: An International Comparison of U.S. and Japanese Plants," *Management Science* 45, no. 5 (2003): 704–721.

3. See Wright and McMahan, "Theoretical Perspectives for Strategic Human Resource Management"; David E. Bowen and Cheri Ostroff, "Understanding HRM-Firm Performance Linkages: The Role of the 'Strength of the HRM System,'" *Academy of Management Journal* 29, no. 2 (2004): 203–221.

4. Bowen and Ostroff, "Understanding HRM-Firm Performance Linkages: The Role of the 'Strength of the HRM System.'"

5. For example, see Rachel Curtis, *District of Columbia Public Schools: Defining Instructional Expectations and Aligning Accountability and Support* (Washington, DC: The Aspen Institute, 2011), http://www.aspeninstitute.org.

6. Propel added a ninth school in the 2013–2014 school year.

7. See Dan Goldhaber, "Into the Looking Glass: Teacher Quality Research over the Next Decade," chap. 10 this volume.

8. For example, see Cassandra Guarino, Lucrecia Santibanez, and Glenn A. Daley, "Teacher Recruitment and Retention: A Review of the Recent Empirical Literature," *Review of Educational Research* 76, no. 2 (2006): 173–208; Hamilton Lankford, Susanna Loeb, and James Wyckoff, "Teacher Sorting and the Plight of Urban Schools: A Descriptive Analysis," *Educational Evaluation and Policy Analysis* 24, no. 1 (2002): 37–62.

Chapter 4

I thank the editors and my Relay GSE colleagues for their thoughtful and constructive feedback on earlier drafts of this chapter.

1. William J. Hussar and Tabitha M. Bailey, *Projections of Education Statistics to 2020* (Washington, DC: Government Printing Office, 2011).

2. For example, Common Core State Standards, http://www.corestandards.org/.

3. For ease of comparison, I use *2.0* here to denote a departure from traditional schools of education. While to date most of those schools, with the noted exception of High Tech High, have prepared teachers to enter 1.0 classrooms, the characteristics they embody are a promising template for a vision of future preparatory institutions that would serve 2.0 schools.

4. Arne Duncan, "Teacher Preparation: Reforming the Uncertain Profession" (speech, Teachers College, Columbia University, New York, October 22, 2009), http://www2.ed.gov/news/speeches/2009/10/10222009.html.

5. Eddy Ramírez, "What You Should Consider Before Education Graduate School," *U.S. News and World Report*, March 25, 2009, http://www.usnews

.com/education/blogs/on-education/2009/03/25/what-you-should-consider-before-education-graduate-school.

6. Frederick M. Hess, Andrew J. Rotherham, and Kate Walsh, eds., *A Qualified Teacher in Every Classroom? Appraising Old Answers and New Ideas* (Cambridge, MA: Harvard Education Press, 2004).

7. National Council on Teacher Quality, *Teacher Prep Review 2013: A Review of the Nation's Teacher Preparation Programs*, 2013, http://www.nctq.org/dmsView/Teacher_Prep_Review_2013_Report.

8. Steven G. Rivkin, Eric A. Hanushek, and John F. Kain, "Teachers, Schools, and Academic Achievement," *Econometrica* 73, no. 2 (2005): 417–458.

9. Matthew M. Chingos and Paul E. Peterson, "It's Easier to Pick a Good Teacher Than Train One: Familiar and New Results on the Correlates of Teacher Effectiveness," *Economics of Education Review* 30, no. 3 (2011): 449–465.

10. Sean P. Corcoran, William N. Evans, and Robert M. Schwab, "Changing Labor-Market Opportunities for Women and the Quality of Teachers, 1957–2000," *American Economic Review* 94, no. 2 (2004): 230–235.

11. Drew H. Gitomer, *Teacher Quality in a Changing Policy Landscape: Improvements in the Teacher Pool*, Educational Testing Service, 2007, http://www.ets.org/Media/Education_Topics/pdf/TQ_full_report.pdf.

12. U.S. Department of Education, *Preparing and Credentialing the Nation's Teachers*, http://www2.ed.gov/about/reports/annual/teachprep/2011-title2report.pdf.

13. Dan Goldhaber, Stephanie Liddle, and Rodney Theobald, "The Gateway to the Profession: Assessing Teacher Preparation Programs Based on Student Achievement," *Economics of Education Review* 34 (June 2013): 29–44; Cory Koedel, Eric Parsons, Michael Podgursky, and Mark Ehlert, "Teacher Preparation Programs and Teacher Quality: Are There Real Differences across Programs?" (working paper, Department of Economics, University of Missouri, Columbia, July 2012); National Council on Teacher Quality, *Teacher Prep 2013*.

14. U.S. Department of Education, *Race to the Top Program Executive Summary*, 2009, http://www2.ed.gov/programs/racetothetop/executive-summary.pdf.

15. Edward Crowe, *Race to the Top and Teacher Preparation: Analyzing Strategies for Ensuring Real Accountability and Fostering Program Innovation*, Center for American Progress, 2011, http://www.americanprogress.org/wp-content/uploads/issues/2011/03/pdf/teacher_preparation.pdf.

16. National Council for Accreditation of Teacher Education, *Transforming Teacher Education through Clinical Practice: A National Strategy to Prepare Effective Teachers*, 2010, http://www.ncate.org/LinkClick.aspx?fileticket=zzeiB1OoqPk%3D&tabid=715.

17. Council for the Accreditation of Educator Preparation, *CAEP Accreditation Standards and Evidence: Aspirations for Educator Preparation*, 2013, http://caepnet.files.wordpress.com/2013/02/commrpt.pdf.

18. Clayton M. Christensen, Michael B. Horn, and Curtis W. Johnson, *Disrupting Class: How Disruptive Innovation Will Change the Way the World Learns* (New York: McGraw-Hill, 2008).

19. James Fraser, *Preparing America's Teachers: A History* (New York: Teachers College Press, 2007).

20. Sidney Trubowitz and Maureen Picard Robins, *The Good Teacher Mentor: Setting the Standard for Support and Success* (New York: Teachers College Press, 2003).

21. Madeline Hunter, *Enhancing Teaching* (New York: Macmillan, 1994).

22. Karen Seashore Lewis, Kenneth Leithwood, Kyla L. Wahlstrom, and Stephen E. Anderson, *Investigating the Links to Improved Student Learning* (New York: Wallace Foundation).

23. Doug Lemov, Erica Woolway, and Katie Yezzi, *Practice Perfect: 42 Rules for Getting Better at Getting Better* (San Francisco: Jossey-Bass, 2012).

24. Donald J. Boyd, Pamela L. Grossman, Hamilton Lankford, Susanna Loeb, and James Wyckoff, "Teacher Preparation and Student Achievement," *Educational Evaluation and Policy Analysis* 31, no. 4 (2009): 434.

25. Suzanne M. Wilson, Robert E. Floden, and Joan Ferrini-Mundy, *Teacher Preparation Research: Current Knowledge, Gaps, and Recommendations*, Center for the Study of Teaching and Policy, 2001, http://depts.washington.edu/ctp-mail/PDFs/TeacherPrep-WFFM-02-2001.pdf; U.S. Department of Education, *Preparing and Credentialing the Nation's Teachers: The Secretary's Eighth Report on Teacher Quality; Based on Data Provided for 2008, 2009 and 2010*, 2011), http://title2.ed.gov/Public/TitleIIReport11.pdf.

26. National Council for Accreditation of Teacher Education, *Transforming Teacher Education through Clinical Practice*.

27. Boston Teacher Residency, http://www.bostonteacherresidency.org/about-faq/.

28. YES Prep Teaching Excellence, http://www.yesprep.org/careers/teaching-excellence.

29. Doug Lemov, *Teach Like a Champion: 49 Techniques that Put Students on the Path to College* (San Francisco: Jossey-Bass, 2010); Robert J. Marzano and John L. Brown, *Handbook for the Art and Science of Teaching* (Alexandria, VA: Association for Supervision and Curriculum Development, 2007).

30. TeachingWorks, http://www.teachingworks.org/.

31. Steven Cantrell and Thomas J. Kane, *Ensuring Fair and Reliable Measures of Effective Teaching*, Bill & Melinda Gates Foundation, 2013, http://metproject.org/downloads/MET_Ensuring_Fair_and_Reliable_Measures_Practitioner_Brief.pdf.

32. edTPA, http://edtpa.aacte.org/.

33. Hilda Borko, "Professional Development and Teacher Learning: Mapping the Terrain," *Educational Researcher* 33, no. 8 (2004): 3–15.

34. Miriam Gamoran Sherin and Sandra Y. Han, "Teacher Learning in the Context of a Video Club," *Teaching and Teacher Education* 20, no. 2 (2004): 163–183.

35. Nicole B. Kersting, Karen B. Givvin, Francisco L. Sotelo, and James W. Stigler, "Teachers' Analyses of Classroom Video Predict Student Learning of Mathematics: Further Explorations of a Novel Measure of Teacher Knowledge," *Journal of Teacher Education* 61, no. 1/2 (2010): 172–181.

36. Brian Marsh, Nick Mitchell, and Peter Adamczyk, "Interactive Video Technology: Enhancing Professional Learning in Initial Teacher Education," *Computers and Education* 54, no. 3 (2010): 742–748.

37. Jian Wang and Kendall Hartley, "Video Technology as a Support for Teacher Education Reform." *Journal of Technology and Teacher Education* 11, no. 1 (2003): 105–138.

38. David F. Labaree, *The Trouble with Ed Schools* (New Haven, CT: Yale University Press, 2006).

39. Anthony S. Bryk and Louis Gomez, *Ruminations on Reinventing an R&D Capacity for Educational Improvement* (paper, American Enterprise Institute conference "The Supply Side of School Reform and the Future of Educational Entrepreneurship," Washington, DC, October 25, 2007), http://www.carnegiefoundation.org/sites/default/files/DED_paper_0.pdf.

40. Ernest L. Boyer, *Scholarship Reconsidered: Priorities of the Professoriate* (San Francisco: Jossey-Bass, 1990), 15–25.

41. Arthur Levine, *Educating School Teachers* (Washington, DC: The Education Schools Project, 2006).

Chapter 5

1. Eliot Freidson, *Professionalism: The Third Logic* (Cambridge, MA: Polity Press, 2001).

2. For an extended discussion of education as a profession, see Jal Mehta, *The Allure of Order: High Hopes, Dashed Expectations, and the Troubled Quest to Remake American Schooling* (New York: Oxford University Press, 2013).

3. Andrew Abbott, *The System of Professions* (Chicago: University of Chicago Press, 1988).

4. Measures of Effective Teaching Project, "Gathering Feedback for Teaching," Gates Foundation, 2012, http://www.metproject.org/downloads/MET_Gathering_Feedback_Research_Paper.pdf.

5. Michael Barber and Mona Mourshed, *How the World's Best-Performing School Systems Come Out on Top*, McKinsey & Company, 2007, http://mckinseyonsociety.com/downloads/reports/Education/Worlds_School_Systems_Final.pdf.

6. Organisation of Economic Co-operation and Development, *Strong Performers and Successful Reformers in Education: Lessons from PISA for the United States*, 2010, http://www.oecd.org/dataoecd/32/50/46623978.pdf.

7. Irving Kristol, *Neoconservatism: The Autobiography of an Idea* (New York: Free Press, 1995).

8. Paul Starr, *The Social Transformation of American Medicine* (New York: Basic Books, 1984).

9. For more detail, see Mehta, *The Allure of Order*.

10. Jack Schneider, *From the Ivory Tower to the Schoolhouse: Understanding How Scholarship Becomes Common Knowledge in Education* (Cambridge, MA: Harvard Education Press, 2014).

11. Frederick M. Hess, *Spinning Wheels: The Politics of Urban School Reform* (Washington, DC: Brookings Institution, 1998).

12. On effective schools, see Stewart C. Purkey and Marshall S. Smith, "Effective Schools: A Review," *Elementary School Journal* 83, no. 4 (1983): 426–452; on Catholic schools, see Anthony S. Bryk, Valerie E. Lee, and Peter Blakeley Holland, *Catholic Schools and the Common Good* (Cambridge, MA: Harvard University Press, 1993); on high-performing charter schools, see David Whitman, *Sweating the Small Stuff: Inner-City Schools and the New Paternalism* (Washington, DC: Thomas B. Fordham Institute, 2008).

13. On the importance of this kind of infrastructure, see David Cohen and Susan Moffitt, *The Ordeal of Equality: Did Federal Regulation Fix the Schools?* (Cambridge, MA: Harvard University Press, 2009).

14. Michael Huberman, "The Model of the Independent Artisan in Teachers' Professional Relations," in *Teachers' Work: Individuals, Colleagues, and Contexts*, ed. Judith Warren Little and Milbrey W. McLaughlin (New York: Teachers College Press, 1993), 11–50.

15. Ted Kolderie, "Where National Policy Goes Next—To Succeed" (working paper, Education Evolving, Saint Paul, MN, 2012).

16. Cass Sunstein, *Republic.com* (Princeton, NJ: Princeton University Press, 2001).

Chapter 6

1. Marcus A. Winters, *Teachers Matter* (Lanham, MD: Rowman & Littlefield, 2012); Robert Maranto and Michael Q. McShane, *President Obama and Education Reform: The Personal and the Political* (New York: Palgrave/Macmillan, 2012); Steven Brill, *Class Warfare: Inside the Fight to Save America's Schools* (New York: Simon & Schuster, 2011).

2. Terry M. Moe and John E. Chubb, *Liberating Learning: Technology, Politics, and the Future of American Education* (San Francisco: Jossey-Bass, 2009); and Tom Vander Ark, *Getting Smart: How Digital Learning Is Changing the World* (San Francisco: Jossey-Bass, 2012).

3. Informant, Pennsylvania Coalition of Public Charter Schools, personal communication, June 25, 2013.

4. Michael Podgursky and Dale Ballou, "Personnel Policy in Charter Schools," Thomas B. Fordham Foundation, 2001, http://www.edexcellencemedia.net/publications/2001/200108_personnelpolicyinsharterschools/personnel_policy.pdf.

5. Dave Eggers and Ninive Clements Calegari, "The High Cost of Low Teacher Salaries," *New York Times*, April 30, 2011.

6. A nod to Frederick Hess, *Revolution at the Margins: The Impact of Competition on Urban School Systems* (Washington, DC: Brookings Institution, 2002).

7. Everett M. Rogers, *Diffusion of Innovations*, 5th ed. (New York: Free Press, 2003).

8. These sorts of structural difference are described in Bryan Hassel, Emily Ayscue Hassel, and Sharon Kebschull Barrett, "Staffing Design: The Missing Key to Teacher Quality 2.0," chap. 2 this volume.

9. Marcus A. Winters, *Teachers Matter* (Lanham, MD: Rowman & Littlefield, 2012).

10. Dennis Beck, Robert Maranto, and Wen-Juo Lo, "Parent Involvement and Student/Parent Satisfaction in Cyber Schools," in *Research Highlights in Technology and Teacher Education 2013* (Chesapeake, VA: AACE).

11. Robert Maranto, "Tough Teacher Evaluation and High Morale?" *Educational Leadership* 71, no. 5 (2014), [forthcoming]; W. James Popham, *Evaluating America's Teachers: Mission Possible?* (Thousand Oaks, CA: Corwin, 2013).

12. Maranto, "Tough Teacher Evaluation and High Morale?"

13. Podgursky and Ballou, "Personnel Policy in Charter Schools"

14. Einar M. Skaalvik and Sidsel Skaalvik, "Teacher Self-Efficacy and Teacher Burnout: A Study of Relations," *Teaching and Teacher Education* 26, no. 4 (2010): 1059–1069; Daniel Muijs and David Reynolds, "Teachers' Beliefs and Behaviors: What Really Matters?" *Journal of Classroom Interaction* 37, no. 2 (2002): 3–15; Lynn S. Fuchs, Douglas Fuchs, and N. Bishop, "Instructional Adaptation for Students at Risk," *Journal of Educational Research* 86, no. 2 (1992): 70–84; Thomas R. Guskey, "Teacher Efficacy, Self-Concept, and Attitudes toward the Implementation of Instructional Innovation," *Teaching and Teacher Education* 4, no. 1 (1988): 63–69; Charles M. Payne, *So Much Reform, So Little Change* (Cambridge, MA: Harvard Education Press, 2008); Lynn S. Fuchs, Douglas Fuchs, and N. Bishop, "Instructional Adaptation for Students at Risk," *Journal of Educational Research* 86, no. 2 (1992): 70–84; Anita E. Woolfolk and Wayne K. Hoy, "Prospective Teachers' Sense of Efficacy and Beliefs about Control," *Journal of Educational Psychology* 82, no. 1 (1990): 81–91; and Thomas R. Guskey, "Teacher Efficacy, Self-Concept, and Attitudes toward the Implementation of Instructional Innovation," *Teaching and Teacher Education* 4, no. 1 (1988): 63–69.

15. Daniel Muijs and David Reynolds, "Teachers' Beliefs and Behaviors: What Really Matters?" *Journal of Classroom Interaction* 37, no. 2 (2002): 3–15.

16. Maranto, "Is Evaluating Teachers a Mission Possible?"

17. Richard E. Ferdig, Cathy Cavanaugh, Meredith DiPietro, Erik Black, and Kara Dawson, "Virtual Schooling Standards and Best Practices for Teacher Education," *Journal of Technology and Teacher Education* 17, no. 4 (2009): 479–503; Kathryn Kennedy and Leanna Archambault, "Offering Preservice Teachers Field Experiences in K–12 Online Learning: A National Survey of Teacher Education Programs," *Journal of Teacher Education* 63, no. 3 (2012): 185–200.

18. Jason LaFrance and Dennis Beck, "Mapping the Terrain: Educational Leadership Field Experiences in K–12 Virtual Schools," *Educational Administration Quarterly* (forthcoming).

Chapter 7

1. As Susan Moore Johnson and Susan M. Kardos write in "Reform Bargaining and School Improvement," in *Conflicting Missions? Teachers Unions and Educational Reform,* ed. Tom Loveless (Washington, DC: Brookings Institution, 2000): "By all accounts collective bargaining for teachers meant more standardized schools, leaving principals with less latitude to run their schools. Not only could they not tell teachers what to do, but uniform, districtwide

rules limited their management options and thus reduced their schools' responsiveness and independence" (p. 18). For discussions of the ways in which CBAs limit principals' discretion and ability to implement necessary reforms, see C. R. Perry and W. A. Wildman, *The Impact of Negotiations in Public Education: The Evidence from the Schools* (Worthington, OH: Charles A. Jones, 1970); Lorraine McDonnell and Anthony Pascal, *Organized Teachers in American Schools* (Santa Monica, CA: RAND, 1979); Julia E. Koppich, "The As-Yet-Unfulfilled Promise of Reform Bargaining," in *Collective Bargaining in Education: Negotiating Change in Today's Schools,* ed. Jane Hannaway and Andrew J. Rotherham (Cambridge, MA: Harvard Education Press, 2006); and Katharine O. Strunk, "Policy Poison or Promise? Exploring the Dual Nature of California School District Collective Bargaining Agreements," *Educational Administration Quarterly* 48, no. 3 (2012): 506–547.

2. National Council on Teacher Quality, *State of the States 2012: Teacher Effectiveness Policies* (Washington, DC: National Council on Teacher Quality, 2012).

3. I use CBAs from districts with four or more schools because many smaller school districts have quite different contracts from their larger neighbors, simply because many contract policies do not affect districts with only a few schools as much as they might their neighbors with a multitude of schools. This sample has substantively similar characteristics as the larger population of California school districts with four or more schools.

4. See Strunk, "Policy Poison or Promise?" for more detail.

5. There is reason to believe that California contracts have many similarities with CBAs from other states. A national sample of contracts collected by the National Council on Teacher Quality highlights many of the same provisions in CBAs from other states. See the National Council on Teacher Quality, Tr3 Teacher Contract Database, http://www.nctq.org/districtPolicy/contractDatabaseLanding.do.

6. PAR is a specific reform that was developed by administrators and unions together to enable master or consulting teachers to help struggling teachers improve.

7. See, for examples, William Koski and Eileen Horng, "Facilitating the Teacher Quality Gap? Collective Bargaining Agreements, Teaching Hiring and Transfer Rules, and Teacher Assignment among Schools in California," *Education Finance and Policy* 2, no.3 (2007): 262–300; and Sarah Anzia and Terry Moe, "Collective Bargaining Agreements, Transfer Rights, and Disadvantaged Schools," *Educational Evaluation and Policy Analysis* (forthcoming).

8. For a more in-depth treatment of reform unionism, see Johnson and Kardos, "Reform Bargaining and School Improvement"; and Koppich, "The As-Yet-Unfulfilled Promise of Reform Bargaining." Also see Charles T. Kerchner and Julia E. Koppich, *A Union of Professionals: Labor Relations in Educational Reform* (New York: Teachers College Press, 1993).

9. Dominic J. Brewer and Jo Smith, *Evaluating the "Crazy Quilt": Education Governance in California* (Los Angeles: Center on Educational Governance, University of Southern California, 2006).

Chapter 8

1. Value-added is one type of growth model; there are different types of models being used in teacher (and school) accountability systems. Nevertheless, in this chapter I use *value-added*.

2. Steven G. Rivkin, Eric A. Hanushek, and John F. Kain, "Teachers, Schools, and Academic Achievement," *Econometrica* 73, no. 2 (2005): 417–458; Daniel Aaronson, Lisa Barrow, and William Sander, "Teachers and Student Achievement in Chicago Public High Schools," *Journal of Labor Economics* 25, no. 1 (2007): 95–135.

3. Douglas N. Harris, "The Policy Uses and 'Policy Validity' of Value-Added and Other Teacher Quality Measures," in *Measurement Issues and the Assessment of Teacher Quality*, ed. Drew H. Gitomer (Thousand Oaks, CA: Sage, 2008).

4. Douglas N. Harris and Tim R. Sass, "Teacher Training, Teacher Quality and Student Achievement," *Journal of Public Economics* 95, no. 7/8 (2011): 798–812; Charles T. Clotfelter, Helen F. Ladd, and Jacob L. Vigdor, "Teacher Credentials and Student Achievement: Longitudinal Analysis with Student Fixed Effects," *Economics of Education Review* 26, no. 6 (2007): 673–682.

5. For example, see Steven Glazerman, Eric Isenberg, Sarah Dolfin, Martha Bleeker, Amy Johnson, Mary Grider, and Matthew Jacobus, *Does Intensive Mentoring Improve Teaching? Results from a Randomized Experiment* (Washington, DC: Mathematica Policy Research, 2010).

6. Kun Yuan, Vi-Nhuan Le, Daniel F. McCaffrey, Julie A. Marsh, Laura S. Hamilton, Brian M. Stecher, and Matthew G. Springer, "Incentive Pay Programs Do Not Affect Teacher Motivation or Reported Practices: Results from Three Randomized Studies," *Educational Evaluation and Policy Analysis* 35, no. 1 (2013): 3–22.

7. National Council on Teacher Quality, *2012 State Teacher Policy Yearbook* (Washington, DC: National Council on Teacher Quality, 2012).

8. Eric A. Hanushek, "Teacher Deselection," in *Creating a New Teaching Profession*, ed. Dan Goldhaber and Jane Hannaway (Washington, DC: Urban Institute Press, 2009).

9. Jesse Rothstein, "Teacher Quality Policy When Supply Matters" (Working Paper No. 18419, National Bureau of Economic Research, Washington, DC, 2012).

10. Dan Koretz, "Limitations in the Use of Achievement Tests as Measures of Educators' Productivity," *Journal of Human Resources* 37, no. 4 (2002): 752–777.

11. Sarah Rosenberg and Elena Silva, *Trending Toward Reform: Teachers Speak on Unions and the Future of the Profession* (Washington, DC: Education Sector, 2012); Public Agenda, *Teaching for a Living: How Teachers See the Profession Today* (Washington, DC: Public Agenda, 2009); William G. Howell and Michael Henderson, *Public Opinion on Merit Pay: Self-Interest vs. Symbolic Politics* (Cambridge, MA: Harvard Program on Education Policy and Governance, 2010).

12. Thomas J. Kane, Daniel F. McCaffrey, Trey Miller, and Douglas O. Staiger, *Have We Identified Effective Teachers? Validating Measures of Effective Teaching Using Random Assignment* (Seattle: Bill & Melinda Gates Foundation, 2013).

13. Thomas J. Kane and Steven Cantrell, *Learning about Teaching: Initial Findings from the Measures of Effective Teaching Project* (Seattle: Bill & Melinda Gates Foundation, 2011).

14. Kata Mihaly, Daniel F. McCaffrey, Douglas O. Staiger, and J. R. Lockwood, *A Composite Estimator of Effective Teaching* (Seattle: Bill & Melinda Gates Foundation, 2013).

15. Raj Chetty, John N. Friedman, and Jonah E. Rockoff, "The Long-Term Impacts of Teacher: Teacher Value-Added and Student Outcomes in Adulthood" (Working Paper No. w17699, National Bureau of Economic Research, Washington, DC, 2011).

16. For example, see C. Kirabo Jackson, *Non-Cognitive Ability, Test Scores, and Teacher Quality: Evidence from 9th Grade Teachers in North Carolina* (Washington, DC: National Bureau of Economic Research, 2012); Jennifer L. Jennings and Thomas A. DiPrete, "Teacher Effects on Social and Behavioral Skills in Elementary School," *Sociology of Education* 83, no. 2 2010): 135–159.

17. Douglas N. Harris, "A Valid Way to Use 'Value-Added' in Teacher Evaluation," *Washington Post*, December 4, 2012.

18. There is evidence, including experimental evidence, that value-added influences principals' views of teachers. For example, see Jonah E. Rockoff, Douglas O. Staiger, Thomas J. Kane, and Eric S. Taylor, "Information and Employee Evaluation: Evidence from a Randomized Intervention in Public Schools," *American Economic Review* 102, no. 7 (2012): 3184–3213.

19. Elizabeth Davidson, Randall Reback, Jonah E. Rockoff, and Heather L. Schwartz, *Fifty Ways to Leave a Child Behind: Idiosyncrasies and Discrepancies in States' Implementation of NCLB* (Washington, DC: National Bureau of Economic Research, 2013).

20. Dan Goldhaber, Joe Walch, and Brian Gabele, *Does the Model Matter? Exploring the Relationship Between Different Achievement-Based Teacher Assessments* (Seattle: Center for Education Data and Research, 2012).

21. Dale Ballou, William Sanders, and Paul Wright, "Controlling for Student Background in Value-Added Assessment of Teachers," *Journal of Education and Behavioral Statistics* 29, no. 1 (2004): 37–65.

22. For additional discussion of model choice and specification, see Dan Goldhaber and Roddy Theobald, *Do Different Value-Added Models Tell Us the Same Things?* (Washington, DC: Carnegie Foundation for the Advancement of Teaching, 2013).

23. For example, see Dan Goldhaber and Michael Hansen, "Is It Just a Bad Class? Assessing the Long-Term Stability of Estimated Teacher Performance," *Economica* (forthcoming); Dan F. McCaffrey, Tim R. Sass, J. R. Lockwood, and Katy Mihaly, "The Intertemporal Variability of Teacher Effect Estimates," *Education Finance and Policy* 4, no. 4 (2009): 572–606.

24. The MET project found that the stability of observation scores, even when multiple observations are conducted, is actually similarly modest as that of value-added.

25. Alternatively, some states and districts, such as Rhode Island, combine measures using matrices that first sort each subcomponent into a performance

rating or score and then assign different final ratings to different permutations of the subcomponent ratings. The matrices also reflect judgments about the importance of each component—in a sense weighting without actually specifying percentages. Moreover, this approach sacrifices a lot of data. A teacher with a score that is way below the cutoff point on a given subcomponent receives the same rating as a teacher who barely misses it.

26. Katie Buckley and Scott Marion, *A Survey of Approaches Used to Evaluate Educators in Non-Tested Grades and Subjects* (Cambridge, MA: National Center for the Improvement of Educational Assessment, 2010).

27. David N. Figlio and Lawrence W. Kenny, "Individual Teacher Incentives and Student Performance," *Journal of Public Economics* 91, no. 5/6 (2007): 901–914; and C. Kirabo Jackson, "Teacher Quality at the High-School Level: The Importance of Accounting for Tracks," *Journal of Labor Economics* (forthcoming).

28. John P. Papay, "Different Tests, Different Answers: The Stability of Teacher Value-Added Estimates across Outcome Measures," *American Educational Research Journal* 48, no.1 (2011): 163–193. Douglas N. Harris, *Value-Added Measures in Education: What Every Educator Needs to Know* (Cambridge, MA: Harvard Education Press, 2011).

29. For a review of the literature and types of SLOs, see Claire Morgan and Natalie Lacireno-Paquet, *Overview of Student Learning Objectives (SLO): Review of the Literature* (Waltham, MA: Regional Educational Laboratory, 2013).

30. At least one "early adopter" district has actually chosen to downweight value-added in favor of these alternative measures. In 2012, the District of Columbia Public Schools announced some changes to its evaluation system, IMPACT, which was among the first of the new evaluations to come online and is often viewed as a model by other states and districts. Specifically, the weight of value-added among eligible teachers was decreased from 50 to 35 percent and replaced by locally designed measures that do not use state assessment data.

31. Rachel Curtis, *Building It Together: The Design and Implementation of Hillsborough County Public Schools' Teacher Evaluation System* (Washington, DC: The Aspen Institute, 2012).

32. Jennifer L. Steele, Laura S. Hamilton, and Brian M. Stecher, *Incorporating Student Performance Measures into Teacher Evaluation Systems* (Santa Monica, CA: RAND, 2010).

33. John Watson, Amy Murin, Lauren Vashaw, Butch Gemin, and Chris Rapp, *Keeping Pace with K–12 Online Learning: An Annual Review of Policy and Practice* (Durango, CO: Evergreen Education Group, 2011).

34. Catherine Fisk Natale, *Teaching in the World of Virtual K–12 Learning: Challenges to Ensure Educator Quality* (Washington, DC: Educational Testing Service, 2011).

35. Matthew M. Chingos, "Questioning the Quality of Virtual Schools," *Education Next* 13, no. 2 (2013): 46–49.

Chapter 9

1. Jonathan A. Plucker, Ronald A. Beghetto, and Gayle Dow, "Why Isn't Creativity More Important to Educational Psychologists? Potential, Pitfalls, and Future Directions in Creativity Research," *Educational Psychologist* 39, no. 2 (2004): 90.

2. We could argue at length about the difference between *creativity* and *innovation*, but we won't. I treat them synonymously in here, as does Plucker, Beghetto, and Dow, "Why Isn't Creativity More Important to Educational Psychologists?"

3. See, for example, the chapter by Dean Keith Simonton, "Chance-Configuration Theory of Scientific Creativity," in *Psychology of Science: Contributions to Metascience*, ed. Barry Gholson, William R. Shadish Jr., Robert A. Neimeyer, and Arthur C. Houts (New York: Cambridge University Press, 1989).

4. James C. Kaufman, *Creativity 101* (New York: Springer, 2009); and Mark A. Runco, *Creativity: Theories and Themes: Research, Development, and Practice* (San Diego: Elsevier, 2010).

5. Rui Yang, "Paradigm Shifts in China's Education Policy: 1950s–2000s," *Italian Journal of Sociology of Education* 1, no. 1 (2012): 29–52.

6. Weiguo Pang and Jonathan Plucker, "Recent Transformations in China's Economic and Education Policies for Promoting Innovation and Creativity," *Journal of Creative Behavior* 46, no. 4 (2013): 247–273.

7. Organisation for Economic Co-operation and Development, *Lessons from PISA for the United States, Strong Performers and Successful Reformers in Education*, 2011, http://dx.doi.org/10.1787/9789264096660-en.

8. See the Holmes Partnership, *The Holmes Partnership Trilogy: Tomorrow's Teachers, Tomorrow's Schools, Tomorrow's Schools of Education* (New York: Peter Lang, 2007).

9. Robert A. Maranto, Gary Ritter, and Arthur Levine, "The Future of Ed Schools: Five Lessons from Business Schools," *Education Week*, January 6, 2010, 16, 25, 36.

10. Targeted outcomes for grades 8–10 are combined; *Curriculum Regulations for General Teacher Education, Pre-School Teacher Education and Practical and Didactic Education* (Oslo, Norway: Ministry of Education and Research, 2010), available online at http://www.regjeringen.no/upload/kilde/kd/pla/2006/0002/ddd/pdfv/235560-rammeplan_laerer_eng.pdf.

11. Jaap Scheerens, "Perspectives on Educational Quality," in *Perspectives on Educational Quality: Illustrative Outcomes on Primary and Secondary Schools in the Netherlands*, ed. Jaap Scheerens, Hans Luyten, and Jan Van Ravens (New York: SpringerBriefs in Education), 3–34. DOI: 10.1007/978-94-007-0926-3_1. For a longer perspective, see Broekhof and Monique Goemans, *Secondary education in the Netherlands* (Strasbourg, France: Council of Europe Press, 1995).

12. Ina V. S. Mullis, Michael O. Martin, Chad A. Minnich, Gabrielle M. Stanco, Alka Arora, Victoria A. S. Centurino, and Courtney E. Castle, eds., *TIMSS 2011 Encyclopedia: Education Policy and Curriculum in Mathematics and Science*, Volume 2: *L–Z and Benchmarking Participants* (Boston: TIMSS and PIRLS International Study Center, Boston College, 2011).

13. Revealingly, the general attitude among my Chinese colleagues is that China needs to move to a system where students spend less time studying for information-recall tests and more time participating in extracurricular activities that develop leadership skills and creativity.

14. See Evan Thomas, *Ike's Bluff: President Eisenhower's Secret Battle to Save the World* (New York: Little, Brown, 2012).

15. INSEAD, and World International Property Organization (WIPO), *The Global Innovation Index 2013: The Local Dynamics of Innovation* (Geneva: Fontainebleau, 2013).

16. Jonathan A. Plucker and David Rutkowski, "Inefficient, Ineffective Reforms," *Education Week*, July 5, 2011, http://www.edweek.org/ew/articles/2011/07/05/36plucker.h30.html?tkn=NRYF39mKSa5eazjlqtz GSPUJtG%2BjmBDZwiZp&cmp=clp-edweek.

17. UNICEF Innocenti Research Centre, *Measuring Child Poverty: New League Tables of Child Poverty in the World's Rich Countries*, Innocenti Report Card No. 10 (2012).

18. The University of Virginia, University of Connecticut, and University of North Carolina–Chapel Hill are all good examples of these institutions making these reforms. See Holmes Partnership, *The Holmes Partnership Trilogy*; and James A. Fraser, "Review of *The Holmes Partnership Trilogy: Tomorrow's Teachers, Tomorrow's Schools, Tomorrow's Schools of Education*," *Teachers College Record* (2007), retrieved from https://tcrecord.org/books/abstract.asp?ContentId=14588.

19. This report is a step in the right direction: National Center for Education Statistics, *U.S. States in a Global Context: Results from the 2011 NAEP-TIMSS Linking Study*, NCES 2013–460 (Washington, DC, Institute of Education Sciences, U.S. Department of Education, 2013), http://nces.ed.gov/pubsearch/pubsinfo.asp?pubid=2013460.

20. Julie Greenberg, Arthur McKee, and Kate Walsh, *Teacher Prep Review: A Review of the Nation's Teacher Preparation Programs, 2013* (Washington, DC: National Council on Teacher Quality, 2013), available online at http://www.nctq.org/dmsView/Teacher_Prep_Review_2013_Report.

21. Ibid.

22. Ibid., 91

23. See http://www.usaid.gov/div.

24. Frederick M. Hess and Michael B. Horn, *Private Enterprise and Public Education* (New York: Teachers College Press, 2013).

Chapter 10

1. Raj Chetty, John Friedman, and Jonah Rockoff, "The Long-Term Impacts of Teachers: Teacher Value-Added and Student Outcomes in Adulthood" (Working Paper No. w17699, National Bureau of Economic Research, Cambridge, MA, December 2011); Thomas Kane and Douglas Staiger, "Estimating Teacher Impacts on Student Achievement: An Experimental Evaluation" (Working Paper No. w14607, National Bureau of Economic Research, Cambridge, MA,

2008); Thomas Kane, Daniel MacCaffrey, Trey Miller, and Douglas Staiger, "Have We Identified Effective Teachers? Validating Measures of Effective Teaching Using Random Assignment" (Seattle: Bill & Melinda Gates Foundation, 2013); and Jesse Rothstein, "Teacher Quality in Educational Production: Tracking, Decay, and Student Achievement," *Quarterly Journal of Economics* 125, no. 1 (2010): 175–214; Dan Goldhaber and Michael Hansen, "Is It Just a Bad Class? Assessing the Long-Term Stability of Estimated Teacher Performance," *Economica* 80 (July 2013): 589–612; Chetty, Friedman, and Rockoff, "The Long-Term Impacts of Teachers"; Daniel McCaffrey, Tim Sass, J. R. Lockwood, and Kata Mihaly, "The Intertemporal Variability of Teacher Effect Estimates," *Education* 4, no. 4 (2009): 572–606.

2. Kata Mihaly, Daniel McCaffrey, Douglas Staiger, and J. R. Lockwood, *A Composite Estimator of Effective Teaching* (Seattle: Bill & Melinda Gates Foundation, 2013); Dan Goldhaber and Joseph Walch, "Strategic Pay Reform: A Student Outcomes-Based Evaluation of Denver's ProComp Teacher Pay Initiative," *Economics of Education Review* 31, no. 6 (2012): 1067–1083.

3. While I do not focus on them here, we might also ask a number of important questions about the behavioral response of administrators to new evaluation systems. For instance, do they strategically assign teachers to their classrooms based on feedback about teacher effectiveness with different types of students? Or, how do administrators deal with legal challenges to evaluations?

4. See, for instance, Roland Fryer, "Teacher Incentives and Student Achievement: Evidence from New York City Public Schools," *Journal of Labor Economics* 31, no. 2 (2013): 373–427; Julie Marsh et al., *A Big Apple for Educators: New York City's Experiment with Schoolwide Performance Bonuses* (New York: RAND, 2012); Matthew Springer et al., *Teacher Pay for Performance: Experimental Evidence from the Project on Incentives in Teaching* (Nashville, TN: National Center on Performance Incentives, Vanderbilt University, 2010). There is, however, some evidence that teachers may respond to the potential loss of a bonus ("loss aversion"); see Roland Fryer, Steven Levitt, John List, and Sally Sadoff, "Enhancing the Efficacy of Teacher Incentives Through Loss Aversion: A Field Experiment" (Working Paper No. 18237, National Bureau of Economic Research, Cambridge, MA, July 2012).

5. There is some evidence that performance feedback can lead to changes in teacher effectiveness. See Eric Taylor and John Tyler, "The Effect of Evaluation on Teacher Performance," *American Economic Review* 102, no. 7 (2012): 3628–3651.

6. See, for instance, Frederick Hess, "Spend Money Like it Matters," *The Effective Educator* 64, no. 4 (2010): 51–54. This workforce composition effect has been shown to be an important way in which pay for performance can influence productivity in the private sector. See, for example, Edward Lazear, "Performance Pay and Productivity," *American Economic Review* 90, no. 5 (2000): 1346–1361; Casey Ichniowski and Kathryn Shaw, "Beyond Incentive Pay: Insiders' Estimates of the Value of Complementary Human Resource Management Practices," *Journal of Economic Perspectives* 17, no. 1 (2003): 155–180.

7. See Clayton Christensen, Curtis Johnson, and Michael Horn, *Disrupting Class: How Disruptive Innovation Will Change the Way the World Learns* (New York: McGraw-Hill, 2008); Paul Hill, "Consequences of Instructional Technology for Human Resource Needs in Education," in *Creating a New Teaching Profession*, ed. Dan Goldhaber and Jane Hannaway (Washington, DC: Urban Institute Press, 2009).

8. John Krieg, "Are Students Left Behind? The Distributional Effects of the No Child Left Behind Act," *Education Finance and Policy* 3, no. 2 (2008): 250–281; Derek Neal and Dian Whitmore Schanzenbach, "Left Behind by Design: Proficiency Counts and Test-Based Accountability," *Review of Economics and Statistics* 92, no. 2 (2010): 263–283.

9. See Marjorie Ragosta, "Computer-Assisted Instruction and Compensatory Education: A Longitudinal Analysis," *Machine-Mediated Learning* 1, no. 1 (1983): 97–127.

10. See, for instance, Lisa Barrow, Lisa Markman, and Cecilia Rouse, "Technology's Edge: The Educational Benefits of Computer-Aided Instruction," *American Economic Journal* 1, no. 1 (2009): 52–74; and Jacob Vigdor and Helen Ladd, "Scaling the Digital Divide: Home Computer Technology and Student Achievement" (working paper no. w16078, National Bureau of Economic Research, Cambridge, MA, 2010).

11. There are of course a host of questions about the impacts that digital engagement tools have on the students who are assigned to them, though this is not, strictly speaking, teacher quality research.

12. Suzanne Simburg and Marguerite Roza, "Innovating Toward Sustainability: How Computer Labs Can Enable New Staffing Structures and New Savings," in *Hopes, Fears, and Reality*, ed. Robin Lake (Seattle: Center for Reinventing Public Education, 2012).

13. Mathew Chingos, "The Impact of a Universal Class-Size Reduction Policy: Evidence from Florida's Statewide Mandate," *Economics of Education Review* 31, no. 5 (2012): 543–562.

14. The reality is that responsibility for students' learning at the elementary level is probably more complex than is typically recognized. See, for example, Heinrich Hock and Eric Isenberg, "Methods for Accounting for Co-Teaching in Value-Added Models" (working paper, Mathematica, Washington, DC, 2012), http://www.mathematica-mpr.com/publications/PDFs/education/acctco-teaching_wp.pdf.

15. The team elements of a 2.0 world lead to some obvious complications for performance evaluations, but digital tools may also make teacher evaluation easier in some respects because there are likely to be more direct computer-based measures of the quality and quantity of work that students are doing.

16. Eugene Kandel and Edward Lazear, "Peer Pressure and Partnerships," *Journal of Political Economy* 100, no. 4 (1992): 801–817.

17. Specifically, Scott Imberman and Michael Lovenheim investigate an incentive pay program in Houston schools and conclude that teacher efforts decline as the effective size of teacher teams increases; see "Incentive Strength and

Teacher Productivity: Evidence from a Group-Based Teacher Incentive Pay System" (Working Paper No. w18439, National Bureau of Economic Research, Cambridge, MA, 2012).

18. Frederick Hess, "The Human Capital Challenge Toward a 21st-Century Teaching Profession," in Goldhaber and Hannaway, *Creating a New Teaching Profession*.

19. For example, see Linda Darling Hammond, "Teacher Preparation Is Essential to TFA's Future," *Education Week*, March 14, 2011, http://www.edweek.org/ew/articles/2011/03/16/24darling-hammond.h30.html.

20. See Billie Gastic, "Closing the Opportunity Gap: Preparing the Next Generation of Effective Teachers," chap. 4 this volume; and Katharine Strunk, "The Role of Collective Bargaining Agreements in the Implementation of Education Reforms: Perils and Possibilities," chap. 7 this volume.

21. John Papay, Martin West, Jon Fullerton, and Thomas Kane, "Does an Urban Teacher Residency Increase Student Achievement? Early Evidence from Boston," *Educational Evaluation and Policy Analysis* 34, no. 4 (2012): 413–434.

22. Note that one of the interesting findings about teachers over the last decade is just how localized they are. See Donald Boyd, Hamilton Lankford, Susanna Loeb, and James Wyckoff, "The Draw of Home: How Teachers' Preferences for Proximity Disadvantage Urban Schools," *Journal of Policy Analysis and Management* 24, no. 1 (2005): 113–132; Michelle Reininger, "Hometown Disadvantage? It Depends on Where You're From: Teachers' Location Preferences and the Implications for Staffing Schools," *Educational Evaluation and Policy Analysis* 34, no. 2 (2012): 127–145. We might expect technology to change this, as it allows school systems using it for distance education to widen their nets when looking for teacher talent.

23. Boyd et al., "Teacher Preparation and Student Achievement"; Dan Goldhaber and Dominic Brewer, "Does Teacher Certification Matter? High School Teacher Certification Status and Student Achievement," *Educational Evaluation and Policy Analysis* 22, no. 2 (2000): 129–145; Steve Glazerman, Daniel Mayer, and Paul Decker, "Alternative Routes to Teaching: The Impacts of Teach for America on Student Achievement and Other Outcomes," *Journal of Policy Analysis and Management* 25, no. 1 (2006): 75–96; Robert Gordon, Thomas Kane, Douglas Staiger, *Identifying Effective Teachers Using Performance on the Job* (Washington, DC: Brookings Institution, 2006); and Thomas Kane, Jonah Rockoff, and Douglas Staiger, "What Does Certification Tell Us About Teacher Effectiveness? Evidence from New York City," *Economics of Education Review* 27, no. 6 (2008): 615–631.

24. For more on the value of experiments, see Grover Whitehurst, "The Value of Experiments in Education," *Education* 7, no. 2 (2012): 107–123.

Conclusion

1. Stu Beitler, "Corning (Gibson), NY Train Wreck, Jul 1912," Newspaper Archive, GenDisasters, http://www3.gendisasters.com/new-york/2700/corning-gibson-ny-train-wreck-jul-1912.

2. Interstate Commerce Commission, "Investigation of Accident on the Delaware, Lackawanna, and Western Railroad Near East Corning N.Y. July 4, 1912," July 30, 1912, http://ntl1.specialcollection.net/scripts/ws.dll?file&fn=6&name=S%3A\DOT_56GB\Railroad\WEBSEARCH\NO071.pdf.

3. Barron Hilton Pioneers of Flight Gallery, "Civilian Aviation: First U.S. Transcontinental Flight," Smithsonian National Air and Space Museum, http://airandspace.si.edu/exhibitions/pioneers-of-flight/online/civilian01.cfm.

4. Jenny Anderson, "Curious Grade for Teachers: Nearly All Pass," *New York Times*, March 30, 2013, http://www.nytimes.com.

5. Lisa Fleisher, "Glimpse of New Teacher Ratings Is Offered," *Wall Street Journal*, June 16, 2013, http://online.wsj.com.

6. U.S. Department of Education, National Center for Education Statistics, Schools and Staffing Survey (SASS), "Public School Teacher Data File," 2011–2012, http://nces.ed.gov/surveys/sass/tables/sass1112_2013314_t1s_001.asp; Bryan C. Hassel and Emily Ayscue Hassel, *Opportunity at the Top: How America's Best Teachers Could Close the Gaps, Raise the Bar, and Keep Our Nation Great* (Chapel Hill, NC: Public Impact, 2010).

7. Hassel and Hassel, *Opportunity at the Top*.

8. Barron Hilton Pioneers of Flight Gallery, "Civilian Aviation."

Acknowledgments

F OR MORE THAN TWO YEARS, we have been exploring a difficult question we think has been sorely missing from today's teacher quality debates: *Will today's reforms hold back tomorrow's schools?* We broached this question with researchers, advocates, teachers, state education leaders, union representatives, and policy makers in private gatherings and at public events. In September 2013 we convened a public research conference at the American Enterprise Institute (AEI) to discuss new papers we commissioned on the subject. What has resulted is a spirited dialogue that has raised as many important questions as it has answers.

The chapters that comprise this volume are the culmination of that discussion, each exploring an important component of the next generation of teacher quality and how it might intersect with our current reform agenda. How might our traditional, twentieth-century definition of teaching evolve with the coming of new school models, such as hybrid virtual schools or innovative school staffing arrangements? How might the attendant structures, like preparation programs, professionalism, and collective bargaining agreements, adjust in order to allow new teaching roles to thrive? What questions should guide a next-generation teacher quality research agenda?

We are indebted to all of those who have been involved in this project and pushed our thinking on these ideas, but we would like to thank especially the following discussants for providing outstanding and concentrated feedback during our 2013 conference: Segun Eubanks of the National Education Association, Heather

Harding of the Education Consortium on Research and Evaluation at George Washington University, Thomas Kane of the Harvard Graduate School of Education, Kate Walsh of the National Council on Teacher Quality, and Daniel Weisberg of TNTP.

We are also indebted to the steadfast support provided by AEI and its president, Arthur Brooks. The Joyce Foundation and Smith Richardson Foundation generously provided financial support for this project, and we are deeply grateful for their involvement and encouragement throughout the process. We thank the terrific staff at AEI, especially Taryn Hochleitner for her work managing and overseeing this project and coordinating the conference, Lauren Aronson and Lauren Empson for their efforts in promoting the ideas, and Daniel Lautzenheiser, KC Deane, and Max Eden for their vital assistance. Finally, we express our gratitude to the Harvard Education Press team, particularly our editor, Caroline Chauncey, who offered skillful and insightful guidance throughout the course of this project.

About the Editors

Frederick M. Hess is resident scholar and director of education policy studies at the American Enterprise Institute. An educator, political scientist, and author, Hess studies a range of K–12 and higher education issues. His books include *Cage-Busting Leadership* (Harvard Education Press, 2013), *Breakthrough Leadership in the Digital Age* (Corwin Press, 2014), *The Same Thing Over and Over* (Harvard University Press, 2010), *Education Unbound* (ASCD, 2010), *Common Sense School Reform* (Palgrave Macmillan, 2006), *Revolution at the Margins* (Brookings Institution Press, 2002), and *Spinning Wheels* (Brookings Institution Press, 1998). He is also the author of the popular *Education Week* blog *Rick Hess Straight Up*. Hess's work has appeared in scholarly and popular outlets such as *Teachers College Record, Harvard Education Review, Social Science Quarterly, Urban Affairs Review, American Politics Quarterly, Chronicle of Higher Education, Phi Delta Kappan, Educational Leadership, U.S. News and World Report, National Affairs, Washington Post, New York Times, Wall Street Journal, The Atlantic,* and *National Review*. He has edited widely cited volumes on the Common Core, the role of for-profits in education, education philanthropy, urban school reform, how to stretch the school dollar, education entrepreneurship, what we have learned about the federal role in education reform, and No Child Left Behind. Hess also serves as executive editor of *Education Next*, as lead faculty member for the Rice Education Entrepreneurship Program, and on the review boards for the Broad Prize in Urban Education and the Broad Prize for Public Charter Schools. He also serves on the boards of directors of the National Association of Charter School Authorizers and 4.0 Schools. A former high school social studies teacher, he teaches or has taught at the University of Virginia, the

University of Pennsylvania, Georgetown University, Rice University, and Harvard University.

Michael Q. McShane is a research fellow in education policy studies at the American Enterprise Institute. He is coauthor of *President Obama and Education Reform: The Personal and the Political* (Palgrave MacMillan, 2012). His scholarship has been published in *Education Finance and Policy* and in various technical reports. He has also contributed to more popular publications, such as *Education Next, Huffington Post, National Review, Chronicle of Higher Education,* and *St. Louis Post-Dispatch.* He is coeditor (with Frederick Hess) of *Common Core Meets the Reform Agenda* (Teachers College Press, 2013). McShane began his career as an inner-city high school teacher in Montgomery, Alabama.

About the Contributors

Sharon Kebschull Barrett is the senior editor with Public Impact, where she edits the *Public Impact* and *Opportunity Culture* blogs, copy-edits Public Impact's reports, and provides research and writing for the firm. Her recent work focuses on extending the reach of excellent teachers, charter schools, and state policy. A former newspaper reporter and copy editor, Barrett is the author of two cookbooks, *Desserts from an Herb Garden* (St. Martin's Press, 1999) and *Morning Glories* (St. Martin's Press, 2000). She has a BA in journalism from the University of North Carolina at Chapel Hill, where she served as editor of the *Daily Tar Heel*.

Dennis Beck is an assistant professor of educational technology at the University of Arkansas, where he teaches courses in instructional design, on integrating technology into the curriculum, and on educational technology research. Beck also has a wealth of experience in the design of online and blended courses in educational and corporate training environments. He has researched and written about K–12 virtual schooling for special-education students and virtual school leaders, as well as about the influence of avatar-based simulations and games on stigma experienced by students and teachers. He is currently working on a study exploring the current professional development experiences of K–12 virtual school administrators. Beck has published in several venues, including the *Educational Administration Quarterly* the *Journal of Educational Research*, and *Computers & Education*.

Rachael Brown is a manager of teacher effectiveness strategy for the District of Columbia Public Schools (DCPS), where she leads teacher retention and recognition policy. Prior to joining DCPS, she worked in thought leadership with Bellwether Education Partners, a national nonprofit organization dedicated to accelerating the achievement of low-income students by cultivating, advising, and placing a community of innovative, effective, and sustainable change agents in public education reform and by improving the policy climate for their work.

Previously, Brown was an associate editor with *The Atlantic* magazine, and her writing has appeared in *The Atlantic, Guardian, New Republic, Smithsonian,* and *New York Times.* She began her career as a high school English teacher and Teach for America corps member, receiving the Symantec Award for Innovation in Teaching in 2007. She holds an MAT from American University and a BFA in writing, literature, and publishing from Emerson College.

Michael DeArmond is a senior research analyst at the Center on Reinventing Public Education, where his research focuses on school district reform, policy implementation, teacher policy, and school district human resource management reform. His published work includes studies of teacher shortages and teacher compensation, as well as the reform of district human resource departments and school-based hiring initiatives. Before working as a researcher, DeArmond was a middle school history teacher.

Matthew Di Carlo is a senior research fellow at the nonprofit Albert Shanker Institute in Washington, DC. His current research focuses mostly on education policy, including teacher evaluation, charter schools, school accountability systems, and teacher compensation. He has also published work on labor markets, social stratification, work and occupations, and political attitudes.

Billie Gastic is the director of research at the Relay Graduate School of Education (GSE). She has also served on New York State's Professional Standards and Practices Board for Teaching since 2012 and was recently reappointed to a four-year term by the state's Board of Regents. Gastic manages Relay GSE's institutional and external research activities and partnerships. She leads a team of staff researchers and research faculty in investigations of effective teaching practices, teacher and school leader preparation, the use of video and online technologies to improve instruction, and the measurement of student achievement growth and character development. Before joining Relay GSE, Gastic was a professor of urban education at Temple University and a professor of public policy at the University of Massachusetts Boston.

Dan Goldhaber is the director of the Center for Education Data and Research and a research professor in interdisciplinary arts and sciences at the University of Washington Bothell. Goldhaber's work focuses on issues of educational productivity, reform, and teacher effectiveness, including the effects of teacher qualifications and quality on student achievement, postsecondary schooling outcomes, teacher governance (e.g., collective bargaining agreements, teacher pensions) and its relationship to student achievement, the development and use of value-added modeling to measure teacher quality, and the impact of teacher pay structure and licensure on the teacher labor market.

Betheny Gross is a senior research analyst and research director at the Center on Reinventing Public Education. For more than ten years Gross has examined evidence and outcomes of district reform across the country and has consulted with districts leaders to formulate strategy and implementation. She is also an authority on teacher quality and labor market issues, investigating teacher policy in both district and charter schools. Recently, Gross coauthored the book *Strife and Progress: Portfolio Strategies for Managing Urban Schools* (Brookings Institution Press, 2012), which documents the portfolio reforms in several urban districts.

Bryan C. Hassel is codirector of Public Impact. He consults nationally with leading public agencies, nonprofit organizations, and foundations working for dramatic improvements in K–12 education. He is a recognized expert on charter schools, school turnarounds, education entrepreneurship, and teacher and leader policy. He leads, with Emily Ayscue Hassel, the Opportunity Culture initiative, which focuses on extending the reach of excellent teachers to all students. Hassel's work has appeared in *Education Next, Education Week*, and numerous other publications. He also blogs for *Education Next* and is a frequent guest blogger on other forums, such as *Education Week*.

Emily Ayscue Hassel is codirector of Public Impact, where she provides thought leadership and oversight to Public Impact's work on teacher and leader policy, organizational change, parental choice of schools, and emerging opportunities for dramatic improvement in preK–12 education. She is leading Public Impact's effort to develop and refine school and staffing models for reaching more students with excellent teachers. Her work has appeared in *Education Week, Education Next*, and other publications; she blogs for *Education Next* and is a frequent guest blogger on other forums, such as *Education Week*. Hassel was named to the inaugural class of the Aspen Teacher Leader Fellows program, designed to cultivate and support teacher leaders who are working to improve the teaching profession and student outcomes. She was previously a consultant and manager for the Hay Group, a leading human resources consulting firm.

Taryn Hochleitner is a research associate in education policy studies at the American Enterprise Institute. Her work focuses on a range of issues, including education technology, efforts to engage parents in public education, and teacher quality. She holds a BA in sociology from American University.

Robert Maranto is the 21st Century Chair in Leadership at the Department of Education Reform at the University of Arkansas. He previously taught at Villanova University and served at the Federal Executive Institute in the Clinton years. In concert with others, he has produced such scholarly books as *President Obama and Education Reform: The Personal and the Political* (Palgrave Macmillan, 2012), *The Obama Presidency* (Routledge, 2011), *Judging Bush* (Stanford University, 2009), *The Politically Correct University* (AEI Press, 2009), *A Guide to Charter Schools* (Rowman & Littlefield Education, 2006), *Beyond a Government of Strangers* (Lexington, 2005), and *School Choice in* *the Real World: Lessons from Arizona Charter Schools* (Westview Press, 2001). He is currently working on a book on the Knowledge Is Power Program and another on Arizona charter schools.

Sara Mead is a principal with Bellwether Education Partners, a nonprofit dedicated to helping education organizations—in the public, private, and nonprofit sectors—become more effective in their work and achieve dramatic results, especially for high-need students. In this role, she writes and conducts analysis on issues related to early childhood education and K–12 education policies and provides strategic advising support to clients serving high-need students.

Jal Mehta is an associate professor in the Harvard Graduate School of Education. His primary research interest is in understanding what it would take to create high-quality schooling at scale, with a particular interest in the professionalization of teaching. He is the author of *The Allure of Order: High Hopes, Dashed Expectations and the Troubled Quest to Remake American Schooling* (Oxford University Press, 2013) and the coeditor (with Robert B. Schwartz and Frederick M. Hess) of *The Futures of School Reform* (Harvard Education Press, 2012). He is currently working on two projects: "In Search of Deeper Learning," a contemporary study of schools, systems, and nations seeking to produce ambitious instruction, and "The Chastened Dream," a history of the effort to link social science with social policy to achieve social progress.

Jonathan Plucker is the Raymond Neag Endowed Professor in Educational Leadership and a professor of educational psychology at the University of Connecticut's Neag School of Education. He was previously a professor of educational psychology and cognitive science at Indiana University, where he was the founding director of the Center for Evaluation and Education Policy. His research, supported by over $30 million in external funding, examines education policy and talent development, with more than 150 publications to his credit. His work defining and studying excellence gaps is part of a larger effort to reorient policy makers' thinking about how best to promote success and high achievement for all children. Plucker is a fellow with the American Psychological Association (APA) and the American Association for the Advancement of Science and is the 2012 recipient of the APA Arnheim Award for Outstanding Achievement for his research on creativity. His past leadership roles include serving as president of Division 10 of the APA and as chair of the Research and Evaluation Division of the National Association for Gifted Children. His work is widely mentioned in the media, including *CNN*, *Wall Street Journal*, *New York Times*, and *Newsweek*.

Andrew Rotherham is a cofounder and partner at Bellwether Education Partners, where he leads the firm's thought leadership and policy analysis work. He is also the executive editor of the forthcoming "Real Clear Education," part of the Real Clear Politics family of news and analysis Web sites, writes the blog *Eduwonk.com*, and is the copublisher of *Education Insider*, a federal policy analysis tool produced by Whiteboard Advisors. Rotherham previously served at the Clinton White House as Special Assistant to the President for Domestic Policy and is a former member of the Virginia Board of Education. He was education columnist for *TIME* and a regular contributor to *U.S. News and World Report*. In addition to Bellwether, he also founded or cofounded two other education reform organizations and served on the boards of several other successful education start-ups. Rotherham is the author or coauthor of more than 250 published articles, book chapters, papers, and op-eds about education policy and politics and is the author or editor of four books on educational policy. He serves on advisory boards and committees for a variety of organizations, including Education Pioneers, The Broad Foundation, and the National Center for Analysis of Longitudinal Data in Education Research (CALDER). He serves on the board of directors for the Indianapolis Mind Trust, is vice chair of the Curry School of Education Foundation at the University of Virginia, and serves on the Visiting Committee for the Harvard Graduate School of Education.

Katharine O. Strunk is an associate professor of education and policy at the University of Southern California. Her research falls into three areas, all under the broad umbrella of K–12 education governance: teacher unions and the collective bargaining agreements they negotiate with school districts, teacher compensation policies, and accountability policies. Her work on these topics centers on the various district-level policy makers and on the ways the structures that are central to district operations and policy can affect these decisions and outcomes. Strunk has served as principal investigator on several foundation-, state-, and federally funded studies and was awarded the National Academy of Education/Spencer Postdoctoral Fellowship in 2011. She has also received distinctions from the American Educational Research Association and the Association for Education Finance and Policy.

Steven Teles is an associate professor of political science at Johns Hopkins University. He is the author of *Whose Welfare? AFDC and Elite Politics* (University Press of Kansas, 1996) and *The Rise of the Conservative Legal Movement* (Princeton University Press, 2008) and is the coeditor (with Glenn C. Loury and Tariq Modood) of *Ethnicity, Social Mobility and Public Policy: Comparing the US and UK* (Cambridge University Press, 2005) and (with Brian J. Glenn) *Conservatism and American Political Development* (Cambridge University Press, 2009). He is currently working on two books, one on the transformation of the field of philanthropy over the last fifty years and the other on why conservatives are changing their positions on mass incarceration.

Index